T0310949

THE CAST OF CHARACTER

This book is concerned with the idea of character and the methods of representing it in ancient and medieval narrative fiction, and shows how late classical and medieval authors adopted techniques and perspectives from rhetoric, philosophy, and sometimes theology to fashion figures who define not only themselves but also their readers.

Ginsberg first tests Ovid's concept of character in the *Amores* and the *Metamorphoses* against the conventions of classical tradition and shows how, although Ovid's idea of character did not change, his technique grew more subtle and complex as his art matured.

Ginsberg then employs the methods of biblical exegesis to show how medieval characters – Gottfried's Tristan, Dante's Farinata, Chrétien's Yvain – both exist as themselves and point to characters beyond themselves, gaining depth and resonance because we see them in this perspective.

Perspective is also a distinguishing quality of the maturing of Boccaccio's art. In the early works his characters seem to be little more than positions in a debate, but as he grew more skilful the strict formalism of binary oppositions gave way to the complexity of experience characteristic of the 'probably true' and culminating in the hundred perspectives of the *Decameron*.

In Chaucer's *Canterbury Tales* the pilgrims are both typical and individual, twice-formed by the tale and by the frame. A character acts, and the reader forms expectations of his acting, and in the process 'character,' the abiding glory of medieval literature, is created.

WARREN GINSBERG is a member of the Department of English at Yale University.

WARREN GINSBERG

The Cast of Character: The Representation of Personality in Ancient and Medieval Literature

UNIVERSITY OF TORONTO PRESS
Toronto Buffalo London

© University of Toronto Press 1983
Toronto Buffalo London
Reprinted 2017
ISBN 978-1-4875-9903-4 (paper)

Canadian Cataloguing in Publication Data

Ginsberg, Warren, 1949–
    The cast of character

Includes index.
ISBN 978-1-4875-9903-4 (pbk.)

1. Characters and characteristics in literature. 2.
Literature, Ancient – History and criticism. 3.
Fiction, Medieval – History and criticism. 4. Ovid,
43 B.C.-17 or 18 – Characters. 5. Boccaccio,
Giovanni, 1313–1375 – Characters. 6. Chaucer,
Geoffrey, d. 1400 – Characters. I. Title.

PN56.4.G55   809'.927   c83-098267-1

Publication of this book is made possible by grants from the Frederick W. Hilles
Publication Fund of Yale University and from the Publications Fund of University of
Toronto Press.

Contents

Acknowledgments

A book of criticism affords its author few pleasures greater than the opportunity to thank the many people whose own criticisms have made it better. Professor Alexander G. McKay opened more avenues for further investigation of Ovid's relation to the classical world than I have had time to pursue. Professors Stephen Barney, Marie Borroff, John Fyler, Thomas Greene, Robert Hanning, David Quint, and Fred Robinson have all read the manuscript or portions of it. Each has made many suggestions that have been incorporated into these pages, much to their benefit. The errors and infelicities that remain are all my own.

A part of the last chapter appeared in *Criticism* 20 (1978), under the title 'And Speketh so Pleyn: The Clerk's Tale and its Teller.' I would like to thank the editors for permission to have it reappear, somewhat altered, here. I am grateful to Doris Nelson, Wanda Fiak, and Diane Repak for their expert help in preparing the manuscript. My thanks are due as well to Yale University for a Morse Fellowship, which allowed me the time to write this book.

There remain two people to whom I owe a special debt of gratitude. Fred Robinson has been a true colleague and friend over the years: knowing him has itself been an education in the fineness of character. And most of all Judith Baskin: no words of dedication can requite what is her due.

THE CAST OF CHARACTER

TO JUDITH

Introduction

Character: the idea is so broad and has undergone such change through the centuries, one book cannot really do much more than interpret certain aspects of its history. There is little here that deals with Greek, Roman, or medieval plays, which might surprise the reader who has been tempted to look beyond the title page. But by limiting myself primarily to ancient and medieval narrative fiction, I have in a sense presupposed the drama rather than ignored it. Although Aristotle based his formulations mainly on the plays he saw, his conception of character looks to the *Rhetoric* and the *Nicomachean Ethics* as well. By their very nature the implications of the *Poetics* extended beyond the stage, as did its influence. By the time of the Augustan poets in Rome, the characters of epic, indeed of all literary genres, obeyed the same general principles of configuration. Different kinds of literature, of course, demanded different modifications in the representation of character, but whether the voice was Ulysses' or that of the narrator of the *Ars Amatoria*, the essential quality of his disposition was revealed in how he acted and in what he said. In Ovid, that disposition often satisfies less the demands of verisimilitude and consistency than those of literary parody; nevertheless, for all their fustian and rhetoric, no character in the *Amores* or the *Metamorphoses*, the two texts studied here in greatest detail, is less a mouthpiece for the typical than Aeschylus's Orestes or Agamemnon.

If by character we understand what Henry James understood, a self-conscious entity whose thoughts and emotions can determine the tone and direction of his narrative, most of Ovid's figures will strike us as simple and one-dimensional. But how much more solid and lifelike his heroes seem compared to the allegories and personifications of medieval literature. Even by ancient standards figures like Raison or Piers Plowman are incomplete: their speech and actions certainly do reveal their moral purpose, but Aristotle's other criteria, propriety, verisimilitude, and consistency, that a character should speak or act in accordance with necessity or probability, render these abstractions characters without substance.[1] So often in the Middle Ages, generic attributes are divorced from the men who act in accordance with them.

Yet there are other figures, Gottfried's Tristan, for instance, or Chrétien's Yvain, Boccaccio's Criseida and ser Ciappelletto, or Chaucer's Canterbury pilgrims, who seem more complex and fully rounded. Each of these characters owes his greater sense of presence to many things: the one aspect I have examined most closely has to do with the way the figure is seen in perspective. As Kenneth Burke has shown us, any character viewed in perspective partakes of the quality of metaphor, since metaphor, like perspective, 'is a device for seeing something *in terms of* something else.' And although it is customary, as Burke continues, 'to think that objective reality is dissolved by such relativity of terms as we get through the shifting of perspectives (the perception of one character in terms of many diverse characters) ... on the contrary, it is by the approach through a variety of perspectives that we establish a character's reality.'[2] My aim has been to show how classical and medieval authors adopted techniques and perspectives from rhetoric, philosophy, and sometimes from theology to fashion figures who define not only themselves but their readers as well. My approach is not new: seeing the particular characters of highly self-conscious poets as products of literary traditions, which inevitably include cultural and rhetorical traditions, finds an ancient analogue in the doctrine of 'genera dicendi,' and a modern counterpart in E.D. Hirsch's vigorous defence of interpretation by reference to the generic.[3] My goal, however, has not been theoretical so much as practical; wherever I could, I have sought to elucidate the poetic in these characters, the 'of-what and how' they are made and mean. Like the poets I study, I have adopted a number of critical perspectives: thus the prominence of literary artifice is emphasized in my treatment of Ovid, the properties of rhetorical debate in Boccaccio, the poetics of exegesis in texts like *Tristan* and *Yvain*, the double manipulation of narrative and topoi in Chaucer's *Canterbury Tales*. These are, let me stress, perspectives in methods of representation more than in the growth and development of the idea of character. Chaucer's Knight would have startled Ovid not because he is the quintessence of knightliness, but because for any Roman the concept of chivalry itself would have been perplexing. Ovid knew as well as Chaucer that 'in sondry landes and sondry ages, sondry been usages'; Latin lovers in the Via Sacra were no less typical than the men and women on the road to Canterbury. Yet Chaucer's techniques of portraying them were quite different from Ovid's, as were the qualities he wished them to represent. Like Chaucer, I do not wish to 'falsen my mateere,' to impose a sense of order or concinnity where neither actually exists. My 'mateere' encompasses different times, languages, and customs; the picture of character that emerges will necessarily be a similar juxtaposition of differing conventions and practices. In the last analysis, any definition of character in ancient and medieval literature will be inductive: beyond shared typicality, it will reflect the qualities of the texts examined. But the contour and dimensions of a mosaic can be discerned even when only fragments have been recovered; taken together these chapters do offer a sense of what character was in the literature from Ovid to Chaucer.

Yet if the representation of character is my subject, my theme is the way character becomes a metaphor for the artist's shaping imagination. Ovid, Chrétien, Dante, Boccaccio, Chaucer all fashion characters whose speeches and actions define not only themselves but central themes or principles of structure or signification as well. I have tried to preserve the integrity of each poet's vision; yet if the purpose and effect of the artistry differs from poet to poet, it is also true that the characters tend to become mirrors of that artistry. This is a concord that binds my diversity of characters into a semblance of harmony; I have emphasized it where I could.

Partly because others have dealt with it so thoroughly, I have been less concerned with what Spitzer called the 'poetical I' and Martin Stevens the 'performing self' than with the obverse phenomenon, the idea of audience as character.[4] One cannot, of course, speak of the audience without speaking of the author when the 'I' of the text is a surrogate for all its possible readers, but in the *Amores* and the *Decameron*, for instance, readers are both like and unlike the narrators in ways that determine the character of each. Even more than by authorial intrusion, however, Ovid, Boccaccio, and Chaucer manipulate their audiences through what a figure in the narrative says or does not say, does or fails to do. This process of shaping the reader's response has been a continuing concern of my investigation.

So too have I been less concerned with the representation of 'individuality,' especially as it appears in twelfth-century romance. The studies of Colin Morris and Robert Hanning have discussed the philosophical, religious, social, and literary aspects of this phenomenon with fine discernment.[5] Hanning in particular has found in the French 'romanciers' a subtle play of multiple perspectives similar to what I argue occurs in Boccaccio. But if poets manipulated viewpoints in independent episodes to reveal personal identity, they also arranged those episodes into a larger order. One of these ordering techniques is what I call literary typology; its juxtaposition of perspectives reveals characters who remain individuals without sacrificing their exemplary significance.

While this study is comparative, it is not per se an inquiry into poetic influence. Ovid's work drew heavily on the traditions of elegy and epic, yet his characters are quite unlike those of Propertius and Virgil. Boccaccio turned to Ovid throughout his career, but the ways his characters differ from his Roman predecessor's are more important than the ways they resemble them. The same is true of Chaucer, who borrowed as much from Ovid and Boccaccio as from anyone else. To understand the idea of character in each of these poets, his entire canon should be considered; in so far as space and time allowed, I have tried to do this. Much of what these authors wrote unavoidably receives only passing attention here, yet I hope that the texts I have selected represent fairly the others I have given shorter shrift. Some major works, like the *Troilus* or the *Elegia di madonna Fiammetta*, are examined only briefly: there was little need for me to linger over masterpieces whose characters have been discussed so much and so well by others. So too with Ovid, a youthful work, the *Amores*, has been given far more attention than poems either better known, such as the *Ars Amatoria*, or of incontestably greater scope and achievement, such as the *Metamorphoses*. So far as I can tell, however, Ovid's techniques of character drawing in his later works do not expand the conception of character one finds in his first. I hope the disproportion of my treatment, if not justified by this fact, may at least be excused by it. In a sense Juvenal's apology for his book can also serve as mine:

> Quidquid agunt homines, votum, timor, ira voluptas
> Gaudia, discursus, nostri farrago libelli est.

What men do: their wishes, fears, anger, pleasures, joys and other pursuits, this is the farrago of my book.

Unless otherwise indicated, all translations in the text are my own.

1

The Idea of Character in Ovid:
The *Amores*

When Ovid begins the fourth book of the *Metamorphoses*, Bacchus has avenged the blasphemies of Pentheus, and the kingship of Thebes has passed to Minyas. The new king had seen enough to persuade him that Bacchus ought to be paid homage; his daughters, however, still scorn the god and his revels. While other women loosen their tresses and roam the mountains with upraised thyrsi, they keep to their palace and ply the distaff. To pass time, they tell stories: first the tragic love of Pyramus and Thisbe, finally the unnatural union of Salmacis and Hermaphroditus. Between these, Leuconoe tells of the Sun's love for Leucothoe, a story she prefaces with a short but revealing account of Venus's adulterous liaison with Mars:

> Hunc quoque, siderea qui temperat omnia luce,
> cepit amor Solem: Solis referemus amores!   170
> primus adulterium Veneris cum Marte putatur
> hic vidisse deus: videt hic deus omnia primus.
> indoluit facto Iunonigenaeque marito
> furta tori furtique locum monstravit, at illi
> et mens et quod opus fabrilis dextra tenebat
> excidit: extemplo graciles ex aere catenas
> retiaque et laqueos, quae lumina fallere possent,
> elimat (non illud opus tenuissima vincant
> stamina, non summo quae pendet aranea tigno),
> utque leves tactus momentaque parva sequantur,   180
> efficit et lecto circumdata collocat arte.
> ut venere torum coniunx et adulter in unum,
> arte viri vinclisque nova ratione paratis
> in mediis ambo deprensi amplexibus haerent.

8 The Cast of Character

Lemnius extemplo valvas patefecit eburnas,
admisitque deos: illi iacurere ligati
turpiter, atque aliquis de dis non tristibus optat
sic fieri turpis: superi risere, diuque
haec fuit in toto notissima fabula caelo.[1]

Love seized him as well, the Sun, who with his shining light regulates all things: I will tell the story of the Sun's love! They say this god was the first to see the adultery of Venus with Mars; this god sees all things first. The deed shocked him, and he revealed to Venus's husband, the son of Juno, the secret love and the place in which they committed it. And Vulcan dropped from his mind and his right hand the work he was designing. At once he fashioned fine chains of brass, and nets, and snares, which no eye could detect. No threads were ever spun more delicate, not those a spider hangs from the highest rafter. He made it so that it would follow the lightest touch, give at the slightest movement, and placed it on the bed, spreading it about with cunning art. When the adulterer and his mate were together in bed, both, caught by Vulcan's art and by the chains prepared for so extraordinary a purpose, cling to each other in the midst of their embrace. The Lord of Lemnos at once threw open the ivory doors and called the gods to come and see. There they lay, locked together, disgracefully, and one of the gods, not the most cheerless, desired that he should be so disgraced. The gods laughed, and for a long time this was the talk of all heaven.   (IV, 169–89)

During his career as Rome's most prolific story-teller, Ovid often contrived to retell the same story in a different manner and with a different purpose. The affair between Venus and Mars is one of these twice-told tales; in the second book of the *Ars Amatoria*, however, Ovid introduces their celestial embarrassment to prove that exposure does nothing to dampen an adulterous relationship:

fabula narratur toto notissima caelo,
Mulciberis capti Marsque Venusque dolis.
Mars pater insano Veneris turbatus amore
de duce terribili factus amator erat;
nec Venus oranti (neque enim dea mollior ulla est)   565
rustica Gradiuo difficilisque fuit.
a, quotiens lasciua pedes risisse mariti
dicitur et duras igne uel arte manus!
Marte palam simul est Vulcanum imitata, decebat,
multaque cum forma gratia mixta fuit.
sed bene concubitus primo celare solebant;

plena uerecundi culpa pudoris era.
indicio Solis (quis Solem fallere possit?)
cognita Vulcano coniugis acta suae.
(quam mala, Sol, exempla moues! pete munus ab ipsa: 575
et tibi, si taceas, quod dare possit, habet.)
Mulciber obscuros lectum circaque superque
disponit laqueos; lumina fallit opus.
fingit iter Lemnon; ueniunt ad foedus amantes;
impliciti laqueis nudus uterque iacent;
conuocat ille deos; praebent spectacula capti;
uix lacrimas Venerem continuisse putant;
non uultus texisse suos, non denique possunt
partibus obscenis obposuisse manus.
hic aliquis ridens 'in me, fortissime Mauors,   585
si tibi sunt oneri, uincula transfer' ait.
uix precibus, Neptune, tuis captiua resoluit
corpora; Mars Thracen occupat, illa Paphon.

The story is told, most famous in all heaven: Mars and Venus captured by the cunning device of Mulciber. Father Mars, driven wild by insane desire for Venus, from terrifying lord of war was made a lover; nor was Venus, since no goddess is more pleasantly agreeable, prudish or captious about Mars's prayers. How often the playful wanton is said to have laughed at her husband's limp and his hands, hardened by work at the forge. When she imitated Vulcan in Mars's presence, it became her: such grace was conjoined with much beauty. At first they were wont to conceal their love-making well: shame was full of retiring modesty. The tattling of the Sun – for who can deceive the Sun – made Vulcan know his wife's affairs. How bad an example you set, O Sun – ask her for favours: if you are silent, you shall have for yourself what she is able to give. Mulciber places hidden snares about and above the bed; the device is too subtle to see. He pretends to go to Lemnos: the lovers hasten to their tryst; both lie naked, entangled in the snare. Vulcan calls the gods: the captives prove a spectacle indeed. They think Venus can scarcely hide her tears; they can't cover their faces, nor can they cover their private parts with their hands. Then someone, laughing, says, 'O Mars, strongest of the strong, if the chains are a burden for you, transfer them to me.' By your prayers, O Neptune, Vulcan with difficulty was persuaded to release the captives. Mars hurries to Thrace, Venus to Paphos.[2]

Parallel versions of stories in Ovid have attracted scholars' attention ever since Heinze delineated the different attributes of elegiac and epic narratives by comparing the accounts of the rape of Proserpina in the *Fasti* and the

Metamorphoses.[3] Heinze found that in elegy, the tone is tender and sentimental, while the stately epic solemnly unfolds, filled with reverence and awe. The elegist interjects offhand remarks throughout his narrative, rapidly passing over a great deal of the action to concentrate on one or two poignant details. The epic, on the other hand, is symmetrical and ordered; the clauses are long, the cola cumulative and the transitions careful.[4]

To account for these differences, many have analysed the nature of the elegiac couplet itself. Continuous hypotactic narration is restricted, rendered almost impossible by a two-line unit that is highly self-contained, end-stopped and almost always circumscribes a completed thought.[5] The further requirement that the ictus coincide with the metre in the last two feet of the pentameter could only impede fluid discourse. Both the demands of the form, therefore, and the narrator's intrusive presence make elegiac couplets a difficult medium for graceful story-telling.

Although Heinze's conclusions have been challenged in some points, the two accounts of Venus and Mars, as Otto Due says, do seem to offer a fine illustration of the difference between epic and elegy.[6] Compared to its counterpart in the *Metamorphoses*, the story in the *Ars* does appear more disjointed and confused. Apart from generic considerations, however, this narrative unevenness is in part due to the absurdity of the point Ovid endeavours to make. A cautionary tale for Odysseus has been converted into an argument that lovers should give up trying to catch their girls when they cheat: 'o iuuenes, deprendere parcite uestras!' (557). Vulcan, Ovid says, gained nothing by his disclosure, since Mars and Venus, once their shame was known to all, did more openly what before they did in secret. Now if this 'praeceptum amoris' is in fact made the point of the story, then Mars and Venus will have to be the primary objects of our attention, and their love recounted in toto. And so we come upon Mars already infatuated ('turbatus amore'), but notice as well that Ovid seems less interested in the god's feelings than in demonstrating that his passion is requited. With a haste only the gods can experience, courtship leads to the couch. After all, a captain of war ought to be no less direct in matters of love: why shouldn't his 'do you want to go to bed' (expressed with wicked civility by 'oranti') have met her equally direct and urbane acquiescence? At any rate, by the next couplet (567–8), Mars and Venus have been together long enough for us to witness a 'jeu d'amour': Venus imitates her husband's gaucheries, and Mars grows even more impassioned watching her.

In light of the intimacy of this glance into their dalliances, it is disconcerting to be told that the godly pair were discreet, driven to conceal their adultery by a sense of shame 'pregnant with retiring modesty' ('plena uerecundi culpa pudoris erat'). We realize with some surprise that Ovid's picture of the gods in love, for all its celestial psychology, is entirely supererogatory to the real subject of the narrative, Vulcan's entrapment. The story should begin, as it does in the *Odyssey* and the *Metamorphoses*, with the Sun's disclosure of the affair. But narration is not the point. Ovid's purpose in the *Ars* is didactic: all characters exist merely to illustrate his precepts of love. Venus's displeasure with her husband, her mockery of his limp and his devotion to his work, together with her concomitant willingness to enter into extra-marital licentiousness, make her a divine exemplar of exactly what Ovid has said married women feel and do in this world. Mars, in turn, becomes the model lover all young men ought to imitate: he sees, he asks, and he conquers. Vulcan, the true protagonist of the tale, is reduced to the stock figure of the bumbling, incompetent husband. The Sun becomes less an agent of discovery than an example of missed opportunities. So flagrantly does this god violate what we might call the rules of amatory decorum that Ovid must instruct him directly about the benefits of blackmail: 'quam mala, Sol, exempla moues! pete munus ab ipsa, / et tibi, si taceas, quod dare possit, habet.' When Ovid finally does tell the story, the phrases are, as Heinze says, exceedingly simple, paratactic and shorn of all ornament. No description of the snare's manufacture, a brief yet salacious look at the naked pair, and almost at once we are returned to what really interested Ovid – not the story itself, but the outrageous meaning he derives from it. No consistent regard for plot or character imparts wholeness, unity, or probability to the passage; Ovid emphasizes only those elements of the story which wit can transmute into hortatory lessons for amatory prowess. In this telling, the poetry's didactic intention accounts for the form of the tale and its relative lack of narrative success.

How different is the account in the *Metamorphoses*. The events unfold smoothly and logically, and a fine rhetorical polish graces the narration: repetition, zeugma, paradox, and conventional poetic conceits are all prominently displayed.[7] The tone is much more proper: all risqué description of enamorment, courtship, and acquiescence, so salient in the *Ars*, has been eliminated. And yet, amid so much propriety, there is wit as well. When we remember the elegiac version, we see that Ovid's epic revision quite appropriately begins not at the beginning, but in medias res. In the *Metamorphoses*, however, all things are connected: Mars and Venus serve as a prologue to the story of the Sun's love for Leucothoe. This latter story, therefore, like those in the *Ars*, is given ab ovo.[8] In fashioning his 'carmen perpetuum,' Ovid both takes and disregards Horace's advice; by transforming elegiac matter into epic structure, Ovid confirms his mastery of both.

Yet it is not the 'epic gravity' of the hexameters, the effective use of enjambment and elegantly balanced periods, or the deliberately elevated vocabulary ('extemplo,' etc.) that most distinguishes the rendering in the *Metamorphoses* from its predecessor. More likely the impression of greater clarity and consistency in the way the story is told results from a significant change in focus: a jovial plan to teach the art of love and its many refinements has narrowed to a single-minded preoccupation with its exposure. As a consequence, unlike the characters in the *Ars*, who are little more than supernal advertisements of the narrator's witty precepts, the Mars, Venus, Vulcan, and Sun who appear in the *Metamorphoses* serve a different, more interesting purpose: they have become the means of delineating their speaker's character.

Consider again the lines in the *Metamorphoses*: the emphasis placed on sight and discovery borders on obsession. The prominence of the Sun, who discovers the tryst, the loving attention given to the nets and the glee at the entrapment, the publication of the discovery and its effect, the multiplication of words that mean or imply look, reveal, see (vidisse, videt, monstravit, lumina fallere, patefecit, admisit, illi iacuere ligati), all point to the fact that beneath her upright priggery, Leuconoe, the narrator, hides the excited fascination of a voyeuse. The Sun's mortification in seeing the crime, Vulcan's shock in hearing it, both mirror Leuconoe's affronted sense of decency in the face of such scandalous passion. She, after all, like Pentheus before her, would rather serve Pallas than Bacchus; for her, the orgiastic obscenities of his rites, indeed, sexual desire of any sort, is disgraceful. In the *Ars*, naturally enough, we are encouraged to think of Mars and Venus's romance as a spirited 'affaire de coeur'; in the *Metamorphoses*, the nature of their activity is clearly labelled: it is 'adulterium,' its participants 'coniunx et adulter.' That Rome's patron deities should comport themselves in such a manner is simply unpardonable.[9]

This high-minded censure of morally reprehensible behaviour makes itself felt throughout the tale, but most clearly in the first few lines. Vulvan has lost his Alexandrian surname of Mulciber; instead he has become 'Iunonigena,' the son of Juno.[10] The mention of Juno, who took such fastidious offence at her husband's adulteries, is exceedingly apt. Like his mother, Vulcan is immediately ready to fashion his revenge: 'extemplo graciles ex aera catenas ... elimat.' But the implications of the epithet extend beyond the narrative as well: Leuconoe, who clearly applauds Vulcan's designs, is also like Juno. Her account of Mars and Venus, we remember, is merely a preliminary for her telling of the Sun's love for Leucothoe, Venus's repayment for his tattling. Both Leuconoe's stories, as well as those her sisters recite, deliberately portray the disastrous consequences uncontrolled desire has for mortals and gods. These worshippers of reason excoriate passion. Indeed, in their last tale, the Salmacis and Hermaphroditus, love has degenerated to the point where it seems a perversion of nature itself. Only women of Juno-like pride could tell such stories, only women who, like Juno, would deny the very existence of Bacchus.

So too only a woman of such lofty moral deportment could commend the actions of the Sun and at the same time imply her superiority to him. The repeated use of chiasmus, 'cepit amor Solis: Solis referemus amores, Primus ... putatur / hic vidisse deus: videt hic deus omnia primus,' lines whose elements are reflections of one another, lends dignity to the god and gravamen to his charge. Yet this Sun, whose eyes, unlike those of Venus and Mars, miss nothing, will himself be blind enough to fall prey to love.[11] The daughters of Minyas, of course, make it quite clear that they will not.

Ovid knew, however, that haughty probity often masks hidden desires. The means of entrapment, which merit only two words in the *Ars* ('obscuros ... laqueos'), now are elaborated over six lines. One almost feels Leuconoe's growing anticipation as she describes the 'fine chains of brass, and nets, and snares,' and praises them for their suppleness and responsiveness to touch, for being finer than any thread man can weave, finer even than the spider's filament. Even the disposition of the web about the bed is praised for its cunning: 'lecto circumdata collocat arte'; in the *Ars*, the snares are merely placed over and about the couch. Leuconoe can hardly wait for the lovers to arrive: there is more than implied haste in the construction 'Ut venere ...' And once they are in bed, the trap is immediately sprung. The rush of triumph we feel as Vulcan immediately ('extemplo') throws open the doors is not his alone: Leuconoe shares the thrill of public vindication as well. 'Illi iacuere ligati, / turpiter,' there they lay, bound together, shamefully. The damning adverb, quite absent in the *Ars*, seems incongruent next to the spondaically emphatic adjective, which fixes the scene with its unblinking detail. The line perfectly captures the character of a woman who can't turn her head from what she so disapproves of seeing.

What in the *Ars* seemed a passing concern for psychological motivation has thus assumed a central importance in the stories of this daughter of Minyas. Ovid implies that suppressed desire disfigures Leuconoe and her sisters; their transformation into bats marries a consonant external form to their true, inner natures. Leuconoe's stories of shady love are actually stories impelled by revenge: Vulcan's on Mars and Venus, Venus's on the Sun-god. It is only fitting, then, that Leuconoe herself be the object of Bacchus's vespertilian vengeance. If Leuconoe would identify herself with Vulcan, Ovid makes sure she feels the truth Vulcan himself utters in the *Ars*:

> saepe tamen demens stulte fecisse fateris
> teque ferunt artis paenituisse tuae

Yet often, you madman [Vulcan], you confess that you acted like a fool, and they say you have repented of your own art. (*Ars* II, 591–2)

The Minyades deny Bacchus, and their stories, in denying the goodness of love, deny Ovid himself. Their transformation is Ovid's revenge as well. Only a poet of his audacity would put his own stories in a moralist's mouth without changing at all the lewdness of their implications.

Yet for all its wit and polish, the most significant aspect of the version in the *Metamorphoses* is the fact that a consistent character emerges from the story Leuconoe was given to tell, and from the way she was made to tell it. To measure Ovid's achievement, we must know what his idea of character and characterization was. A long tradition lies behind him, and, as chief authority on matters of love in the Middle Ages and beyond, his practice would become the model for many poets to come.

Considered formally, the Greek work 'charakter' is an agent noun, one who 'charessei.'[12] Originally, 'charassein' described the act of graving, sketching a mark or inflicting a wound. Later, by a natural progression of meaning, it came to designate the act of writing on wood, stone, or even earth: in every case a marking of the surface, or again, the stamping of an impression upon a coin blank. Eventually, 'charakter' itself was transferred from the agent to the die or stamp with which the act was carried out.

The decisive shift in the word's semantic history, however, was from an active to a passive sense; both agent and instrument became less important than result. By the time 'charakter' first appears in Greek literature, in the *Suppliants* of Aeschylus, it already meant the impression stamped on a coin. This notion of impression still allowed the word to signify many things: to Herodotus 'charakter' was a speech characteristic; to Aristophanes, style as spoken expression; to Euripides, abstract entities like virtue and noble descent; to Plato, an individuating quality. No writer, however, including Plato and Aristotle, employed the term with any thought of that inward individuality we associate with the word today.

For Plato, of course, as citizen of Athens in fact and the ideal Republic in spirit, the question that mattered was, 'what is man, beyond the individual?' Any feeling, such as grief, excessively indulged, will foster in man a disposition contrary to reason: isolated by sorrow, neither the statesman nor the shoemaker will be able to discharge his obligations to the state. And it is precisely because poets by nature imitate this peevish and diverse character, that is, the inclination which makes a man recall his affliction and lament, rather than the more admirable disposition that makes him, in the face of sorrow, turn as quickly as possible to the healing and restoring of what is fallen and diseased, that Plato would exclude poets from his Republic.[13] The poet and the painter depict the more graphic workings of the appetitive soul; they represent that character which has little value for the city, and even less for the truth.

By the time Aristotle was writing, however, Athens had been crippled by Sparta, and discussions of ethics began to examine individual goals apart from their civic context. At the outset of the *Nicomachean Ethics*, as W.D. Ross says, Aristotle describes the good of the state as 'greater and more perfect than that of the individual, and the latter as something with which we may have to put up if we cannot attain the former. But his sense of the individual life appears to grow as he discusses it, and at the end of the work he speaks as if the state were merely ancillary to the moral life of the individual, supplying the element of compulsion which is needed if a man's desires are to be made subservient to his reason.'[14]

For Aristotle, the goal of ethical behaviour was 'well-being': the doing of certain things 'not because we see them to be right in themselves, but because we see them to be such as will bring us nearer to the "good for man." '[15] Thus the 'study of character,' which is how Aristotle refers to his ethical treatises, will in large part be the study of moral virtue – that internal disposition which, 'when it has to choose among actions and feelings, observes the mean relative to us, this being determined by such a rule or principle as would take shape in the mind of a man of sense or practical wisdom.'[16] When Aristotle gives his famous description of the 'great-souled' man in the fourth book of the *Nicomachean Ethics*, both the general qualities, such as indifference to good or bad fortune, openness in love and hatred, in speech and action, an apparently supercilious attitude toward honour, and the specific traits, such as unhurriedness of step, deepness of voice, and deliberateness of speech, are meant to illustrate that magnanimity is the mean between poor-spiritedness and vanity.

In his biological works, Aristotle had classified organisms by their ascending degree of likeness; the virtues are categorized in a similar manner in the *Ethics*. The first of these degrees of likeness is 'the complete identity of type which exists in a single species.'[17] Within a given group of living beings, an impartial observer will accept similarities as essential and differences as insignificant. In the *Nicomachean Ethics* as well, a man assumes individuality in so far as he conforms with the qualities of a virtue whose differentia are well known. A person no longer is defined by what he does in the city, but by his ruling disposition: Agamemnon is, among other things, 'megalopsuchios' because he is disposed to act in a definite and recognizable manner.

The discussion of character ('ethe') in the *Rhetoric* and *Poetics* follows the observations Aristotle made in the *Ethics*. No art, we are told at the beginning of the *Rhetoric*, has regard for the individual case. Medicine does not search for what will cure Socrates, but for that which cures a person or persons of such and such type. Rhetoric, therefore, 'will not consider what seems probable to the individual – to Socrates or to Hippias – but what seems probable to a given class.'[18] In the second book, Aristotle first teaches the orator how to create a favourable impression of his own character, that he is truthful, sincere, a man of integrity and the like. Then, in chapters twelve through seventeen, we learn that when an orator sketches his own or anyone else's character, he must show due regard for a person's age and position in respect to the gifts of fortune. There is a decorum of type the orator must observe if his portrait is to carry conviction.

Similarly, when Aristotle defines character in the *Poetics* as 'that which reveals moral purpose, showing what kind of thing a man chooses or avoids,' we have returned to the generic descriptions of the *Nicomachean Ethics*.[19] In a drama, a character must have four qualities: goodness (that is, he must be endowed with a purpose which is good), propriety, truthfulness to life, and consistency (xv, 1–6: 1454a). In any rendering, the poet should always aim at the necessary or the probable, for only then can poetry display its peculiar excellence, which is its ability to express the universal. By universal, Aristotle means 'how a person of a certain type will on occasion speak or act, according to the law of probability or necessity' (IX, 4: 1451b). The particular, what Aristophanes did or suffered, should interest none but the writer of comedy, but any poet, if he would represent men who are irascible, indolent, or possessed of any other defect of character, should preserve the type and yet ennoble it. In Aristotle's poetics, everyone, from Oedipus to Xanthias, must be a model of his ruling disposition.

It is for these reasons that Aristotle maintains that in tragedy plot necessarily assumes precedence over character. Whatever the objections, no other conclusion can seem as valid if we accept Aristotle's statement in the *Ethics* that 'states of character are formed from similar activities' (*Ethics* 1103, a14–b25, Ross's translation). For Aristotle, moral virtues are produced in us neither by Nature nor against Nature, but by repeated activity, by habit. Action is prior to a man's disposition to act in a particular way: thus the importance of receiving the right kind of education. The aesthetic analogue to such thinking would naturally conceive of plot as character-in-action, and character, when opposed to plot, as 'character-in-so-far-as-it-is-inactive.'[20] In drama, which deals with figures whose dispositions are faits accomplis, any character must depend upon the actions of the plot for the revelation of that disposition. Only if those actions are probable, and the character's reactions consistent, would Aristotle consider the play an artistic success.

Unlike his teacher, Aristotle's disciple Theophrastus was not so predominantly ethical an observer of character. In the collection of some thirty brief sketches called the *Characters*, Theophrastus studies various types of character, such as the pretentious man, the man of petty ambition, the ironic man, the miser, and the spendthrift, each of which, at first glance, seems an aberration of that virtue which is the 'mean relative to us.' But, as Warren Anderson has argued, although Theophrastus is still interested in the types, in the stamp which stamps many coins, not one, he is no moralist. In a markedly discontinuous style, Theophrastus describes what he sees objectively; details exist for their own sake. The figures he portrays are without moorings. Divorced from all civic context, they exist only in the immediate moment, 'for it is from moment to moment that they live, with no constant factor other than the master impulse which characterizes them.'[21]

Many used to think Theophrastus wrote the *Characters* as a kind of prompt-book for Menander. Be this as it may, it nevertheless is only with Menander and the New Comedy that character comes to denote the individual nature of a single person. The stock figures of Attic Comedy are given distinct personalities. For Alfred Korte, Abrotonon in Menander's *Epitrepontes* is not at all the typical hetaera, but a figure as full-rounded and memorable as Goethe's Philine.[22]

Remarkable as Menander's achievement was, however, character did not readily take on the meaning he had given it. 'Charakter' itself only became a common word in the first century BC, but it and other words that expressed the same notion, such as 'ethopoeia,' became for the most part terms of rhetoric which were used to designate a single author's personal style. Cicero's use of the word is typical, showing a natural development of what Herodotus and Aristophanes used the word to mean: 'sed in omni re difficillimum est formam, qui *XAPAKTHP* Graece dicitur, exponere optimi, quod aliud aliis videtur optimum. / But in every case, it is difficult to describe the "form," which is called "charakter" in Greek, of the best, because different people have different notions of what is best.'[23] Cicero uses 'forma' here in the Aristotelian sense; Hubbell translates it as 'pattern.' In any case, it has little to do with individual occurrences; character and character-drawing had become chiefly aspects of style.

As such, in Roman rhetoric and poetics character conformed to the principles of the law of decorum: excess had to be avoided and the mean observed.[24] The orator who pleaded a cause had to consider not only the character of his client and opponent, but his own character and that of his audience as well. In every case this meant that the phrases and sentiments he uttered had to be congruent with the rank, descent, or moral stature of the person he wished to portray.

'Ut quasi mores oratoris effingat oratorio': perhaps the foremost supposition of Roman rhetoric is that the style and tone of any speech reflect the character of its speaker.[25] By using the proper words, the orator gives his speech and 'ethical cast' which ought to persuade his listeners of his integrity, love of honour, and devotion to the public weal. [26] To do this, the speaker would have to consider the character of his audience: before the senate, nothing but the grand style would be appropriate; before a popular assembly, a less finished style would have to be employed. Passionate eloquence full of the artifices of rhetoric will more likely persuade a jury of many than a single judge.

Furthermore, within the body of a speech, any sketch of the defendant, his advocates, or any person connected with the case had to be decorous as well. Cicero and Quintilian, for instance, both followed Aristotle in advising that the way a figure expresses himself should be in keeping with his age. [27] The young love brilliance and exuberance; what they say will be rich with gaudy colours, but lacking in discipline and reserve. With age comes riper judgment; a certain dignity and austerity will mark the mature man's utterances. Cicero could even remark that his own style was growing grey with the years. [28]

By observing such propriety, a speaker may delineate a character in a way that will not seem incongruous to the audience. Indeed, the rhetoricians advised their pupils to introduce striking imitations of life and custom ('morum et vitae imitatio'), since they lend a speech persuasiveness and charm. [29] But for all their vividness, portraits had to emphasize the qualities proper to each man's nature. A false note, something that seemed out of joint with a man's ruling passion, would cause an audience to laugh and impair the effectiveness of his appeal to them.

The law of decorum, to use J.F. D'Alton's words, dogged the orator's every step, and it seems to have held equal sway over poetic theory. [30] Horace insists that Piso's characters be fashioned with propriety:

> format enim Natura prius nos intus ad omnem
> fortunam habitum; iuvat aut impellit ad iram,
> aut ad humum maerore gravi deducit et angit;
> post effert animi motus interprete lingua.
> si dicentis erant fortunis absona dicta,
> Romani tollent equites peditesque cachinnum.

For Nature first shapes us within to meet every change of fortune; she brings joy or impels to anger, or bows us to the ground and tortures us under a heavy load of grief; then, with the tongue for interpreter, she proclaims the emotions of the soul. If the speaker's words sound discordant with his fortunes, the Romans, in boxes or the pit alike, will raise a loud guffaw. (A.P., 107–12) [31]

Whatever the intermediate influences, the Aristotelian presuppositions of this passage are evident. [32] As in Aristotle, character is a matter of disposition: the consistency of attitude in what a man says or does when confronted by the vagaries of fortune. We see this more clearly when Horace tells young dramatists that Medea should be fierce and unyielding, Ino tearful, Orestes sorrowful (*A.P.*, 123–4). Each figure is less an individual than a ruling passion: by each episode, once and for all, Medea defines not herself but 'ferocitas,' Ixion not himself but 'perfidia.' For Horace as much as for Aristotle, character depends upon plot: it is the first way the poet can realize his goal, which is the representation of an action.

In Horace, poetry itself almost seems to be the mediating principle, the tongue that interprets, that provides, as it were, level ground for the movements of the soul as it passes through the extremes of anger, sorrow, and joy. But whether the poetry itself is mesotic or not, it must obey the rules of 'convenientia.' Certain congruence must grace the expression if the poet wants to avoid the groundlings' catcalls. When later in the *Ars Poetica* Horace describes the manners of each age and demonstrates how to give a befitting tone to natures that change with the years (156–78), he follows Aristotle's *Rhetoric* (II, 12–14), even as he invests that old doctrine with his own artistry. Gordon Williams's analysis of the passage reveals that when Horace departs from Aristotle, his changes are poetic, not analytic. Indeed, the *Ars Poetica* is the first attempt we know of to criticize poetry in poetry.[33] So if the matter of the *Ars* is largely traditional, its expression is completely novel, and the idea of character, as we would expect, remains as strongly typical in Horace's poetic as it had been in Aristotle's.

When Ovid began to write, therefore, his notion of what character was would have been shaped partly by philosophy, partly by literary criticism, but mostly, given the nature of his time, his own temperament and training, by rhetoric. Naturally enough, the schoolmasters of Rome had more to say about the character of the speaker and his audience than about the decorum of dramatic personae: Cicero's feeling that the character of the orator be mirrored in his speech was echoed in nearly every orator's manual. Perhaps the one concept of Roman rhetoric that most clearly affected the rendering of this kind of character was that of 'fides,' of sincerity. Once we have examined this, we shall, at last, be able to judge the sophistication and originality of the voice that dominates the *Amores*, and the artistic development of that voice in the *Metamorphoses*.

For any speech to be successful, an orator must persuade his audience that he is sincere.[34] The word 'fides,' which expressed this idea, contained within it, as Heinze has shown, both a subjective and an objective aspect: the former is concerned with sincerity, the latter with persuasiveness.[35] No matter the occasion, the orator will want to convince his audience that he speaks out of devotion to truth, love of honour, a sense of moral integrity; in short, that he is a man worth listening to. According to Quintilian, such a claim in fact must be an intrinsic quality of the speech: 'a bad speech fails to present the character of the speaker properly.'[36] 'Fides' therefore came to mean both good faith on the part of the speaker, that he is the man he presents himself to be, and the audience's acceptance of his claim to speak in good faith.

As the result of persuasiveness, sincerity in Roman discourse was considered a matter of style. For Quintilian, 'it is enough to speak with propriety, pleasantly and convincingly': 'proprie, iucunde, credibiliter dicere sat est,' since such a style reveals the ethos of the speaker most persuasively (VI, 2.19). Similar considerations held in poetry: Propertius could urge his friend Lynceus to turn from epic to elegiac verse by saying

> Incipe iam angusto versus includere torno,
> inque tuos ignis, dure poeta, veni.

Begin now to confine your verses on the narrow wheel, and come, harsh poet, to your own fire.   (II, 34: 43–4)[37]

As A.W. Allen says, for Lynceus to find fitting expression for his fiery passions, he must adopt a style more severe and polished, the narrower ambit of the potter's wheel rather than the expansiveness of epic: 'As epic poet, Lynceus was *durus*, but if he would turn to the theme of love, he would become a *tener poeta* – not simply because he would write as a lover, but because he would write in a style that is *tener* (graceful), in contrast to the *durus* style of epic.'[38] From this point of view, the personality of a poet is determined by his style; in the poetry of love, sincerity is textual, contingent upon propriety even more than upon intensity.

In the *Amores*, Ovid seems to me most subtle and inventive precisely in his manipulation of these ideas of character and sincerity, which is to say, in the making of his style. The *Amores* are often said to chronicle not the impact of love upon an individual, but Love itself, its typical working. This, I think, is true, and what separates Ovid from the other elegists. He alone realized that in such an undertaking, the character of the audience would be as important as the character of the lover he presents in his lines. And in the *Amores* Ovid creates his audience out of the same imaginative cloth from which he fashions his lover.

Consider, for example, the epigram Ovid wrote to introduce the second edition of the *Amores*:

> Qui modo Nasonis fueramus quinque libelli,
> tres sumus: hoc illi praetulit auctor opus.

> ut iam nulla tibi nos sit legisse uoluptas,
> at leuior demptis poena duobus erit.

We who once were five little books of Ovid's now are three; the author preferred the work this way. If still you derive no pleasure from us, the pain at least will be two books lighter.[39]

The unassuming modesty of this prooemium is charming, and, to all appearances, conventional. Besides eliciting the 'good favour,' the 'benivolentia' of the audience, as rhetorical doctrine advised, the understated wit and verbal echoes might have brought to the Roman reader's mind the introduction of a different poet, the dedicatory hendecasyllabics of Catullus:

> Cui dono lepidum nouum libellum
> arida modo pumice expolitum?
> Corneli, tibi: namque tu solebas
> meas esse aliquid putare nugas,
> iam tum cum ausus es unus Italorum
> omne aeuum tribus explicare cartis
> doctis, Iuppiter, et laboriosis.
> quare habe tibi quidquid hoc libelli
> qualecumque; quod (o) patrona uirgo,
> plus uno maneat perenne saeclo.[40]

To whom am I to give this pleasant little volume, just now polished with dry pumice? Cornelius, to you: for you were wont to think my trifles worth something, even now when you, alone among the Italians, have dared to expound the history of all the ages in three learned, o Jupiter, and industrious volumes. Wherefore take this small book, whatever its worth, which, o patroness virgin, may yet be read after more than one century.

Whether this small volume of trifles refers to the entire collection of one hundred sixteen poems, or only to a part of it, Catullus's dedication is the model by which we should read Ovid's.[41] The fine tension of the earlier poem results from the contrast between the insistence with which Catullus deprecates his poetry and the simultaneous implication that the poems are polished works of art which ought to last through the centuries. The dedication opens with Catullus in search of an audience: 'to whom am I to give this pleasant little book [libellum]?' Who would want it, even if the ends of the roll have been polished with dry pumice? Perhaps the poems within, the reader seems to be urged to infer, are as arid and abrasive as the pumice that has spruced up the volume's appearance. Cornelius Nepos, at any rate, is the man, since he appears to have praised Catullu's trifles ('nugas'). And trifles they must be, for by immediately describing the magnitude of Nepos's undertaking, Catullus underscores the slightness of his offering.[42] The multiple qualifications of Catullus's own poetry in the following colon seem well deserved: 'quare ... quidquid hoc libelli / qualecumque,' wherefore 'take this bit of a book,' as Wheeler translates it, 'however poor it may be.'[43]

On this note of diffidence and reservation we expect the poem to end; how unexpected, then, even though it ostensibly seems only a hope, is the pride one senses in the poet's concluding prayer for his book. Worthy to call the Muse its patroness, Catullus hopes his poems will be immortal. Beneath the self-deprecatory humility, we realize that a deeper feeling of achievement sanctions this request for literary permanence under the sponsorship of the goddesses of poetry and wisdom. And this intimation of pride forces us to read the poem again, this time with the end in mind from the beginning. What once was modest to the point of disparagement now seems more confident and assured of its value. 'Lepidum,' 'explolitum,' 'doctis,' words that at first seemed mocking references to the paltriness of Catullus's poetry, now appear to be words of unqualified praise.[44] Irony that once seemed directed at the poet now threatens to be extended to his audience. After all, Nepos, a man unique not only in Rome but in all Italy, a man who in his *Chronicles* compiled the wisdom of all ages, thinks Catullus has value.[45] The compliment to Nepos becomes an admonition to other readers: their perception, and ours, will be measured and judged by our reactions to what we read. Catullus's poem is a fine instance of a poet creating and interpreting his audience.

The blush that suddenly transforms itself into a ruby of self-esteem is precisely the alchemy Ovid perpetrates in his epigram, but by methods more arch and self-consciously literary. Here, the books speak, not the poet, and what they say is elegant and disarming. But whereas Catullus is simultaneously diffident and proud, Ovid's modesty has struck many as the merest pretext for his books' wit. This goes beyond the feeling that if the two books taken away were anywhere near as sprightly as the description of their removal, their loss is great indeed. More than a hint of disagreement colours the phrase 'hoc illi praetulit auctor opus.' Perhaps the author's preference is ill advised; had the books had their own way, there might well be the original five before us now.

The conceit of books politely deferring to the literary editorship of their author, all the while intimating that his decision to abridge was questionable, is quite humorous and effective. By separating the work from himself, Ovid could accede with grace to the criticism we infer the first edition received, yet at the same time imply that the critics were wrong. The fact that the books speak is itself startling: loquacious tombstones, statues, chaplets, and locks of hair were common in ancient poetry, but never before, certainly not in elegy, had the 'libelli' spoken for themselves.[46] Even while pruning them, Ovid accords his volumes a singlular honour, which makes their hinted-at difference with him all the more witty and pointed.

In the end, of course, Ovid and his books are one; far from being ashamed of them, Ovid is utterly proud. His poems, for all their lubricity, are not nugatory; despite the numerous conventional laments over the lightness of the pentameter, Ovid never in his amatory poetry calls his elegies trifles ('nugae') or playthings ('lusi').[47] The slightest of the *Amores* proclaims its self-conscious artistry, for even the epigram, as any Roman with the rudiments of rhetoric would have recognized, introduces the collection by cunningly masking its faults.

According to the author of the *Rhetroica ad Herennium*, the most appropriate exordium to a cause depends on the nature of that cause, whether it is honourable, discreditable, doubtful, or petty.[48] There are two kinds of Introduction: the Direct Opening ('principium'), in Greek called the 'prooemium,' and the Subtle Approach, called the 'ephodos.' The purpose of the Direct Opening is 'to enable us to have hearers who are attentive, receptive and well disposed' (I, iv. 6); the *ad Herennium* approves its use for all causes except the discreditable.[49] If, for example, our cause is doubtful, that is, partly honourable and partly discreditable, which is, in fact, the pose Catullus adopts in his dedication, then to obtain the audience's good will a prooemium is recommended in which one may discuss, among other things, one's own person, provided that 'we praise our services without arrogance ... and likewise if we set forth our disabilities ...' (I, v. 8).[50] This again seems a fair summary of Catullus's method: to a rhetorician, his introductory poem would seem a finished example of the Direct Opening.

If, however, one's cause is discreditable ('turpe'), or the audience has been won over by previous speakers, or has been wearied by listening to what has already been said, the Subtle Approach is called for.[51] On all three accounts, Ovid would have found the appeal of the 'insinuatio' irresistible. The subject matter of the *Amores* would definitely strike some as disreputable; at the beginning of the second book, Ovid gaily admits the charge by telling the crabbed upright who will take offence to go away:

> Hoc quoque composui Paelignis natus aquosis
> ille ego nequitiae Naso poeta meae;
> hoc quoque iussit Amor; procul hinc, procul este, seueri:
> non estis teneris apta theatra modis.

This also I have composed, I, Naso, born among the watery Paeligni, that poet of my own worthless ways. This also Love ordered: get you hence, you stern and severe. You are not a fit audience for delicate strains.   (II, i: 1–4)

But at the head of his collection, before he can be sure of his audience, Ovid would want to cultivate their consideration and good will. Augustus's attempts to legislate morality might well have disposed those who heard Ovid to view his ribaldry more dimly than that of his predecessors: the wit with which this difficulty is dodged is just the counterbalancing touch of ingenuity Ovid would need to emphasize, and the more understanding delighted to see. To the censorious, the epigram might seem to imply that the naughtier sections of the first edition had been pruned; to those who enjoyed the bravado of the original five books, the epigram might seem to announce a subtle counter-challenge, a retraction in which one suspects very little will be retracted. Either reader will be attentive, if not fully well disposed; neither, I think could resist the temptation to read further.

Besides the immodesty of his subject matter, however, Ovid's belatedness as elegist gave him equally compelling reasons to use the Subtle Approach. Following as he does Gallus, Tibullus, and Propertius, Ovid knew his work would be derivative and run the risk of redundancy; would an audience respond to him which Propertius had already moved? Or, a question even more pressing for the poet: would the reading public out of sheer surfeit, not bother at all to read yet another account of one more lover's amorous doings? As Martial says, 'non scribit, cuius carmina nemo legit / he doesn't write whose poems no one reads.'[52]

In true rhetorical fashion, Ovid's epigram speaks obliquely to both concerns, chiefly by distracting our attention from them. 'If the hearers have been fatigued by listening,' the ad Herennium advises that we 'open with something that may provoke laughter' (I, vi. 9).[53] A list of eighteen means of provoking laughter then follows, some of which include irony, ambiguity, banter, a pun, or an unexpected turn. Ovid's humorous epigram has something of all of these; we smile, and are beguiled into reading further. In contrast to Catullus, then, the introduction to the Amores seems to be an example of the Subtle Approach. What is simple and charming is also full of innuendo and implication. Why, a rhetorician might have asked, would this poet who knew quite well the techniques of persuasion, begin his volume with an elegant 'insinuatio' if what follows has nothing scurrilous or discreditable about it?[54] The wit of Ovid's epigram has its serious side as well: as much as Catullus, it creates its audience even as it makes itself independent of them, appearing humble even as it affirms its own worth. Ovid has in fact gone beyond Catullus in making his poetry seem independent even of him.

But what is really new and remarkable about Ovid's introductory and programmatic poems is the way they manipulate their audience. Just when we think our inclinations have been gracefully deferred to, we are defined, delimited, in effect made a character in what we will read. Ovid's apparent humility may make us placable and well disposed, and our delight in his wit can certainly make us feel witty and delightful ourselves, but our inclusion in his audience reveals to us our ruling disposition: we are gayer, less captious, younger, more sophisticated than most: in a word cultured, and as such, proleptic enunciators of the authorial voice.[55] For these are precisely the traits we will discover in the Ovid who speaks the *Amores*. Indeed, this collocation of poet and audience is implicit in the epigram. Ovid doesn't address us, his books do, and what they say is directed as much to Ovid as to us. We are both audience. If our response to the *Amores* seems our own, we shall have to remember that it has been carefully anticipated, even to the point of having been predetermined. And the fact that Ovid makes us so charming might have much to do with why he was so immediately popular among his Roman readers.

It is necessary to stress again that this sort of pre-conditioning of the audience is the result both of rhetoric and something beyond rhetoric. As we have seen, from at least Aristotle on, orators were advised to base their arguments not on 'any and every premise that may be recognized as true, but from opinions of a definite sort – the opinions of the audience, or else the opinions of authorities they accept' (II, 22).[56] Persuasion must begin with what an audience already feels: the speaker will either encourage advantageous preconceptions or try to overcome harmful prejudices. Through his art, the orator gradually seeks to make his listeners party to his feelings, impressing on them the stamp of his character as he speaks.

This is not quite the same thing as what Ovid does. In the *Amores*, the thoughts, emotions, indeed the character of the audience are not only presumed, but are to a certain extent prefabricated. When Ovid began to prepare his second edition, public response to the *Amores* was a matter of record. Ovid could, therefore, employ oratorical techniques to persuade now those who had been critical before. The manner in which the epigram does service as a species of Subtle Introduction is, I think, a step in this direction.

But although Ovid may have thought as a rhetorician, he wrote as a poet. Those critical reactions to his poetry are not challenged, pleaded with, or cajoled; they are simply changed, made a priori to feel the effects of persuasion by fiat of the imagination. A new group, witty, in love, and lovers of Ovid's poetry, has been given its voice. There are, in fact, two audiences of the *Amores*, which sometimes overlap, sometimes are tangential. One was actual, the reading public, as well as those smaller private gatherings of good friends, the 'dulcia convictus membra ... mei' Ovid read and listened to.[57] The other is fictional, the audience created for the second edition of the *Amores*, the audience which speaks in Ovid's voice:

> ... me legat in sponsi facie non frigida uirgo
> et rudis ignoto tactus amore puer;
> atque aliquis iuuenum, quo nunc ego, saucius arcu
> agnoscat flammae conscia signa suae
> miratusque diu 'quo' dicat 'ab indice doctus
> conposuit casus iste poeta meos?'

For my readers I want the girl not cold at the sight of her promised lover's face, and the untaught boy touched by love for the first time. And let some youth who is wounded by the same bow as I am now know in my lines the signs of his own flames, and, long wondering, say, 'From what tell-tale has this poet learned, that he has put in verse my own misadventures?' (II, i: 5–10)

This specially chosen audience is not limited to infatuated youngsters: in it as well are those cultured sophisticates who appreciate Ovid's artistry. Once again, the emotions of these adolescent Romans are anticipated and given their shape by the words of the poem. Ovid insists that the youth's passion and his verse are coeval and, ultimately, interchangeable. Any young lover can relive his or her experience by reading the *Amores*. This is essentially the stance of Propertius, who says at the end of his first elegy

> quod si quis monitis tardas adverterit aures,
> heu referet quanto verba dolore mea!

For if any should turn his ears too late to my warning, ah! with how much pain will he repeat my words. (I, i: 37–8)

But Ovid goes further. Ovid's verse, rather than the persona of Ovid's lover, claims universality: only by referring to it will the boy's particular passion seem valid and real. The individual reactions or feelings of any member of the external audience are made to seem like 'high shadows on the screen of categories,' to adopt W.K. Wimsatt's fine phrase about the imagery of Samuel Johnson.[58] In effect, individuality of any sort has been eliminated: the youth's response, as well as his experience, are not so much his own, as subjunctive, contingent for their articulation upon Ovid's poetry: 'quo ... ab indice doctus / conposuit casus iste poeta meos?' And in Ovid, as we shall see, articulation is the final reality, the object of all representation. We know nothing of what the youth did or felt except that it has been expressed in Ovid's perfect elegiac couplet. The form of our experience in love, and Ovid's, is the love poetry he writes.

This fundamental conceit, that the poetry itself is not accidental, a reflection of the private experiences of that native of Sulmo, P. Ovidius Naso, in Rome, but essential, generic, prior to any personal encounter with love, is the principal fiction of the *Amores*. It is also what is most poetical, the thing most 'made' in the work, and what distinguishes it most from rhetoric. In order to authenticate its claims, however, the *Amores* must forswear mimesis, must refuse to imitate the reality, particular or universal, of nature and experience. Beyond Corinna's torn locks, beyond the poet's self-aware laments outside her door, Ovid will strive to represent his own poetry's artifice, for by making the incidents of the *Amores* commonplaces of elegiac tradition, Ovid can suggest, through subtle self-reference and allusion, that his reworking is not the copy but the model of all the others.

In this regard, the elegies of Propertius, whose concerns and techniques were closest to Ovid, are again instructive. The nervous energy and tension of Propertius's poems in large part springs from the confrontation of two irreconcilable forces: the poet's fervent desire that Cynthia be the ideal woman and their companionship the pattern of all love, and the immutable fact of Cynthia's infidelity, with the anger and despair it causes. In portraying particular incidents, Cynthia asleep, for example, or Cynthia at Baiae, Propertius could represent the universal quality of what he feels. By his actions and responses, a 'dispositio amantis' is revealed, the form and anatomy, as it were, of any love.[59]

In Ovid, however, the figure of the lover takes second place to the verse that describes his experience. Consider again the line in which Ovid asks the youth to acknowledge the passion of his verse: 'agnoscat flammae conscia signa suae.' A strange metamorphosis occurs here: not only does the youth's identity begin to be lost in Ovid's, Ovid's begins to coalesce with his poetry. The import of the line is clear enough – let the youth recognize when reading me the signs of his own passion – but a literal translation of the line is more difficult. Perhaps something like 'let the youth recognize the signs of his flames, signs I know and share with him' comes close, but the connotations of 'conscius,' 'to know in common,' 'to participate,' 'to bear witness to,' 'to conspire with,' are too great to convey except in extended paraphrase. Similarly it is impossible to recapture in English the remarkable blending and balancing of meaning and diction Ovid achieves by chiastically surrounding 'conscia signa' with 'flammae ... suae.' The passion delineated here is simultaneously the youth's, Ovid the poet's, and the verse's.

But certainly the most striking thing about the line is the artificiality of the passion itself. Few readers would have failed to recognize the allusion to the words that introduce the most famous love story in Latin literature, Dido's 'agnosco veteris vestigia flammae / I know the signs of the old flame.'[60] Here, where Ovid offers his readers what purports to be a mirror of their own experience, we find not an instance of Ovid's own ardour, but an allusion to Virgil.[61] As speaker Ovid would liken himself to Aeneas, whose words excite his listeners till they, like Dido, recognize the signs of their own love. As poet, Ovid at the same time advances his claim that he is the Virgil and his collection the *Aeneid* of Elegy, a contention we shall see implicitly maintained throughout the first poem of the second book of the *Amores*.[62] As a result, youth, speaker, audience, and book alike all seem to have become pawns in a poetic strategy whose object is the exaltation of Ovid's verse. But even as the poetry aspires to the condition of epideictic oratory, its characters and audience, figures we were ready to invest with a local habitation and a name, become airy nothing: they cease to be the objects of attention, becoming instead the means by which Ovid represents his own artistic accomplishment. For how could Virgil, Dido, Aeneas, Ovid, a 'rudis puer,' and 'uirgo non frigida' be implicated in the same passion unless the 'forma,' the character of that passion has somehow been represented? Love in the *Amores* is literary; those who feel it become poetic creations. By design Ovid would claim he's most original precisely where he seems to be most derivative.

This is why the books themselves speak the epigram, and why Ovid's programmatic poems, unlike those of Propertius and Tibullus, are so preoccupied with writing and literature. This is why so many situations in the *Amores* are completely conventional; it is also why readers of the *Amores* have often felt the lack of intimacy, the absence of a deeply felt passion, which we so value in a Catullus or Propertius. Given the nature of their subject, the elegists would tend toward the personal, but the *Amores*, as Hemann Fränkel has said, are 'the Story of Love ... the comprehensive image of what a young man's existence is like when it is dominated by a passionate attachment.'[63] That image, however, is not drawn from life as much as it is from literature; its character is the style of a state of being.

'To forge in the smithy of his soul the uncreated conscience of his race': Joyce recognized a kindred craftsman in Ovid, and it is not accidental that a line from the *Metamorphoses*, 'et ignotas animum dimittit in artes / And he turns his mind to unknown arts,' stands as the epigraph to *A Portrait of the Artist as a Young Man*.[64] In many ways, Joyce's title could be the epigraph to the *Amores*. To make the correspondence more exact, however, one might read 'A Portrait of the Passion as a Young Man,' or 'A Portrait of the Artifice as a Young Man.'

Propertius's elegies emphatically begin with Cynthia, his love, and the inspiration of his genius:

> Cynthia prima suis miserum me cepit ocellis
> contactum nullis ante cupidinibus.

Cynthia, woe is me, first seized me with her eyes: I had never felt passion till then.   (I, i: 1–2).

The *Amores*, however, begin with an account of how they came to be written, with an allusion, rather than with a lover:

> Arma graui numero uiolentaque bella parabam
> edere, materia conueniente modis.

Arms and violent wars in weighty numbers I was making ready to sound forth, the matter suiting itself to the metre.   (I, i: 1–2)[65]

The recall of the opening line of the *Aeneid* is blatant, as if Ovid were embarking on a work that would rival Virgil's. The inference is warranted, for with this, the first of many references to Virgil in the *Amores*, Ovid introduces a constant motif we have already seen repeated in the first poem of the second book: to write of the war of love is to write the love epic. The earlier elegists drew the traditional comparison between lover and warrior. Ovid also plays with the likeness, especially in I, ix, but always translates the battle into literary terms as well.

Virgil, however, is not the only poetic rival; in the first pentameter Ovid playfully nods to Horace, chief spokesman for 'convenientia' in poetry.[66] The subject matter of this first poem, Ovid's consternation at Cupid's intervention in his epic, is actually a discussion of stylistic impropriety. Love's foray into measures suited for 'tristia bella' violates all sense of decorum:[67] it would be as if Venus were to ply Minerva's bow, or Minerva luxuriate on Venus's couch (I, i: 7–8). The incompatibility would be like that of Horace's painter:

> Humano capiti cervicem pictor equinam
> iungere si velit, et varias inducere plumas
> undique collatis membris, ut turpiter atrum
> desinat in piscem mulier formosa superne,
> spectatum admissi risum teneatis, amici?

If a painter wished to join the neck of a horse to a human head, and to spread feathers of many colours over limbs picked up now here, now there, so that what at the top is a lovely women ends below in a black fish, could you, my friends, permitted to see such a thing, keep from laughing? (*Ars Poetica*, 1–5)

Later in Ovid's poem, Cupid remedies the situation by giving the poet a subject fit for lighter numbers: '"quod" que "canas, uates, accipe," dixit, "opus" / "Receive, o bard, the matter which you will sing," he said,' but Ovid has already alerted us that in his elegies, style will take precedence over content. Indeed, the style is the matter. We still do not know with whom Ovid has fallen in love, nor do we learn her name before the fifth poem. The point seems clear: Ovid falls in love with poetry before he falls in love with Corinna.[68]

All this is done, of course, with that special cheek and humour which so distinguish Ovid's verse. To suborn the high seriousness of the most eminent Augustans with wit enough to excuse the offence, to engage Virgil in laughing poetic rivalry, all the while maintaining the artistry of his verse: these are surprising motifs to find in the first poem of a book called *Amores*, the poem in which we expect the poet to declare his love. How much more surprising, then, to find that this poem so preoccupied with establishing its status as literature has been cast as a 'recusatio,' a poem in which the poet ponders, in Horace's words, 'what his shoulders should refuse, and what they may bear.[69]

The 'recusatio' was the ancient forerunner of that widespread phenomenon in medieval poetry which Curtius calls the 'modesty topos.' Callimachus, reacting to a proliferation of tedious, wooden epics, seems to have invented the concept: in the prologue to his *Aitia*, he refuses to write a long continuous poem that deals with kings and heroes and shop-worn myths. Apollo, Callimachus claims, has commanded him to keep his Muse thin, and to sing for those who love not the braying of asses but the shrill voice of the cicada.[70] In Rome, however, Virgil, Horace, and even Propertius refashioned these ideas, whose occasion, import, and concern were exclusively artistic, in a way that, as Gordon Williams says, would have disgusted their Alexandrian precursor.[71] The Latin poets similarly regret that their poor talents cannot rise to great subjects, but these are not the Trojan War and old tales from mythology, but the events of recent Roman history, particularly the deeds of Augustus. Nothing could be more foreign to Callimahus than the political bais of such an attitude.

With characteristic cunning, Ovid returns the 'recusatio' to its original provenance. The sublime heights Cupid disallows the poet are hardly the recent events of Roman history, although the phrase 'arma ... violentaque bella' is ambiguous enough to hint at the Civil Wars. In light of the allusion to the *Aeneid*, one would more likely think of the Trojan War and its aftermath, but this tried subject again is not what Ovid will refuse to write about.[72] Rather, Cupid's theft deprives us of the splendour of what would have been Ovid's epic:

> cum bene surrexit uersu noua pagina primo,
> attenuat neruos proximus ille meos.

With the first verse the new page began well; that next one, by your doing, vitiates the vigour of my work.   (I, i: 17–18).

As in Callimachus, Ovid's refusal is purely a literary statement, but unlike Callimachus, Ovid pictures himself already engaged on the epic divine interference now prevents him from completing.[73] And this is no trot-work of some hellenistic hack; as Ovid implies, an epic, had he written it, certainly would have been worth reading. In any case, Ovid intimates that neither he nor his reader will in fact sacrifice anything, since the work Love now charges him to write in lieu of an epic is, as we have seen, the epic of elegies. When Ovid objects to Cupid's invasion into his poetry by saying 'Pieridum uates, non tua, turba sumus / We bards are the Muses' company, not yours,' he significantly designates himself (for the second time in the poem) a 'vates,' a member of that almost priest-like fraternity of poets devoted to the Muses. The word 'vates' was an archaic term Virgil and Horace resurrected to confer a sense of dignity, seriousness, and prophetic importance to the poet's utterance.[74] Ovid shares in the pride, the near arrogance of this novel conception of the poet's place and function in society. He too would write of great deeds; certainly he has no intention of dallying in something so low as love.

Or so it would seem. When he receives his mission from Cupid, the god himself, as we have seen, calls Ovid 'uates': ' "quod" que "canas, uates, accipe" dixit "opus." ' Is this mere pretentiousness, Ovid deflating the pomposity of his great predecessors through mockery by association? Partly it is, but this poet is most happy when he can take what he seems to refuse. Ovid also appropriates for himself the artistic gravity and pre-eminence claimed by the vatic Augustans, elevating love poetry to the same position as epic or poems of political consequence. As much as any ode, each of the *Amores*, Ovid seems to claim, will be worthy of the Muse.

This is perhaps the reason why so much space and effort in the next poem, *Amores* I, ii, is given to 'Amor Triumphator,' to a mock triumph of Love that is replete with political overtones. As the poem unfolds, we see that in Ovid, cause is made to follow effect: having been commanded to write love poetry, the poet is now in love:

> Esse quid hoc dicam, quod tam mihi dura uidentur
> strata, neque in lecto pallia nostra sedent,
> et uacuus somno noctem, quam longa, peregi,
> lassaque uersati corporis ossa dolent?

What shall I say this means, that the couch seems so hard to me, and the blankets will not stay on the bed, and I pass the whole night long without sleep, and the weary bones of my body ache from tossing and turning? (I, ii: 1–4)

Ovid's uncertainty here is humorous; hardly smitten by the passion that overwhelms Propertius, the poet passes his feelings in review under the calm scrutiny of reason.[75] Surely he'd know if it were love, or is love a cunning god, who works, like Ovid, 'tecta … arte,' with concealed art (5–6)? This must be the answer, Ovid convinces himself, and so, because love is so overpowering in Gallus, Tibullus, and Propertius, Ovid *decides* his love is as well:

> sic erit: haeserunt tenues in corde sagittae,
> et possessa ferus pectora uersat Amor.

That will be it: the subtle arrows have fixed themselves in my heart, and Love torments the breast he possesses. (7–8)

The previous equivocation renders these sentiments exaggerated and a pretence, a parody of the passion that traditionally seized the elegiac lover. But Ovid does more than offer a burlesque of love and its effects; he subordinates the humour to his art. Throughout the poem, falling in love, accepting his 'servitium,' has been expressed as a skirmish beween reason and desire, a battle the poet, of course, is only too happy to decide in desire's favour. Following the remarkably intellectual realization that he is in love, Ovid first coolly adduces three well-balanced illustrations which demonstrate the advisability of surrendering to love (11–16), and then capitulates unconditionally (17–22). In the second half of the poem (23–48), Ovid describes Love's triumphant procession through Rome, Amor as Caesar leading his conquered foes, Mens Bona and Pudicitia, their hands tied behind their backs, and displaying his weapons, Blanditia, Error, and Furor. It is true, as John Barsby says, that the military metaphors of Ovid's surrender neatly anticipate the subsequent triumph.[76] But beyond the local relevance, the military imagery ought to remind us that in this poem love is a species of war, and the elegy that describes it a mock epic. The bipartite structure of the poem reflects its theme; as if arrayed in opposing camps, the first twenty-two lines describe Ovid's deliberations whether he should yield to love, the next twenty-six the consequences of his surrender. Even within the first half of the elegy there is balanced conflict between the intellect and the emotions: the opening description of the poet's emotional condition (1–4) is followed by his questioning analysis of the situation (5–6); the decision that he is in love ('sic erit': 7) is followed in the same couplet by a report of the depth of his feeling. The three epigrammatic exempla that follow are not merely instances of Ovid's fondness for witty paradox; the very dispassion with which they examine a supposedly consuming emotion is the poem's point. Nor is the actual description of the triumph an example of over-elaboration, of Ovid's not knowing when to stop. Besides being an attempt at sustained description, so important a feature of Virgil's epic style, the sheer length of the account stands as a narrative analogy to the immensity of love's power.[77] Everywhere in this poem about falling in love, instead of intensity we find measure and equipoise, an art that represents love not as felt experience but as literary metaphor. Love battles against reason – such is the elegiac tradition – and although Amor seems to carry the day, *Amores* I, ii really bears witness to art's triumph.

Experience in the *Amores*, then, is always poetic experience; this has, of course, been said before, as often to accuse Ovid of insincerity as to admire his brilliance as a parodist. Yet in a work so concerned with art, we ought to take seriously Ovid's own pretensions to art. The final couplet of *Amores* I, ii is a witty, political joke:

> aspice cognati felicia Caesaris arma:
> qua uicit, uictos protegit ille manu.

Consider the fortunate battles of your kinsman Caesar: he protects the conquered by the hand with which he conquered them. (51–2)[78]

Augustus is Cupid's kinsman since as a member of the Julian family his line stems from Iulus, son of Aeneas, whose mother, Venus, was Cupid's mother as well. Beyond the audacity of this wit, however, beyond the paradox, striking in itself, of the appeal for protection from the hands of the conquerer, stands Ovid's seemingly unabashed intention of incorporating the politics of contemporary Rome into his love poetry. The *Amores*, Ovid appears to announce, are my Roman Elegies, my *Carmen Seculare*. If the parody seems subversive, it nevertheless is completely characteristic. It could be, as E.J. Kenney has argued in a different context, that Ovid mocks not so much Horace and Virgil as his own pretensions.[79] But Ovid's humility often seems the cutting edge of his pride: witness the epigram. The 'arma Caesaris,' as we have seen, were considered subjects only the highest poetry was fit to describe. By alluding to Augustus's lineage the way he does, Ovid encourages his reader to recall the founding of Rome, which few Romans would do without thinking of the *Aeneid*. The literary challenge sounded in the first poem is reissued here; politics, like everything else in the *Amores*, becomes only a pretext for poetry.

The epigram and first two poems of the *Amores* define the character of the work and the character of the persona who is its central subject. The book is itself a character, we must realize, whose disposition, in the Aristotelian sense, naturally enough is bookishness. This may seem an arid tautology – Ovid has been regularly accused of being a most tautological poet – but Ovid gathered many benefits from making convention its own virtue. The idea, first of all, is strikingly original, something that immediately separates the *Amores* from Tibullus and Propertius, even though reliance on earlier models had always been a common feature of Latin poetry. Never before had the Book, had Art spoken in its own voice; only in Ovid could Elegia and Tragoedia dispute each other's claim to the poet's voice (III, i). Furthermore, the whimsy of the idea is designed to enchant; just the sort of thing to delight a Roman public that, in Sandys's phrase, 'relieved from the fears, and inevitably disappointed of some hopes, which had been excited by the great revolution, desired chiefly to be entertained and amused.'[80] But the book qua character is as well a poetic strategy that allows Ovid his measure of seriousness. The reader becomes concerned not only with the lover, who himself is a parody, but also with the art of the *Amores*, about which Ovid is fully earnest. The puffed-up pretentiousness, 'l'esprit et l'humour chez Ovide,' to use the title of Frécaut's book, in this respect is subtle and devious, the kind of laughter a rhetorician would try to evoke.[81] Nothing can belie great aspirations more than making light of them:

> Mantua Vergilio gaudet, Verona Catullo;
> Paelignae dicar gloria gentis ego,
>
> ...
>
> atque aliquis spectans hospes Sulmonis aquosi
> moenia, quae campi iugera pauca tenent,
> 'quae tantum' dicet 'potuistis ferre poetam,
> quantulacumque estis, uos ego magna uoco.'

Mantua rejoices in Virgil, Verona in Catullus; I shall be called the glory of the Paelignians ... and some stranger, pondering the walls of watery Sulmo, which guard the few acres of her plain, will say, 'O you who were able to beget such a poet, however small you are, I call you great.'   (III, xv: 7–8; 11–14)[82]

Certainly there is a large element of bravado in this self-assessment, but who will say the prophecy that concludes the *Amores* is uttered with anything less than full conviction?

> inbelles elegi, genialis Musa, ualete,
> post mea mansurum fata superstes opus.

Unwarlike elegies, genial Muse, farewell, work that shall endure after I am no more. (III, xv: 19–20)

Propertius ends his first book with a declaration of who he is, his rank and lineage, his place of birth. Ovid ends his with a declaration of the immortality of his poetry:

> ergo etiam cum me supremus adederit ignis,
> uiuam, parsque mei multa superstes erit.

Therefore, even when the last flames have devoured me, I shall live, and the great part of me shall endure. (I, xv: 39–40)

In Ovid's restatement, poetry occupies the place the poet held in Propertius; the poem's the thing Ovid celebrates in all its shades and nuances.

The lover of the *Amores* is equally literary in that he is a poet, and the situations he relates, as well as his reactions, are almost entirely determined by literary tradition. In the second poem, for instance, we have seen the poet gaily welcoming the 'servitium' of love, an emotional enslavement which caused Propertius such anguish. The tone here and wherever the lover loves is light-hearted; in the place of passionate involvement there is a fondness for ingenuity and paradox. The lover is, as many have described him, a parody of the lover in earlier elegiac poetry. Thus we find witty innovations or reversals of commonplace motifs: a 'paraclausithyron' (I, vi), in which the doorkeeper, rather than the door itself, is addressed; a poem, the so-called 'propemptikon' (II, xi), expressing Ovid's dread at the prospect of Corinna going to sea, and his joyful relief on her safe return (II, xii). Of course, when the parallel situation occurs in Propertius, the poet himself is the one who sets sail (I, 17). At no time does Ovid even hint that he shares Propertius's devotion:

> seu mare per longum mea cogitet ire puella,
> hanc sequar, et fidos una aget aura duos.

Or should my love think to sail great stretches of sea, I will follow her, and one breeze shall propel two faithful ones. (Propertius, II, xxviA: 29–30)

On the contrary, it is Ovid's own fear of the sea that gives his poem its life. He may say his heart grows faint with concern for Corinna, but we know neither she, the gods, nor Love itself could move his cold feet from solid ground:

> sero respicitur tellus, ubi fune soluto
> currit in inmensum panda carina salum

Too late do you look back at the land, once the cable has been untied, and the curved keel rushes out to the immense deep. (II, xi: 23–4)

The shiver is almost audible as the 'panda carina' is nearly swallowed by the surrounding 'inmensum ... salum.'

Similarly, Ovid must give us his lament on the death of Corinna's parrot (II, vi, with apologies to Catullus), and his reproaches of Corinna now that her hair has fallen out because she treated it with too much dye (I, xiv: compare Propertius I, ii, II, xviiiB, and Tibullus I, viii). In every case, where other poets communicate an emotion, from which we can deduce the character of the speaker, Ovid presents a burlesque, emotions divorced from feelings, sorrow without grief, anger without resentment. In consequence, the lover in the *Amores* lacks character, in the sense that no passion seems to dominate him the way desire and despair dominate Propertius. Ovid's lover, in short, is a voice, more an echo of sensation than a fictional incarnation of it and its effects: a remarkable figure to cast as the protagonist of a collection of love poetry.

Yet the voice we hear in the *Amores* is nothing if not bright, charming, urbane, and polished; this voice, however, is not the lover's, but the poet's. It is, of course, something of a sophistry to separate the lover from the poet; even when Ovid seems most emotional, the event is described with poetic detachment. Ovid's elegies are almost entirely monologues: Corinna never speaks,[83] and the other briefly heard voices belong to conventions (the 'lena' Dipsas in I, viii, the augur in III, v), to personifications (Cupid in I, i, Tragoedia and Elegia in III, i, and the rivers in III, vi), or to characters in Tibullus's poetry (Delia and Nemesis in III, ix). The range and verisimilitude in Propertius is much greater: Cynthia is independent enough to utter her own accusations (I, iii), and we hear the voices of Roman lovers (I, vii), mariners (I, viii), and friends (II, xxiv). Ovid's monotone rendering of all experience does have its point: it is precisely this curious union of aloofness and participation that makes the *Amores* uniquely universal. When Ovid's lover describes a noon-time assignation (I, v), or the remorse that followed a fit of insane madness, during which he struck Corinna (I, vii), we respond less to his passion than to how it has been managed. We recognize the theatricality of the setting in the first poem, the staged hyperbole of the raving in the second, and delight in the robust wit that has revitalized tired fare with such élan. Consider the setting of *Amores* I, v, a poem often praised for the sincerity of its atempt to portray a genuine experience.[84] Ovid clearly wishes to create a 'sylvan scene' in his bedroom:

> Aestus erat, mediamque dies exegerat horam;
> …
> pars adaperta fuit, pars altera clausa fenestrae,
> quale fere siluae lumen habere solent,
> qualia sublucent fugiente crepuscula Phoebo
> aut ubi nox abiit nec tamen orta dies

It was sultry, and the day had passed its middle hour … One window shutter was opened, the other closed – just the kind of light woods often have, the kind of twilight that glimmers when the sun sets, or when night has gone but day has not yet arisen.   (I, v: 1, 3–6)

Charles Segal has demonstrated that midday heat was considered dangerous in pastoral. Through the figure of Menaclas, for instance, Virgil suggests in the fifth eclogue that, as Segal puts it, 'song can conquer the *aestus* of midday heat as part of the ultimate triumph of art and spirit over passion and violence.'[85] Ovid agrees, yet turns Virgil's moral inside out by practising a kind of pathetic fallacy in which the proper literary setting is made to reflect his own feelings. The scene has exchanged bucolic simplicity for urban intrigue. Like his rustic counterpart, Ovid feels a passion of violent propensity; thus he rips Corinna's dress from her. But unlike Menaclas, Ovid has no wish to substitute his art for his desire; instead he will consummate his desire through his art. We are engaged not by the quality of the passion, but by the artifice that prompted it. In the *Amores*, particulars of any sort, emotions, Corinna herself, are significant only in so far as they provide the opportunity for the poet's sophisticated reworking of conventional occasions and responses.

The poet and the book are the most complex characters in the *Amores*. Indeed, they are the only characters who matter: Corinna, about whom so much has been written, seems loved less as a person than as the occasion for Ovid's poetry about her. Her status as real or fictional creature ultimately is beside the point: why else would Ovid delay her entrance until the fifth poem? The first two poems of the collection, as we have seen, are concerned with the art of writing love poetry; the third appears to be a monologue the poet rehearses to himself, in which he enumerates his merits.[86] Naturally enough, chief among them is the fact that he is a poet: how should a poet woo except by his poetry?

> nos quoque per totum pariter cantabimur orbem
> iunctaque semper erunt nomina nostra tuis.

We as well shall be sung in like manner throughout the world, and my name shall be joined to yours forever. (I, iii: 25–6)

Unfortunately, the company Ovid promises Corinna will join includes Io, Europa, and Leda: three women violently raped, famous more for their subsequent suffering than for their happiness in love. These women have been chosen less for any likeness they may bear to Corinna than for Ovid's own self-aggrandizement: he fancies himself a second Zeus, granting through his poetry immortal fame to himself and anyone else he chooses.[87] The elegy advertises itself, not Corinna. Not a word has been uttered to this point in praise of her beauty, her grace, her charm, or her manners; to Ovid, the means, the how-to, the poetry of love is more important than the possession of any particular woman.

This is perhaps the reason why in the fourth poem we learn the lady has a 'vir.' Much has been said about his status as well, but whether husband or merely another lover, the significant fact about him is that he is an obstacle.[88] Yet this man is not vilified so much as he is made the excuse for a small 'ars amatoria.' The joy and subject of *Amores* I, iv is not Corinna or love, but methods of deception, which in the course of the work comes to be almost synonymous with love.[89] Thus when in the next poem Corinna finally does appear by name, she has been trifled with and ignored to such an extent that Ovid must introduce her with a rhetorical flourish:

> ecce, Corinna uenit tunica uelata recincta,
> candida diuidua colla tegente coma,
> qualiter in thalamos formosa Sameramis isse
> dicitur ét multis Lais amata uiris.

Behold, Corinna comes, dressed in loosened tunic, with her parted hair covering her white neck, just as they say lovely Semiramis looked going to her marriage bed and Lais loved by many men. (I, v: 9–12)

To be associated with the licentious Semiramis and the adulterous Lais does little to benefit Corinna's reputation, but by this time, she must have been grateful for any mention at all. 'Ecce,' behold, indeed: we were wondering when Ovid would ever get to her.

In the last analysis, Corinna is like her lover, a parody, the lady who does not fascinate Ovid nearly as much as his poetry about her does. Unlike Lesbia or Cynthia, Corinna's fatal fault isn't her infidelity; rather it is the fact that she isn't a figure large enough to satisfy all of Ovid's poetic ambitions. Ovid deserts her before she can leave him:

> denique quas tota quisquam probat Vrbe puellas,
> noster in has omnis ambitiosus amor.

For whatever girls anyone praises in all Rome, my love would seek the favours of them all. (II, iv: 47–48)

In the second book of the *Amores*, Ovid often poses as both a Don Juan and an Everylover; for the one, a woman could be no more than an opportunity to display technique, for the other, an idea one can court in a fine romance. Ovid in fact deserts Corinna three times: once when he pursues all the other women in Rome, again when he writes elegies on subjects other than her, and finally when he ceases to write elegy at all. Corinna's real rivals are Elegia and Tragoedia: she certainly ceases to exist for Ovid once limping pentameter has been left behind.

In this regard, we can perhaps see Ovid at his most sophisticated by examining the characterization in a poem I have already quoted in parts, the elegy that introduces the central book of the *Amores*:

> Hoc quoque composui Paelignis natus aquosis
> ille ego nequitiae Naso poeta meae;
> hoc quoque iussit Amor; procul hinc, procul este, seueri:
> non estis teneris apta theatra modis.
> me legat in sponsi facie non frigida uirgo   5
> et rudis ignoto tactus amore puer;
> atque aliquis iuuenum, quo nunc ego, saucius arcu
> agnoscat flammae conscia signa suae
> miratusque diu 'quo' dicat 'ab indice doctus
> conposuit casus iste poeta meos?'   10
> ausus eram, memini, caelestia dicere bella
> centimanumque Gyen (et satis oris erat),
> cum male se Tellus ulta est ingestaque Olympo
> ardua deuexum Pelion Ossa tulit:
> in manibus nimbos et cum Ioue fulmen habebam,   15
> quod bene pro caelo mitteret ille suo.

clausit amica fores: ego cum Ioue fulmen omisi;
excidit ingenio Iuppiter ipse meo.
Iuppitter, ignoscas: nil me tua tela iuuabant;
clausa tuo maius ianua fulmen habet.   20
blanditias elegosque leuis, mea tela, resumpsi:
mollierunt duras lenia uerba fores.
carmina sanguineae deducunt cornua lunae
et reuocant niueos solis euntis equos;
carmine dissiliunt abruptis faucibus angues   25
inque suos fontes uersa recurrit aqua;
carminibus cessere fores, insertaque posti,
quamuis robur erat, carmine uicta sera est.
quid mihi profuerit uelox cantatus Achilles?
quid pro me Atrides alter et alter agent,   30
quique tot errando quot bello perdidit annos,
raptus et Haemoniis flebilis Hector equis?
at facie tenerae laudata saepe puellae
ad uatem, pretium carminis, ipsa uenit.
magna datur merces: heroum clara ualete   35
nomina: non apta est gratia uestra mihi;
ad mea formosos uultus adhibete puellae
carmina, purpureus quae mihi dictat Amor.

This also I have composed, I, Naso, born among the watery Paeligni, that poet of my own worthless ways. This also love ordered: hence, get you hence, you stern and severe, you are not a fit audience for my delicate strains. For my readers I want the girl not cold at the sight of her promised lover's face, and the untaught boy touched by love for the first time. And let any youth who is wounded by the same bow as I now am know in my lines the signs of his own flames, and, long wondering, say, 'From what tell-tale has this poet learned, that he has put in verse my own misadventures?' I had dared, I remember, to sing of celestial wars, and of hundred-handed Gyas – my verse was quite good – when the Earth ill avenged herself, and steep Ossa, hurled with sloping Pelion, was piled on Olympus. I had in hand the storm clouds and the lightning bolt with Jove, which he would hurl for the good of his own heaven. My beloved slammed her door; I let fall the lightning with Jove. Jupiter himself was knocked from my mind. Jupiter, forgive me. Your bolts were of no avail to me: the closed door is a thunderbolt greater than yours. I have taken up again my own bolts: light and charming elegies – gentle words have softened hard doors. Poetry brings down the horns of the blood-red moon, and recalls the snow-white steeds of the setting sun. By poems snakes are split open, their jaws burst apart, and waters rush back to their sources. Doors have yielded to poetry, and the bolt inserted in the post; even though it was oak, the bolt was conquered by poetry. What will it profit me to have sung of swift Achilles? What will the one or the other son of Atreus do for me, or he who lost as many years wandering as in war, or the lamented Hector, dragged by Haemonian horses? But a delicate girl often praised for her beauty comes herself to the poet as reward for his poems. The compensation is great indeed! Farewell, famous names of heroes: your gratitude is not the kind I want. Turn, o girls, your beautiful faces to my poems, which robust Love dictates to me.

Ovid appears in all his guises here, as lover, as poet, and as book. Formally, the poem divides into two sections. In the first, Ovid, identifying himself as much by the salacious nature of his subject as by his birth-place, addresses his audience (1–10).[90] In the second, we learn that Ovid had been writing an epic gigantomachia when his 'amica' shut her door to him: Jupiter and epic were laid aside (11–20). To win her back, Ovid will resume writing elegies, since they can work miracles, including the opening of closed doors (21–8). Epic little profits someone in Ovid's situation, while love poetry gets the girl; therefore farewell epic and welcome elegy (29–38).

In the first couplet of the poem, two voices saying things only slightly different seem to speak at once. Both, of course, are the poet's, but the first speaks subjectively, 'hoc composui ... ego ... Naso,' while the second acknowledges the poet's fame, 'ille ... nequitiae ... poeta meae.' 'Ille' carries resonances that go beyond its primary meaning of 'the well-known ... poet'; there is a hint of independence, of detachment: that poet of the first book of the *Amores*, as opposed to this ('hoc') second. That book, though of the narrator's scandals, has its own destiny; ought it not, by the dictates of logic, to have its own words as well? Book begins to separate from poet here; the line nicely anticipates the complete division between book and poet in the epigram: 'hoc illi praetulit auctor opus.'

That 'ille,' in fact, thrives on ambiguity: it paradoxically implies continuity and disjunction at the same time. Like the epigram, it offers, if for an instant, the chance, however slight, that this book will be less morally offensive than the last. When placed in opposition to 'hoc,' 'ille' can refer to something inferior in degree as well as to something more distant in space: could the poet, who clearly labels his matter 'nequitia,' have recognized his folly and mended his manners? Not at all likely; 'quoque' in the first line argues against it, but by entertaining the hope, however remotely, Ovid will make his subsequent defiance all the more pointed. For in the next couplet, Ovid wears his 'nequitia' like a badge, dispatching his fastidious critics with impunity: 'procul hinc, procul este, seueri.' Ovid first establishes the authority of his own poetry, primarily by referring to himself: with the mention of the deified Amor, the reader is meant to recall the first poem of the *Amores*. He then undercuts Virgil's. 'Procul, o procul este, profani' (VI, 258): these are the famous words the Sibyl shouts to Aeneas and his followers at the mouth of the cave that leads to the underworld. Light raillery replaces awe and solemnity as Ovid refashions himself an Aeneas and those whose morals exclude them from his audience a profane troop unworthy to enter the temple of his poetry. Elegiac poetry, 'tener modus,' elevates itself to the status of sibylline prophecy, an utterance whose implications concerned nothing less than the founding of Rome. The rivalry with Virgil announced in *Amores* I, i is taken up again; nothing has changed. And lest we overlook the quotation from Virgil, in verse eight Ovid quotes again, this time echoing the words of Dido.

Not only in its subject matter, then, but also in its ideas and themes will this second book of the *Amores* resemble the first. And so, the opening poem of each book chronicles the poet's inspiration. Propertius's may be Cynthia, Tibullus's Delia, but Ovid's is Amor, which is to say not Corinna but his own poetry. Ovid certainly had Propertius in mind here, for his predecessor's second book also began with an elaborate disquisition on the source of his poetic genius. Unlike those of Ovid, however, Propertius's many songs of love (Propertius's word is 'amores') were dictated by no deity except his own beloved:

> non haec Calliope, non haec mihi cantat Apollo,
> ingenium nobis ipsa puella facit.

Not Calliope nor Apollo sings these things to me: the girl herself is my genius.   (II, i: 3–4)

This poetic apotheosis of Cynthia was a rather startling innovation on Propertius's part; Ovid seems to return to convention, but instead of a divine woman or Muse, we find parody of epic and allusion to his own celestial poetry. Quintilian has said Ovid was too infatuated by his own wit ('nimium amator ingenii sui'); a perfect description, rather than judgment, of *Amores* II, i.[91]

Part of the charm of this poem undoubtedly springs from the fact that the haughty implications of this first section are at such great odds with the form of the second. As in *Amores* I, i, Ovid again writes a 'recusatio,' always with his witty proviso in mind: 'et satis oris erat.' There is much playful inventiveness in the description of Ovid's turning aside from epic; here is one case of the thunder, Corinna's slamming her door, preceding Jove's lightning. This thunder, however, is rumbling of a special sort. 'Clausit amica fores'!: the sentence, for all its dactylic, alliterative crackling, is, of course, not reportage but a metaphor, a way of saying that the girl denied the poet her favours. Ovid was not at his writing desk when he heard a door banged shut. The crash never actually occurs except in the poetry, yet in the poem it is clothed with the literalness of fact. The verisimilitude of this incident is the verisimilitude of a metaphor, a conventional metaphor at that. Like her door, Corinna's 'being' is less than that of the fiction she appears in: the description of her actions depends less on her feelings or character than on the fact that Ovid had reached that point in his poem where Jove stood poised with his lightning. In this sense, Corinna is like her audience, the 'apta theatra' of line four, whose responses have been made fit by the work they read. All are props, elements of stagecraft, each assigned its role in the production of Ovid's poetry.[92]

When Ovid knits up his elegy, he recalls the opening of the poem. Achilles, Odysseus, all the heroes of Greece and Rome are of little use to him in love: 'heroum clara ualete / nomina; non apta est gratia uestra mihi' (35–6). 'Apta theatra; apta … gratia': the audience, Corinna, the great characters of epic, Ovid as lover himself, all seem reflections of one another, or, to give the figure a slightly Dantesque turn, a circle of mirrors designed to reflect the poetic artifice at the centre. The poem closes with a remarkable request:

> ad mea formosos uultus adhibete puellae
> carmina, purpureus quae mihi dictat Amor.

This is not a simple metonymy in which Ovid refers to himself by his poems. The same bifurcation between poet and book, between literal and metaphoric reality, that we sensed at the poem's beginning is present here. Both the grammatical and the thematic centre of the line is 'carmina'; it is the thing the girls should turn towards and the thing Love dictates. But how can anyone, much less the 'puellae' (the plural is itself surprising), turn her face, beautiful or otherwise, to a poem unless either she is herself like a poem, that is, a fictional creation, or the poem is itself animate and possesses literal sensibilities? The line sanctions both inferences, and through them Ovid defines the character of his poetry: a place where convention and metaphor are real. We resist reading the line literally because the notion it expresses seems absurd. Even Grant Showerman, the Loeb translator, expands the Latin: 'turn hither your beauteous faces as I sing the songs …' But as it stands, the effect of the line is to make Ovid's audience once again characters in his poem.

It may seem naive or oversubtle to take the line at face value, but Ovid's insistence throughout the *Amores* on the autonomy of his poetry persuades me that to do so is neither. *Amores* II, i, after all, is an unabashed celebration of 'blanditias elegosque leuis.' The triple repetition of 'carmen' in successive couplets (23–8), each beginning with a differently declined form of the word (a variation Romans thought quite elegant), extols the virtues of the form, while the following two couplets deprecate the value of epic. And this, we remember, is a 'recusatio'! The tradition, and especially Propertius's expression of it, has been turned on its head. For in the introductory poem to his second book Propertius had said that were it his destiny to write epic, he would not sing of the Titans, 'nor of Ossa piled on Olympus so that Pelion might be a path to heaven' (II, i: 19–20), but of the deeds of Augustus. Ovid's response is clear: not politics but poetry, for poetry is its own 'imperium.'

If asked, therefore, what this 'Programmgedicht' imitates, we would have to say, in the last analysis, itself. Mimesis in the *Amores* is poetic self-reflection: characters seem lifelike in proportion to how metaphorical or conventional they are. The longest poem in the *Amores*, and in many ways one of the most important, is the overheard monologue of the bawd Dipsas. The poem stands in the exact centre of the first book (I, viii); is is often recalled in other poems of the collection. No other character in the *Amores* is described in greater detail, no other character is allowed to speak at such length in her own voice, and no character, including Corinna, arouses in Ovid the same pitch of emotion. Yet Dipsas, of course, is the 'lena,' the go-between come straight from the pages of Menander and the New Comedy, Greek mime, Plautus, Tibullus, and Propertius. Ovid's description of her is purposefully fantastic; as John Barsby says, the poet 'has unmistakably left the world of reality for the world of literary convention.'[93] Precisely the case: yet is there anyone in the *Amores* who seems half as vivid or commanding as Dipsas?

Consider some of the powers Ovid ascribes to the witch:

> illa magas artes Aeaeaque carmina nouit,
> inque caput liquidas arte recuruat aquas;
> ...
> cum uoluit, toto glomerantur nubila caelo;
> cum uoluit, puro fulget in orbe dies.
> sanguine, si qua fides, stillantia sidera uidi;
> purpureus Lunae sanguine uultus erat.

She knows the magic arts and Aeaen spells, and by her art she turns back flowing waters toward their sources ... When she wants, clouds gather over the whole sky; when she wants, the day dazzles in clear heaven. I have seen the stars, believe it or not, dripping with blood; the face of the Moon was ruddy with blood. (I, viii: 5–6; 9–12)

This list is admittedly selective, but the resemblance to the virtues Ovid claims for elegy in II, i is too great to overlook:

> carmina sanguineae deducunt cornua lunae,
> et reuocant niueos solis euntis equos;
> carmine …
> inque suos fontes uersa recurrit aqua   (II, i: 23–4; 26)

And, Ovid adds, his poems, which 'purpureus Amor' dictates, can force the hardest doors to yield. By juxtaposing these poems, we sense that Ovid's intense desire to calumniate Dipsas hardly springs from his disgust at her immorality, greed, or profession, but rather from his chagrin that the procuress has appropriated both the letter and the spirit of his words in her attempt to seduce Corinna:

> haec sibi proposuit thalamos temerare pudicos;
> nec tamen eloquio lingua nocente caret.

This woman has set herself to corrupt a pure marriage; yet her tongue does not lack a pernicious persuasiveness.   (I, viii: 19–20)

Dipsas, in short, is the poet's rival, matching his intent and even his means. All Ovid's contumely, his barefaced charges of supernatural skullduggery, stand as an overwrought prelude to Dipsas's very practical, earthy advice. The poet doth protest too much, as well he might, since he himself follows the precepts of Dipsas's 'ars amatoria' even more than does Corinna. The bawd counsels her charge not to admit infidelity:

> et quasi laesa prior nonnumquam irascere laeso:
> uanescit culpa culpa repensa tua.

Sometimes, when you have wronged him, be angry, as if wronged first. His grievance, countered by yours, fades away.   (79–80)

In the Cypassis poems (II, vii and viii), we see Ovid, not Corinna, translating this advice into action. When Dipsas says poets should be rich, 'surda sit oranti tua ianua, laxa ferenti / let your door be deaf to prayers, but open to the gift-bringer,' we recall not only Ovid's lament at Corinna's door (I, vi), but still more the tenth poem of Book I. Here Corinna seems to have heeded Dipsas's advice, for she has asked Ovid for presents. The effect this has on the poet is devastating:

> Qualis ab Eurota Phrygiis auecta carinis
> coniugibus belli causa duobus erat,

qualis erat Lede, quam plumis abditus albis
callidus in falsa lusit adulter aue,
qualis Amymone siccis errauit in Argis,
cum premeret summi uerticis urna comas,
talis eras: aquilamque in te taurumque timebam
et quicquid magno de Ioue fecit amor.
nunc timor omnis abest animique resanuit error,
nec facies oculos iam capit ista meos.

Such as she was, borne away from the Eurotas on Phrygian ships, the cause of war for two husbands, such as was Leda, whom the cunning adulterer, disguised in white feathers, deceived in the guise of a bird, such as was Amymone, who wandered in dry Argos when the urn pressed the hair on the top of her head, so you were, and for you I feared the eagle and the bull and whatever form love has made mighty Jupiter take. Now all fear is gone and my mind's delusion cured; no longer does that beauty of yours seize my eyes.   (I, x: 1–10)

The gay mockery in deflating the epic dimensions of Ovid's disillusionment is infectious: three similes in full dress just to reflect Ovid's disapproval of his girlfriend's request for a gift. Beyond the bombast, however, Ovid implies that Corinna's mercenary impulses hardly befit a heroine of literature, yet, as we have seen, a literary heroine is exactly what Ovid had promised his verse would make Corinna: 'nos quoque per totum pariter cantabimur orbem' (I, iii: 25). No, Corinna here seems instead to act more like a real person: what Roman courtesan would not ask her lover for some keepsake? But however real her actions may seem, we remember that by asking, Corinna is following the advice of Dipsas, that most stereotypical bawd. There is a strange propriety in Corinna's behaviour: since she does something an epic heroine never would do, she ought to resemble an elegiac rather than an epic prototype, a Dipsas rather than a Helen. In any case, there is little verisimilitude: Ovid either berates Corinna for failing to live up to the literary standards he has imagined for her, or chastises her for associating with characters of the literary demimonde.

But such, alas, are the brazen ways of the world. Ovid recognizes this and so begins his denunciation of feminine cupidity by parading before Corinna the invaluable presents he can give. Ovid's gift is his poetry, and so long as Corinna recognizes its worth, Ovid can second Dipsas's rules:

nec tamen indignum est a diuite praemia posci:
munera poscenti quod dare possit habet.

Yet it isn't unbecoming to ask the rich for presents: he has the gifts he can give to the girl who asks. (I, x: 53–4)

Ovid ends by prostituting his poetry completely; his art out-Dipsases Dipsas in a tour de force of amatory casuistry.

Corinna and the man who loves her are parodies, figures without character; Dipsas a convention who takes her life from her very conventionality. The poet is a more complicated creation, compacted partly of parody, partly of convention, but mostly of art. He is the focal point of our response: all of us and none of us at once. The book he appears in is a character as well, ruled by its own disposition, a vocal embodiment of all the differentia of bookishness. In bald summary, the dramatis personae sound almost as if they were the models of the characters in one of Ring Lardner's nonsense plays. Yet besides the facetiousness and levity, there is purpose and design. Every figure of the *Amores* celebrates the poetry that has made him what he is. Throughout his career, Ovid took his poetry seriously: with how much greater earnestness would he have presented the first work of his youth, the book with which he announced, 'This is a poet'! We do Ovid a disservice if we feel he would have been content only to mock his own pretensions. The *Amores*, and not least through its characters, achieves something more enduring than parody or pretence would allow: the conviction that, despite appearances, love's laughter can be significant if it appears in a true work of art.

2

The Representation of Character in Ovid:
The *Metamorphoses*

As we saw in the last chapter, characterization in the *Amores* is complex. A figure like Corinna, herself a parody, appears in a poem spoken by a narrator we call Ovid, who is her lover. As lover, this Ovid is a parody of the traditional elegiac lover, but the persona has a second aspect as well: Ovid the poet, highly conscious that the amatory situations he finds himself in are commonplaces of literary convention. This figure, it seems, is the 'auctor operis'; after all, the books of the *Amores* hold him responsible for their abridgment. Yet as readers we know that books don't talk, except in metaphor, and that these poems were not written by one of their creations: behind all these fictions stands the historical Ovid, artfully manipulating each.

Something more than fondness for intricacy accounts for this bewilderingly involved concatenation. As we move from subjective to increasingly objective reality, from literature to life, each link in Ovid's chain of awareness authenticates the one it succeeds. Corinna seems more real because her Ovid is a poet, conscious not only of her but of the competing claims of tragedy. She is lent, as it were, a certain sense of presence by association. The poet in turn seems more palpable because his voice is not synonymous with that of his books. The *Amores* exist apart from the poet who says he wrote them, responding directly not only to him, but to the public that reads them as well. And finally, we authenticate the books by the very fact that we hold and read them. But the books we do hold are not the books who are the self-professed speakers of their artificer's fictions: in Ovid, books are characters as well as things. Nor are we the same audience the 'tres libelli' of the epigram address; besides us there is a fictional audience of the *Amores*. Of all Ovid's major figures, only Corinna is a monotype: the narrator is poet and lover, the book fiction and object, the audience character and us. Removed from all these involutions, complex enough to remind one of the *Book of the Duchess* or *A*

Midsummer Night's Dream, stands Ovid the maker. His many surrogates speak, but neither one particular creation nor any congregation of them speaks his voice. With characteristic wit, the Ovid who writes the *Amores* has adopted the distance of an epic poet from his narrative.

None of Ovid's other elegiac works presents nearly so complicated or sophisticated a fictional situation as the *Amores*, primarily because none exploits the possibilities of juxtaposition nearly so well. By artfully arranging poems related to one another more by occasion than by content, the *Amores* suggests narrative unity without sacrificing elegiac individuality. In this Ovid learned much from Propertius, whose three books also seem to chronicle the course of an affair. At first, a number of poems portray through different episodes the poet deeply in love with Cynthia, then abjectly disillusioned by her infidelity, and finally bitterly resigned to his experience. Yet Propertius's poems are in fact a series of discrete incidents, not, for the most part, bound to each other by causal or logical connections. Because associations are only intimated, not articulated, each reader is relatively free to furnish the temporal or other links he will. This is why those who have laboured to establish the chronology of Propertius's liaison with Cynthia have built structures that rest ultimately on their own inferences, and why those who place one or another of the *Amores* in the first or second edition argue what cannot be proved.[1] Both Propertius and Ovid beguile their readers into filling the gaps between elegies, into establishing a continuity the poets themselves thought it unnecessary to provide. *Amores* I, v, a joyful midday mingling in love, ends with Ovid's fond hope for many more days that will match this: 'proueniant medii sic mihi saepe dies!' *Amores* III, v, a solitary nighttime premonition of Corinna's adulterous betrayal, ends with Ovid waking into metaphorical darkness and death: 'gelido mihi sanguis ab ore / fugit et ante oculos nox stetit alta meos / The blood fled from my frozen face, and profound night stood before my eyes' (45–6). By arranging these poems in analogous positions, Ovid encourages the reader to feel the ebb and flow of his relationship with Corinna, the early happiness, the final sundering. We bring to these distinct moments a sense that time has passed, and fill the interstices between the poems with the continuity of our own experience. Certainly *Amores* III, v could not have preceded its counterpart in the first book, yet in the very next poem of that book (I, vi) we hear Ovid's laments on the threshold of Corinna's locked door. In *Amores* I, viii we learn from Dipsas that Corinna has already attracted the attention of a rich admirer. Based on its content alone, *Amores* III, v could easily be placed in the first book. But if it had been, the poem would not resonate as richly as it does. With greater distance, the reader can hear a far greater range of overtones. By inviting the reader to make firm connections where connections, if they exist at all, had been only implied, by providing space for his readers to enter his fiction, Ovid conveys in the *Amores* both the singularity of love and reality and a sense of their underlying order. Ovid's affair with Corinna becomes both the spoken subject and the unspoken frame of the *Amores*.

It is precisely this interplay between specific elegy and overarching frame, implied or actual, that allows Ovid to create characters who are more than one-dimensional. The importance of a framing device for the representation of character becomes clear if we compare the *Amores* to the *Heroides*. These fifteen letters, written by heroines of myth to the lovers who either have abandoned them or are separated from them, together with the three double letters sent between Paris and Helen, Leander and Hero, and Acontius and Cypidde, are Ovid's most sustained effort at character-drawing. Despite the varying dispositions of the women, whose monologues sometimes reveal the deeper workings of their souls, nothing really allows Penelope to be more than the picture of faithfulness, Oenone a verbal incarnation of offended pride, or Medea the terrifying spectacle of passion feeding a growing desire for revenge. There is no interaction, no chance for development or change; each woman is captured in the same moment of isolation. Although their reactions differ, the cause for each remains the same: unable to speak to anyone but themselves, their characters are static, limited by the confines of the letter itself. They are twenty solitary voices, each crying in her own wilderness.

Yet Ovid embraces these apparent defects and does what he can to make virtues of them. The *Heroides* often are called 'suasoriae' in verse; what Roman would have failed to recognize the similarity of the letters to those overwrought attempts at persuasion practised in the schools of rhetoric?[2] But how can persuasion succeed when it has been deliberately robbed of its immediacy? When Ovid declaimed his own school 'suasoriae,' his object was to convince his listeners that his arguments were the most plausible. The figures the ladies of the *Heroides* seek to persuade, however, are absent, and nothing lessens an argument's effectiveness like distance. How much easier to ignore an indignant letter than an affronted woman. Nor does Ovid allow his heroines to prevail upon his readers. Since the audience knows that Ulysses does return to Penelope, all Penelope's efforts to persuade him to return will strike us as redundant before the fact. Perhaps we feel sympathy for Penelope's plight, but her arguments cannot move us. The *Heroides* may employ ecphrasis, adynaton, and all the other rhetorical techniques of the 'suasoria,' but the *Heroides* deny their rhetoricity: they are not a work of oratory, but of poetry. By divorcing the poems from every intent to persuade, Ovid has left the schools and given us a Roman equivalent of Theophrastus's *Character-Sketches*. And of the two, the *Heroides* is the more pleasing, since Theophrastus's catalogue is descriptive while Ovid's is dramatic. His heroines reveal their dispositions, as Aristotle advises, through what they say. As in the *Amores*, the focus is directed exclusively toward poetic art, but unlike the *Amores*, the *Heroides* lacks a central narrator. To remain faithful to its ideal, the work prohibits the participation, and sometimes the interest, of its readers.

Despite its different form, much the same can be said of the *Fasti*. Here, for the first time in Ovid, the frame has been made an integral part of the poem, but the Roman calendar proved so unpoetic a structure, that it stands completely unintegrated with the stories it orders. The most famous tale in the *Fasti*, the rape of Proserpina, starts abruptly, for no reason other than the happenstance that Romans celebrated the games of Ceres on 14 April: 'Exigit ipse locus raptus ut virginis edam / The day itself demands that I recount the rape of the virgin' (LV, 417).[3] As Heinze and others have shown, the narrative unfolds in the discursive, elliptical manner of elegy:[4] Ovid devotes eight lines to the enumeration of the flowers Proserpina and her companions pick, but only two to her actual rape by Pluto. The softer emotions, sorrowful lamentation and pity, are emphasized throughout: the sentimental pathos of Ceres' visit to the hut of Caeleus is touching.

As we saw in the story of Venus and Mars in the *Ars Amatoria*, however, not every digression from the narrative can be attributed to elegiac circuity. Consider the lilies of the field and the girls who gather them:

> praeda puellares animos prolectat inanis,
> et non sentitur sedulitate labor.
> haec implet lento calathos e vimine nexos,
> haec gremium, laxos degravat illa sinus:
> illa legit calthas, huic sunt violaria curae,
> illa papavereas subsecat ungue comas:
> has, hyacinthe, tenes; illas, amarante, moraris:
> pars thyma, pars rorem, pars meliloton amat.
> plurima lecta rosa est, sunt et sine nomine flores;
> ipsa crocos tenues liliaque alba legit.

The delicate booty enticed their girlish minds, and they were too busy to feel fatigue. One fills a basket twined with supple osier, another weighs down her lap, a third the loose folds of her robe; One gathers marigolds, violets catch the attention of another; one breaks off poppy heads with her nails; some, o hyacinth, you attract; others, o amaranth, you cause to linger. Some love thyme, others rosemary, others melilot. Many roses were gathered, and flowers without a name. Proserpina herself gathers delicate crocuses and white lilies. (IV, 433–42)

At first glance, this catalogue seems a delightful excursus, reverberating with the music of spring, but at best only marginally related to the story. We can, of course, say that the spirit of exuberant life here will subsequently make Ceres' grief all the more poignant, but amid such delicacy, the point will seem forced. Even the narrator is carried away by the joy of this abundance, addressing as he does the hyacinths and amaranths directly. Charming, personal, yet hardly to the point: in every way the passage exhibits all the supposed characteristics of elegy.

But are these flowers merely rhetorical embellishment? Before he begins his account of Proserpina, Ovid enumerates at length the bounties of Ceres (IV, 396–416); that there be a profusion of flowers befits the generous nature of the goddess Ovid now celebrates. Ceres' gifts, however, are corn and spelt, the foodstuffs man needs to survive in this age of bronze. Flowers are more the profitless treasure of a child. The violets, roses, hyacinths, and melilots, then, are external manifestations of Proserpina's character: there are so many of them because she is her mother's daughter. Ovid himself encourages us to associate the landscape with the child who wanders in it: 'Praeda puellares animos prolectat inanis / the delicate booty [i.e. the flowers] lured their girlish minds.' Proserpina, Pluto's 'praeda ... inanis,' is like a flower that blooms and dies, but appears again next spring.

The shape of Ovid's narratives, therefore, the order in which they develop and the way they are elaborated, can sometimes be determined by considerations of plot, sentiment, or character. Ovid seems particularly able to do any number of these things at once, to make a rhetorical amplification of a setting a character sketch as well. Ovid can be most artful precisely when he seems most rhetorical: these are the occasions when our attention must be keenest.

Many of the stories in the *Fasti* are artistically sophisticated, but none of its characters appears to be any more complicated than Proserpina. Ovid's object, of course, is etiology: in explaining how, for instance, the feast of Anna Perenna came about, the full articulation of her ruling passion would not necessarily be a major concern. Indeed, the deified Anna seems to have left behind the complexities of blood and mire, becoming instead a beautifully flowing paronomasia:

amne perenne latens Anna Perenna vocor.

Hiding in the perennial river, Anna Perenna I am called.   (III, 653)

The characters in the *Fasti* are simple, subordinated completely to the narratives they appear in. What development there is is indirect, often the incidental result of rhetorical elaboration of some aspect of the plot. The stories themselves are discrete and self-contained, fixed by their position in the calendar, as isolated from one another as Penelope is from Helen in the *Heroides*.

The narrator of the *Fasti*, however, sometimes seems more interesting than his material. Throughout the poem the narrator's voice never does supersede the calendar as the agent of continuity; often the poet and the calendar are indistinguishable. When this is so, Ovid proves less than fascinating:

> Dicta Pales nobis, idem Vinalia dicam,
> una tamen media est inter utramque dies

I have spoken of Pales; now I will tell of the Vinalia, but there is one day interposed between the two.   (IV, 863–4)

But not every festival is so mechanically introduced. At times, Ovid will frame the entry with an account of how he learned the pertinent facts. This story can be no more than a simple vignette: walking the streets of Rome during the feast of Vesta, Ovid suddenly saw a matron walking barefoot. An old woman saw him perplexed and so explained the custom (VI, 395ff). When there are conflicting interpretations, however, the rival etymologies of April, May, and June, for instance, Ovid can produce a marvellous entr'acte.

Before he describes how he was sitting in a grove pondering the origin of June, Ovid informs his reader that there are a number of different explanations, and he may choose the one he pleases. Ovid will tell them all, and tell them truly: 'facta canam.' A curious disclaimer then follows:

> ... sed erunt qui me finxisse loquantur
> nullaque mortali numina visa putent.
> est deus in nobis; agitante calescimus illo:
> impetus hic sacrae semina mentis habet.
> fas mihi praecipue voltus vidisse deorum,
> vel quia sum vates, vel quia sacra cano.

But some will say I have lied, who think no deities were ever seen by mortals. There is a god in us; we grow warm when he stirs us; it is his impulse that sows the seeds of inspiration. I especially have the right to see the faces of the gods, because I am a poet, because I sing of sacred things.   (VI, 3–8)

Suddenly goddesses appear, not those Hesiod, the 'praeceptor arandi' (the teacher of ploughing) saw, nor those Paris was asked to judge, but Juno and Hebe; the narrator grows pale, and to calm him, Jove's sister and wife endorses the privileges he claimed as poet:

> ... 'o vates, Romani conditor anni,
> ause per exiguos magna referre modos,
> ius tibi fecisti numen caeleste videndi,
> cum placuit numeris condere festa tuis.'

O poet, author of the Roman year, who has dared to tell of great things in slender couplets, you have won for yourself the right to see a celestial divinity since you wished to celebrate the festivals in your poems. (21–4)

Each goddess then tells why June is named for her: disharmony threatens until Concordia appears to explain that June is named for the junction of the peoples of Tatius and Quirinus. Ovid concludes by refusing to choose:

> ite pares a me. perierunt iudice formae
> Pergama; plus laedunt, quam iuvat una, duae.

Go from me as equals. Pergamum perished when Paris judged the beauty of the goddesses. Two of them do more injury than one may remedy. (99–100)

As a chronicler of antiquity, Ovid would have made Varro blanch, but the *Fasti* were never intended to be a work of historical scholarship. Rather they were to be the fulfilment of the promise of Propertius's fourth book, a work to rival Callimachus's *Aetia*. Establishing the true explanation of the origin of June seems to concern Ovid far less than establishing his truthfulness as a vatic poet. Perhaps someone will characterize the celestial sources of Ovid's evidence as the fanciful fictions of an overactive imagination, which, of course, is just what they are. Only the poet sees the faces of the gods, and Ovid proves he is a poet, involving himself in another judgment of Paris and rendering in the process a verdict more judicious than his Trojan ancestor's. The 'aetion' per se was unimportant when compared to the art with which it was presented. And so, in explaining the possible origins of the name June, Ovid fashions a fourth etiology, the story we have just read, whose status as factual evidence is as verifiable as any of the others. By making the goddesses their own advocates, Ovid intentionally undercuts the plausibility of each interpretation: how could a scene so highly fictitious disclose the truth of the matter? But in this case, Ovid's fiction is coterminous with the truth: no one knows the actual origin of June; Ovid refuses to choose among the explanations. His tableau is a poetic analogy to the facts of the case, concerned not with origins so much as with conclusions: an unbiased report, as it were, of the present state of research. The frame may prevent any book of the *Fasti* from being more than a month's worth of unrelated stories, but each day can itself be a poetic festival.

By dubbing Hesiod the 'praeceptor arandi,' Ovid playfully reminds his reader of his tenure as 'praeceptor amandi' in the *Ars Amatoria*. Indeed, the entire jeu d'esprit that opens the sixth book of the *Fasti* is a gloss on Ovid's earlier claim that his instruction in love was based on his own experience:

> non ego, Phoebe, datas a te mihi mentiar artes,
> nec nos aeriae uoce monemur auis,
> nec mihi sunt uisae Clio Cliusque sorores
> seruanti pecudes uallibus, Ascra, tuis;
> usus opus mouet hoc: uati parete perito;
> uera canam. coeptis, mater Amoris, ades.

Phoebus, I will not lie and say that you have taught me my art, nor am I instructed by the calls of airborne birds, nor have I seen Clio and her sisters while tending sheep in your valleys, O Ascra; experience promotes this work. Make way for a poet who is expert. I shall sing the truth; mother of Love, favour my undertaking.   (*Ars* I, 25–30)[5]

Ovid's 'usus,' not only his experience, but his skill, practice, employment, and pleasure as well, is his poetry. The poet who puts his knowledge at our disposal is expert ('peritus') not only in love affairs, but in his skill, training, and practice. Thus when Ovid refers to himself in the *Ars*, he often recalls situations from the *Amores*: how he tore his mistress's hair (*Ars* II, 169ff, cf *Amores* I, vii), or how a maid took her mistress's place in Ovid's bed (*Ars* III, 665ff, cf *Amores* II, viii). The narrator in all Ovid's elegies is a man whose character never changes: the spokesman of his own artifice, he is the lie that laughs because he speaks the truth.

For many it was in the *Ars Amatoria* and the *Remedia Amoris* that Ovid found the material best suited to his technical brilliance. The *Amores* ingeniously parodies the elegiac lover without leaving his traditional métier; how much greater the wit and irony if ungovernable love were codified into a system and cast in the form of a didactic poem. Gods and heroes without distinction could haunt the Roman demimonde. In the last chapter we saw how Ovid makes Mars and Venus model pupils, the Sun-god and Vulcan gauche spoilsports in his school for scandal. But the most interesting character in the *Ars* is, of course, the narrator. He has been discussed at length and with insight by Durling, Solodow, and Fyler among others; all emphasize how through him Ovid is able to equate amatory prowess with poetic virtuosity.[6] For my purposes, I would only underline a point that is implicit in their discussions. The *Ars* and the *Remedia* were the first continuous narratives Ovid produced; already he has seen that a story interpolated in them could either, as in the case of Venus and Mars, be outrageously slanted to illustrate a point, or, as in the case of Daedalus and Icarus, reveal with some subtlety the ethos of the speaker. In his reading of this latter tale, Durling readily demonstrates that the narrator's truest love is his art. By introducing tales into a larger framework, Ovid discovered that he did not have to sacrifice any of the sophistication his juxtaposition of poems produced in the *Amores*: a figure's disposition now could be revealed by the kind of story he tells and the way he tells it. This artistic lesson of the *Ars* Ovid learned well; he employs the same techniques with similar success in the *Metamorphoses*.

The characters of the *Metamorphoses* are uncomplicated. In the words of Brooks Otis, 'each is governed by one simple emotion: vengeance, *libido*, conjugal devotion, the simple desire to possess the beloved.'[7] Simplicity, however, does not mean artlessness, as Otis well knows: by his definition the characters of Ovid's earlier elegiac poetry were also 'rude mechanicals,' lovers ruled by passion, poets by poetry. Yet few, I think, would maintain that the idea of character in these works, or the methods of representing them, are anything but complex. Through thematic or narrative juxtaposition, Ovid's characters do more than be; they mean. The Proserpina of the *Fasti*, to take the simplest case, is not only a young girl, but also a flower: we are shortsighted if we ignore the implications of the comparison. In the *Metamorphoses* as well, seeming digressions or prolonged descriptions of some event in the narrative will often be metaphorical extensions of the protagonist's character. Something like this occurs in the story of Ceyx and Alcyone. As in his earlier works, however, Ovid's narrators are the figures who attract the greatest attention. But in this 'carmen perpetuum,' narrators are also characters, figures like Orpheus or the Minyades who tell stories yet at the same time are involved in different, framing fictions. In both these cases, my concern will be to see whether a sense of ethos is reflected in the texture of the narrative, in what is said, and, equally important, in how it is said. It is this aspect of 'ethopoeia' that makes the characters of Ovid's epic interesting.

The story of Ceyx and Alcyone dominates the eleventh book of the *Metamorphoses*; after the Phaeton, it is the longest episode of the poem. The most conspicuous feature of the story is the ninety-nine-line description of the storm which drowns Ceyx, an elaborate ecphrasis that was clearly meant to recall and rival the great storms of the *Aenied* and *Odyssey*. In Ovid's sources, this tempest is an act of divine retribution, sent as chastisement for Ceyx and Alcyone because they had the effrontery to call themselves Zeus and Hera and act accordingly. But in Ovid, as Otis says, Ceyx and Alcyone are pious and devoted to each other, and the gods have nothing to do with their tragedy.[8] In the place of divine vengeance we find the inanimate powers of nature: ultimately the story is concerned with 'the cosmic sympathy or antipathy that exists between man and nature.'[9]

In some respects Otis' reading of the episode is convincing, but I wonder whether Ovid's tempest represents the forces of a disinterested nature alone. It is true that the gods stand at the periphery of this rendering of the story, but that does not mean that the storm will have ceased to have anything to do with Ceyx and Alcyone themselves. Even in Ovid's sources, after all, the gods are only the efficient, not the final cause of the hurricane. The very scholium on the *Birds* of Aristophanes that preserves the version Ovid most probably followed makes the storm punishment for the couple's impiety. In Ovid, the whirlwind is summoned up not so much by overweening pride as by excessive love.

Even before Ceyx leaves her, Alcyone has made clear her overwhelming concern for her husband's safety. As he was preparing to join Peleus in his hunt for the terrible wolf, Alcyone implores Ceyx not to go:

> ... sed Alcyone coniunx excita tumultu
> prosilit et nondum totos ornata capillos
> disicit hos ipsos colloque infusa mariti,
> mittat ut auxilium sine se, verbisque precatur
> et lacrimis, animasque duas ut servet in una.

But Alcyone his wife, aroused by the commotion, rushed in, and tore loose the hair she had not yet entirely made up, and threw her arms about her husband's neck. She begs with words and tears that he send aid but not go himself, and so save two lives in one. (XI, 384–8)

Her prayers are granted, not because Ceyx heeds them, but because Peleus intervenes to say that no arms at all should be taken up on his behalf. He prays to the sea-nymph Psamathe, Thetis intercedes, and the wolf is turned to marble in mid-flight.

Soon afterward, Alcyone must again beseech her husband to remain home. Ceyx, it seems, has been so disturbed by his brother's fate and other strange things that have happened since Daedalion was transformed into a hawk that he decides he must consult the sacred oracles at Claros. When he reveals his intention to his wife, Alcyone's reaction is immediate: she is chilled to the marrow of her bones, her face grows pale as boxwood, and her cheeks are wet with tears. Three times she tries to talk; three times tears prevent her. Finally she is able to say

> 'quae mea culpa tuam,' dixit, 'carissime, mentem
> vertit? ubi est, quae cura mei prior esse solebat?
> iam potes Alcyone securus abesse relicta?
> iam via longa placet? iam sum tibi carior absens?'

What fault of mine, o dearest husband, has turned your mind to this? Where is that care for me which used to be foremost? Can you now be apart from your abandoned Alcyone without a thought of her? Do you now want to take a long journey? Am I now more dear absent? (421–4)

Not yet aware of her husband's specific destination, Alcyone derives some comfort from supposing that Ceyx will travel by land: even to think of venturing on the sea makes her die of fright. She is Aeolus's daughter, and knows that once the winds have been let loose over water, 'nil illis vetitum est / nothing can check them.' She knows, for she has seen the winds raging when she was a child. But if Ceyx is still determined to go, Alcyone has one final request – let him take her:

> ... certe iactabimur una,
> nec, nisi quae patiar, metuam; pariterque feremus,
> quidquid erit, pariter super aequora lata feremur.'

For certainly we shall be tossed [by the storm] together, nor shall I fear beyond what I now suffer, and whatever comes we will bear equally, and together we shall be borne over the wide sea. (441–3)

Alcyone's love really seems a species of fear; any physical separation from her husband, as Otis says, is for her a premonition of death.[10] The questions that open her answer to Ceyx are heartfelt: Alcyone actually believes that Ceyx, since he would leave her, must have ceased to love her. Later we see this same sense of insecurity when Alcyone petitions Juno to keep the now drowned Ceyx safe:

> utque foret sospes coniunx suus utque rediret,
> optabat, nullamque sibi praeferret; at illi
> hoc de tot votis poterat contingere solum.

And she prays that her husband may be unharmed, and that he return, and that he love no woman more than her. But of all her prayers, only this last could be granted. (580–2)

Even more than they characterize the quality of her love, however, Alcyone's effusive tears and protracted supplications identify her as her father's daughter. Aeolus, Alcyone herself tells us, is the god 'who may hold in check the strong winds, and, when he pleases, calm the sea / qui carcere fortes / contineat ventos, et, cum velit, aequora placet' (431–2). Alcyone is continually crying her prayers ('verbisque precatur et lacrimis,' 388; 'lacrimisque genae maduere profusis ... fletibus ora rigavit / singultuque pias interrumpente querellas,' 418–20; 'lacrimasque emisit obortas,' 458; 'quaerente moras Ceyce,' 461; 'umentes oculos,' 464); we are encouraged to think her devotion is as boundless as the sea, as intense as a sudden wind.

Indeed, Ovid uses lineage itself to reflect the suppressed tension of Ceyx and Alcyone's relationship. Ceyx clearly has inherited his father's attributes: he is introduced as 'the son of Lucifer, and bearing his father's brightness in his countenance' (271–2; the phrase 'son of Lucifer' is repeated at 346), but the consanguinity is most evident in Ceyx's own actions and words. It seems natural that he should swear to return to Alcyone 'per patrios ignes / by his father's fires.' Even more telling, however, is his initial reaction to Alcyone's pleading:

> talibus Aeolidis dictis lacrimisque movetur
> sidereus coniunx; neque enim minor ignis in ipso est.
> sed neque propositos pelagi dimittere cursus
> nec vult Alcyonen in partem adhibere pericli

The starborn husband is moved by these words, and by the tears of Aeolus's daughter, nor is the fire of love any less in him, yet neither is he willing to abandon his proposed journeys on the sea nor to make Alcyone a party to such danger. (444–7)

Ceyx and Alcyone clearly love one another, yet one senses that underlying their affection is an incompatibility as elemental as that between fire and water.

Ceyx's motives for undertaking the voyage seem unexceptionable, yet one cannot help feeling that he remains so adamant in the face of his wife's petitions because be needs to escape the smothering protectiveness of her love. Although he is peaceful by nature, Ceyx is not inert: he quickly dons armour to aid Peleus, and is ready to take action to secure the well-being of his kingdom. Alcyone's adoration would inundate Ceyx; to preserve no more than his manhood he would have to set off on his voyage.

Yet love this vast is not so easily forestalled. No sooner does Ceyx leave his wife than the storm rises. Otis has analysed the structure and 'leitmotiv' of the passage.[11] The tempest, he says, is described not from Ceyx's point of view, but from that of the captain, the sailors, and above all, the wind and the waves. The elements are at war with men. Unlike Homer, however, whose armies are compared to waves and the wind, Ovid likens the wind and the waves to warriors besieging a stronghold. By this shift, Ovid 'literally animates the inanimate and reveals the malicious intention of the sea-storm.'[12]

This is certainly true: lines like 'spoliisque animosa superstes / unda velut vicatrix sinuataque despicit undas / one last wave, like a conqueror, eager for spoils, curving at its crest looks down upon the other waves' (552–3) make it clear that this storm meant to kill. But why should inanimate nature be malicious? Though she is nowhere present, the storm is actually described from Alcyone's point of view: its meanness is the counterpart to her fears; it is described at such length because her love is equally vast; it engulfs Ceyx even as her overflooding love would. Like Proserpina's gathering of flowers, the storm is a narrative ecphrasis that is also a metaphorical characterization of Alcyone's love. The raging winds and angry sea battle against the ship: Ovid has emphasized Alcyone's descent from Aeolus not so that we should notice the absence of the god, but so that we should associate his daugher with the hurricane. The suddenness with which it rises recalls Alcyone's reaction when Ceyx first told her of his plans: 'cui protinus intima frigus / ossa receperunt / immediately she was chilled to the very marrow of her bones' (416–17); and its fury finds an analogue in the tenacity of her devotion. As Ceyx embarks, Alcyone exchanges signs of love with him;

> ubi terra recessit
> longius atque oculi nequeunt cognoscere vultus,
> dum licet, insequitur fugientem lumine pinum.
> haec quoque ut haud poterat spatio summota videri,
> vela tamen spectat summa fluitantia malo;
> ut nec vela videt, vacuum petit anxia lectum

When land grew more distant, and her eyes could not make out his face, while she could she followed the fleeing ship with her gaze. When this was also so distant that it could no longer be seen, still she watched the sails billowing at the top of the mast, and when she could not even see the sails, anxious she sought her empty bed. (466–71).

And it is fitting that love be shown here in all its destructive potential, since the Ceyx and Alcyone, together with the brief story of Aesacus that follows, are Ovid's segue to the Trojan War, the greatest of all conflicts, fought for a love that in its excess was suicidal.

But as much as Alcyone and the storm are metaphors of each other, they are also executors of Ovid's craft. The storm, as many have noticed, is full of epic conceits: full-dress similes straight from the *Iliad* abound – the wind and waves charge ('ibat in arma') against the ship

> utque solent sumptis incursus viribus ire
> pectore in arma feri protentaque tela leones

like fierce lions who, gaining strength in their breast as they attack, are wont to rush against arms and extended spears   (510–11)

– the ship is likened to a city besieged and overrun (515ff, 535, 553), and so forth. Ceyx and Alcyone lived in the generation before the Trojan War. By situating his storm at this time, and within the story of Ceyx and his wife, Ovid rather brazenly asserts the priority of his storm to those described by Homer and Virgil, just as he subordinates their epics to the theme of his more encompassing epic. After all, the final books of Ovid's poem concern themselves with the greatest of all metamorphoses, the transformation of Troy into Rome. Even as Virgil assimilated the *Iliad* and the *Odyssey*, Ovid now refashions Homer *and* Virgil. Thus, from Ovid's point of view, even as Achilles will, some years from now, all ablaze battle the Simois, so now the sea extinguishes Ceyx the son of Lucifer. And even as Aeneas will escape a tempest at sea to face the burning love of Dido in Carthage, so now Ovid restyles the progress of the epic. In the *Amores*, the characters consistently drew attention away from themselves and toward Ovid's art. In the *Metamorphoses*, not only the characters but the narrative itself does this as well. The idea hasn't changed, but the techniques of representation have grown much more complex.

Most of Ovid's stories, of course, are not nearly so elaborate as the tale of Ceyx and Alcyone, nor is the disposition of every character represented in so oblique and subtle a way. Often figures in the *Metamorphoses* are purely a matter of style. The insistent repetitions that mark the story of the Raven and Crow in Book II, to cite one example, constitute the birds' sum and substance.

Juno has convinced Ocean and Tethys that they should deny Arcas and his mother, newly translated to the heavens, their pure waters as a resting place. The goddess then returns to her palace, and Ovid begins the story of the garrulous raven:

> ingreditur liquidum pavonibus aethera pictis,
> tam nuper pictis caeso pavonibus Argo,
> quam tu nuper eras, cum candidus ante fuisses,
> corve loquax, subito nigrantes versus in alas.
> nam fuit haec quondam niveis argentea pennis
> ales, ut aequaret totas sine labe columbas
> nec servaturis vigili Capitolia voce

cederet anseribus nec amanti flumina cygno.
lingua fuit damno: lingua faciente loquaci,
qui color albus erat, nunc est contrarius albo.

She is borne through the pure ether by her coloured peacocks, by peacocks recently painted with the eyes of the dead Argus, at that time when you also were suddenly changed to black, o talkative raven, though you once were white. For the raven was once a silvery bird with snow-white wings, who could rival pigeons without blemish, who would not yield to the geese destined to save the Capitol with their vigilant cries, nor to the river-loving swan. Talking too much was his undoing; by making his tongue talk too much, the talkative bird who once was white now is white's opposite. (II, 532–41).

Ovid here is purposely redundant. He talks too much about talking too much, repeats too often that the raven was turned from white to black. Although he is much more lavish in his use of colour than Callimachus, whose *Hecale* was the source of the story, Ovid's range is emphatically limited to black and white.[13] Yet in this case, wordiness is a virtue: not only does such verbosity demonstrate the raven's chief fault, it also prepares the audience for the crow's tale, a tale which, of course, is a mirror image of the raven's. Together, the stories ask a flippant question: how does one distinguish a raven from a crow, anyhow? Ovid answers, 'you can't, you can't,' and makes the second response as delightful as the first.

Besides this kind of stylistic characterization, as well as the characterization through narrative amplification of the Ceyx and Alcyone, the story a narrator chooses to tell often gives us a sense of his character. The most obvious examples of this are Orpheus's stories in Book x. Angry with the gods and dejected over the loss of Eurydice, Orpheus abstained from contact with any woman for three years, 'seu quod male cesserat illi, / sive fidem dederat / either because love had come to such a bad end for him, or because he had so pledged his faith' (x, 80–1). Instead, he gave his love to young boys, 'plucking the brief springtime and first flowers of their youth / aetatis breve ver et primos carpere flores' (85).[14]

By revealing the nature of Orpheus's condition following his bereavement, the succeeding stories qualify the alternative explanations of his avoidance of women. Even before he speaks, however, Ovid lets us know that Orpheus's apparent misogyny, with its consequent homosexuality, though understandable, is self-defeating. With the mention of the brief springtime and first flowers of youth, we recall Proserpina; Orpheus's love of boys, however, can never result in return or rebirth of any sort, only in the inevitable loss of a beauty that by nature must quickly pass. Similarly, Ovid hints that with the loss of his mate, Orpheus perhaps becomes a kind of Dido, keeping faith with a spouse he dearly loved, but someone he feels betrayed him by dying. Orpheus's three-year abstinence, then, like Dido's vows of celibacy, is in the end a form of self-immolation, a harbinger of his ultimate fate.

That Orpheus's grief should seem as much a literary allusion as a deeply experienced emotion will come as no surprise to the reader of the *Amores*. Indeed, the stunned coldness Orpheus feels the moment Eurydice slips from him is rendered indirectly, through a series of similes:

> non aliter stupuit gemina nece coniugis Orpheus,
> quam tria qui timidus, medio portante catenas,
> colla canis vidit; quem non pavor ante reliquit,
> quam natura prior, saxo per corpus oborto;
> quique in se crimen traxit voluitque videri
> Olenos esse nocens, tuque, o confisa figurae,
> infelix Lethaea, tuae, iunctissima quondam
> pectora, nunc lapides, quos umida sustinet Ide.

Orpheus was dumbstruck by the double death of his wife no differently than was that fearful man who saw the three-necked dog, the middle one chained about, whom fear did not leave before his former nature, his body having turned to stone; nor than were Olenos, who took the offence upon himself and wished to seem guilty, and you, unfortunate Lethaea, so confident of your beauty, once two hearts most closely joined, now stones which wet Ida holds.   (x, 64–71)

For Ovid, a poet's reactions can hardly be anything but the devices of poetry. All three similes tell us Orpheus was so dumbfounded by his loss that he turned to stone, but like marble in Pygmalion's hands, Ovid shapes these seemingly lapidary comparisons and brings them to life. The similes catalogue Orpheus's feelings in much the way his subsequent stories will. His devotion to Eurydice, as well as his sense of failing her, make Orpheus another Olenos, the loving husband unable to do anything but turn to stone with his wife. Yet Orpheus's feeling that Eurydice somehow betrayed him also finds expression: Lethaea, Olenos's wife, who boasted of her beauty, has brought punishment not only upon herself, but upon her guiltless husband as well. Moreover, in his terror and frustration, Orpheus is both the man petrified at the sight of Cerberus and the Hercules who dragged the creature from the underworld, with little profit for himself. Indeed, Orpheus's subsequent anger at women in general, his desire to sing of 'inconcessibusque puellas / ignibus attonitas meruisse libidine poenam / girls seized by illicit passions paying the penalty for their lust' (x, 153–4), initially makes Cerberus a savage surrogate for Eurydice.

Even Orpheus, however, will sense the injustice of the association, for his anger will be tempered by his enduring love for Eurydice. The landscape itself, the hill where many trees gather to hear Orpheus's songs, reflects how truly divided his soul is. Among the trees is the cypress, who once was the youth Cyparissus. This boy, beloved by Apollo, by evil chance shot a deer he deeply loved, and was so disconsolate at its death that he wept, despite the god's attempts to cheer him, until he became the mourning cypress. The story nicely mirrors Orpheus's abiding love for Eurydice, his refusal to be comforted, and his anger at himself for her loss.[15]

Orpheus, however, doesn't tell this story; Ovid does. The son of Apollo's first tale is the rape of Ganymede, a short, brutal account which takes a spiteful joy in its utter denial of tenderness and affection:

> Rex superum Phrygii quondam Ganymedis amore
> arsit, et inventum est aliquid, quod Iuppiter esse,
> quam quod erat, mallet, nulla tamen alite verti
> dignatur, nisi quae posset sua fulmina ferre.
> nec mora, percusso mendacibus aere pennis
> abripit Iliaden, qui nunc quoque pocula miscet
> invitaque Iovi nectar Iunone ministrat.

The king of the gods once burned with love for Phrygian Ganymede, and something was found which Jupiter would rather be than what he was. Nevertheless, he would not deign to be turned into any bird other than the one that could bear his thunderbolts. Without delay, he beat the air with his lying wings and stole the Trojan boy away, who even now, though against Juno's will, mixes the nectar and keeps the cups of Jove. (x, 155–61)

Love here is nothing but naked force and the cause of enmity and distance between husband and wife. Orpheus's first utterance is full of anger, anger at the cruel and deceitful gods, anger at the forced sundering from his wife, anger at himself for losing Eurydice. Because the account is so abrupt, the rape seems savage and heartless. Jupiter is unbearably haughty, and his love expresses itself in curiously negative and unlovely forms. Because he burns with love, the god prefers to be something other than what he is. He does not deign to transform himself into any bird other than the royal eagle. The shape he assumes is 'lying,' and the phrasing of the rape itself, 'abripit Iliaden,' inexorably foreshadows a second ravishment, which will bring war and death to the race of

Tros. Underlying every detail of the story there is a harsh denial of sensitivity, of regard for another, of love. Each element in the tale reflects Orpheus's resentment.

Anger, though, is not the only emotion that grips the bereaved. With the next story, of Apollo and Hyacinthus, we see that rage can quickly turn to poignant self-reproach:

> Phoebus ait 'videoque tuum, mea crimina, vulnus.
> tu dolor es facinusque meum: mea dextera leto
> inscribenda tuo est. ego sum tibi funeris auctor.
> quae mea culpa tamen? nisi si lusisse vocari
> culpa potest, nisi culpa potest et amasse vocari.'

And Phoebus says, 'I see your wound and my guilt. You are my grief and my crime. Your death must be ascribed to my hand. I am the cause of your funeral rites. Yet how am I at fault, unless to have played with you can be called a fault, unless to have loved you can be called a fault.' (197–201)

Hyacinthus, Apollo continues, will be with him forever, both in his songs and in the flower the youth has become.

Orpheus has given his father words whose significance he can readily apply to himself. Like Apollo's arts ('nil prosunt artes,' 189). Orpheus's songs have failed him: the craft of neither god nor poet can revive his beloved. Hyacinthus has clearly become Eurydice's surrogate: not only is he called the Taenarian youth (183), but even as Orpheus began his quest for Eurydice by passing through the gate of Taenarus, Hyacinthus's death itself recalls Eurydice's. Apollo's discus descends but, hitting the earth, flies up, striking Hyacinthus in the face. So Orpheus descends but loses his wife in the ascent. Orpheus's stories are undoubtedly cathartic, yet again we note that they do not express his feelings so much as they poeticize them. Orpheus's sense of the delicate fragility of his love for Eurydice once more finds its clearest formulation in a self-conscious, highly literary simile (cf *Iliad* VIII, 306ff; *Aeneid* IX, 435ff):

> ut, siquis violas riguoque papaver in horto
> liliaque infringat fulvis horrentia linguis,
> marcida demittant subito caput illa gravatum
> nec se sustineant spectentque cacumine terram,
> sic vultus moriens iacet ...

Just as if someone in a well-watered garden breaks off violets, poppies, or lilies bristly with yellow pistils, the head weighed down they suddenly droop, withered, and cannot hold themselves straight, and gaze at the ground with their tops, so the dying head [of Hyacinthus] lies. (190-4)

The same identity of form and experience that describes the dying Hyacinthus in terms of the flower he has not yet become characterizes the relation between Orpheus and his tales. In the face of death, love is like spring flowers, beautiful, but passing. Yet Apollo's songs do reaffirm his love for Hyacinthus even after the youth has died; by singing, Orpheus has also, we sense, moved closer to the mercies of consolation.

Orpheus's first two stories set the pattern of vacillation between the flower and the stone, between, that is, the love that lives after death and the anger of bereavement, which continues throughout the book. Two brief tales follow, each concerned with hardened men and women. In the second, the Propoetides, first to prostitute their bodies and their fame, are turned to stone by an angry Venus. Ovid's account has received much perceptive comment; for my purposes its central importance to the depiction of Orpheus is clear. With Pygmalion, homosexual love has yielded to an idealized love between man and woman. If Orpheus was petrified by Eurydice's death, his songs give living form not only to himself but to the memory of his wife as well. Orpheus's songs, we see, are a way of coming to terms with his wife's death. They present a general movement from anger to reconciliation that is effected primarily through the good graces of his art. Many have noted that Orpheus undergoes no transformation, but Orpheus is his own metamorphosis. In his songs we see him in the process of change, for the stone becomes a flower. After three years, complete resignation to the loss of his wife is impossible; Orpheus's anger again surfaces in the story of Cinyras and Myrrha. Nor is love ever far from the fear of danger and the frustration of death: the book ends with the story of Venus and Adonis. But by the end, tenderness has joined with perception; death's wound, though unhealed, is far less angry. In his final description of the anemone, the flower Adonis has become, Orpheus reaffirms his love for Eurydice, fully aware of the inevitability of his loss:

> ... brevis est tamen usus in illo;
> namque male haerentem et nimia levitate caducum
> excutiunt idem, qui praestant nomina, venti

But brief is the season for enjoying the flower, for the winds, which give it its name, shake the anemone that clings so tenuously and is doomed so easily to fall. (737-9)

Orpheus is ready to rejoin Eurydice in the fields of the blessed.

Taken together, Orpheus's florilegium of tales reveals the dimensions of his character. He is not an individual, but an emblematic figure whose stories represent our many responses to the death of someone we love. In them we feel our anger, our suffering, and our frustration, but intimations of our eventual resignation as well, and our reaffirmation of the goodness of what has been taken from us. Orpheus is a poet; though his end is brutal and tragic, he everywhere shows a poet's far-reaching compassion. His experience is poetic and inclusive, even in his death: torn apart by Maenads, his dismembered head was washed ashore at Lesbos. Here a savage serpent was about to attack it when Apollo appeared

> et in lapidem rictus serpentis apertos
> congelat et patulos, ut erant, indurat hiatus

and he freezes into stone the open and yawning jaws of the serpent, just as they were, and hardens the opened mouth. (XI, 59–60)

The second death Orpheus would figuratively suffer here is exactly like the first death Eurydice actually suffered, even as the snake now literally experiences the metaphorical petrification Eurydice's death had caused Orpheus. Orpheus is the songs he sings; how could Ovid not have characterized this artist through the stories he tells?

From these examples we see that stories in the *Metamorphoses* consistently convey a sense of ethos by the way they are told. Sometimes, as in the case of Leuconoe, a portrait emerges which seems psychologically consistent. Only a prig, the kind of woman Dipsas describes as chaste because no one asked, could tell the story of Mars and Venus the way she does. As I said in the last chapter, love to Leuconoe is less a matter of the heart than an instrument of revenge, just deserts for having submitted reason to desire. The remarkable use of paronomasia in her transition from the story of Mars and Venus to the story of the Sun-god, Leucothoe, and Clytie makes this clear:

> exigit indicii memorem Cythereia poenam
> inque vices illum, tectos qui laesit amores,
> laedit amore pari. quid nunc, Hyperione nate,
> forma colorque tibi radiataque lumina prosunt?
> nempe, tuis omnes qui terras ignibus uris,
> ureris igne novo, quique omnia cernere debes,
> Leucothoen spectas et virgine figis in una,
> quos mundo debes, oculos.

But the goddess of Cytherea did not forget the one who had spied on her, and took revenge. She in turn betrayed him equally in love who had betrayed her secret love. What now, O son of Hyperion, does your beauty, brightness, and radiant light profit you? For you who heat all lands with your flames burn with a strange fire. And you who ought to behold all things, gaze at Leucothoe, and fix on one girl eyes you owe to the world. (IV, 190–7)

How unlovely love seems when Leuconoe talks of it; Molière's Arsinoe could not speak with more heavy-handed condescension and disapprobation. Love, Leuconoe takes pains to point out, again and again, disrupts the natural order, creates physical and social chaos, since the Sun fails to discharge his proper duties. Why, the god must have been blind to fall in love with Leucothoe; clearly he wasn't seeing straight at the time, for to love Leucothoe would give Venus the chance to avenge her humiliation. Or so the burden of Leuconoe's insinuations runs.

And yet, for all this censorious disapproval, how suggestive is the name of the god's beloved: but for a letter, it could have been Leuconoe. Bömer tells us that Ovid invented the name Leuconoe for this daughter of Minyas;[16] at least it appears in no known source that mentions these women. Its resemblance, however, to the name of the woman whose father buries her alive to punish her adultery is striking. Leucothoe also is a name which, so far as one can tell, never was associated with the story of the Sun's love.[17] Ovid, I think, meant us to associate the two, not only by their sound, but by their condition. Leucothoe is buried for a love she did not choose; Leuconoe sits deep within her palace to escape a form of love she cannot accept. Her scorn surfaces with her jealousy as she lists each of the Sun's unregarded paramours: not Clymene, Rhodos, not the most beautiful mother of Aeaean Circe ('Aeaeae genetrix pulcherrima Circes,' IV, 205), not even Clytie could attract the Sun's attention. Even Leucothoe is looked on with this same mixture of envy and disparagement. Her beauty is evident, but by describing Leucothoe as more beautiful than her beautiful mother ('sed postquam filia crevit, / quam mater cunctas, tam matrem filia vicit,' 210–11), Leuconoe not too subtly implies that this tender thing is no more than another Circe, an enchanting witch. Clytie, angry and jealous, exposes the adultery ('adulterium'), and Leucothoe's father then executes his terrible punishment. The Sun would never again visit Clytie, who, still crazed with passion, withers until she is changed into a flower. Love indulged or love spurned: both lead to death. For Leuconoe, it is better not to have loved at all. Yet her stories actually demonstrate that when desire is suppressed, uglier promptings, jealousy, vengeance, and senseless cruelty will emerge. By indicting love Leuconoe indicts herself of the far worse crime of denying it.

Like the stories of Orpheus, then, the tales of the Minyades are thematically related: each derogates uncontrolled desire to a greater degree. Among mortals, love leads only to death; among the gods, to humiliation and disgrace. The sentiment and pathos of the Pyramus and Thisbe, told by an unnamed narrator, quickly disappears as Leuconoe fixes on the more repellent aspects of human relations, on revenge, on malice, on the barbarity of a father burying his daughter alive. The tales culminate in Alcithoe's tale of Salmacis and Hermaphroditus, an eerie, disturbing affair that ultimately suggests love is a perversion of nature.

Salmacis is the sexual impulse gone wild. Her desire is so great, it makes her woo like a man: in her attempt to seduce Hermaphroditus, she adopts the blandishments Odysseus addressed to Nausikaa (IV, 315–28; cf *Odyssey* VI, 150ff). Indeed, her passion rivals that of Jupiter himself when he is about to rape Europa:

> gaudet amans et, dum veniat sperata voluptas,
> oscula dat manibus, vix iam, vix cetera differt.

The lover rejoices and gives kisses to the hands, in hope that other pleasures may come; with difficulty now, with difficulty does he keep himself from taking the rest. (II, 862–3)

Salmacis first saw Hermaphroditus while she was gathering flowers: 'puerum videt, visumque optavit habere, / nec tamen adiit, etsi properabat adire / she saw the youth, and what she saw, she wanted to have, yet still she did not approach, although she would have hurried to approach' (IV, 316–17). For all her masculine forwardness, however, Salmacis is vain, preening, and self-centred in a way that immediately reminds us of Ovid's elegiac women. Her sister nymphs scold Salmacis for not accompanying them and Diana, for refusing to mingle with her leisure the hardships of the chase. Seeing Hermaphroditus, Salmacis adjusts her dress, fixes her face, makes herself pretty. Alcithoe makes it perfectly clear Salmacis is everything she is not. And yet, because Salmacis's character is androgynous, even before she meets Hermaphroditus, she becomes Alcithoe's reflection. For even as Bacchus is the most feminine of the gods, the Minyades who deny him are the most masculine of women. The Minyades are Maenads in reverse, as the similar sounds of their names serve to tell us. If the followers of Bacchus, in the frenzy of their devotion, unwittingly commit acts of inhuman cruelty, the daughters of Minyas, in the name of reason, harbour within themselves an inhumanity equally disfiguring. Alcithoe compares Salmacis's clasping the unyielding

Hermaphroditus to a serpent that coils about an eagle's talons, to the ivy that wraps itself around tree trunks, to the tentacles of the sea-polyp as they close about their prey (362–7). A more gruesome picture of love can hardly be imagined; to the Minyades, sexual appetite, like eating or fighting, is one of the primitive instincts common to the lowest orders of life. Yet a moment before, Alcithoe's description of the naked Hermaphroditus reveals her undeniable attraction:

> tum vero placuit nudaeque cupidine formae
> Salmacis exarsit: flagrant quoque lumina nymphae,
> non aliter, quam cum puro nitidissimus orbe
> opposita speculi referitur imagine Phoebus,
> vixque moram patitur, vix iam sua gaudia differt.

Then Salmacis truly rejoices and burns with desire for his naked beauty: the eyes of the nymph blaze, not unlike when Phoebus most resplendent with his clear orb is reflected in a mirror, and only with difficulty does she delay, only with difficulty does she now defer her joy. (346–50)

As Ovid's simile suggests, Salmacis and the woman who tells her story are mirror images of each other.

These few examples describe what seem to me the major techniques of 'ethopoeia' in the *Metamorphoses*. His characters may seem facile, but Ovid's methods of characterization are not. Yet despite the increased sophistication of Ovid's later works, the figures of the *Ars*, *Fasti*, and *Metamorphoses* only make us realize in retrospect how original the conception of character is in the *Amores*. Here, for the first time, all the devices of rhetoric and poetry were enjoined to render less the portrait of a lover than the portrait of his creation. This was a new idea of character, something unheard of in elegy before, and the characters in Ovid's other works are little more than adaptations of this idea to the formal and stylistic demands of different kinds of poetry. Ovid's characters are all the stylish spokesmen of their maker's craft, and the brilliant wit they bespoke was heard throughout the Middle Ages.[18]

But other ideas were heard as well. Essentially Ovidian characters love and do battle in many medieval works; indeed, when we turn to Boccaccio and Chaucer, we shall again see characters transmuted into metaphors of the artist's shaping fiction. In the next chapter, however, we shall examine other figures who drew their breath from a different tradition, modelled in part on the techniques of biblical interpretation, a tradition I call literary typology.

3

Literary Typology and
the Medieval Idea of Character

Not very far into Gottfried von Strassburg's *Tristan*, a curious episode, apparently unconnected with the development of the plot, seems to interrupt the narrative. We have already seen how the young Tristan, though kidnapped from his native Parmenie by Norse merchants, quickly gains the admiration of King Mark and all the people of Cornwall through his mastery of the art of venery. Very soon, Rual li Foitenant, true to both his name and his duty as Tristan's guardian, will discover his charge and be welcomed by him as a true parent: the moment he sees Rual, Tristan says:

> 'nu müeze unser trehtîn
> iemer gebenedîet sîn,
> vater, daz ich dich sehen muoz!'[1]

Now may our Lord be sanctified forever, father, that I am allowed to see you.   (3937–9

After their meeting, father and son remain in Cornwall for Tristan's investiture into knighthood; both then return to Parmenie.

Between Tristan's entrance into Mark's court and his reunion with Rual, Gottfried informs us that Tristan plays the harp with surpassing skill. The sorrow the youth had had earlier in mastering the instrument now turns to joy: hearing him, King Mark says,

> ... Tristan, gâ her!
> der dich dâ hât gelêret,
> der sî vor gote geêret
> und dû mit ime! daz ist vil wol.

dîne leiche ich gerne hoeren sol
underwîlen wider naht,
so du doch niht geslâfen maht.
diz tuostu wol mir unde dir.

Tristan, come here. May he who has taught you so be honoured before God, and you with him! This is very good. I would like to hear your lays sometimes at evening when you cannot fall asleep. You will do this for me, and for yourself as well? (3646–53)

With Tristan's acceptance, his high place in Mark's court is assured.

The scene is not lengthy, but both in what it says and does not say, this incident exemplifies much that is significant for an understanding of medieval fiction. Unlike the abduction, the hunt, or the reunion with Rual, nothing happens here which overtly affects the course of Tristan's life. Of course, no one would claim that everything that happens in a medieval romance happens to further the plot. Exactly the opposite: consider the Roman de la Rose, where digression seem to be cultivated for its own sake. Today we find medieval poems most annoying precisely where they are most digressive: one reason Tristan's harping bothers us so little is that it's so quickly done. But although the episode may be hard to defend for its relevance to the plot, it certainly can be justified as an exposition of character. Tristan here proves himself a perfect practitioner of courtesy's active and esthetic arts. A master huntsman and a master musician, the young Tristan already shows the accomplishments of a most seasoned chevalier.

At first glance, the description of Tristan's musicianship would appear to function in much the same way the description of the storm did in Ovid's Ceyx and Alcyone. In each case, amplification of some element in the narrative reveals an important quality or disposition in one of its protagonists. In Ovid, however, the characterization was metaphorical and indirect: the storm's meanness was made the poetic counterpart to Alcyone's obsessive fear for Ceyx's safety, and the tempest was described at such length because her love was equally vast.

In Gottfried, on the other hand, the characterization is allusive: we learn about Tristan not so much from the way his story is told as from his similarity to other figures. By emphasizing the effects of Tristan's harping, the fact that many a man listening to him 'sin selbes naman vergaz: / dâ begunden herze und oren / tumben unde toren / und ûz ir rehte wanken / forgot his own name: his heart and ears began to trick and deceive him, and turn from their proper functions' (3592–5), the youth from Parmenie does seem, as W.T.H. Jackson says, another Orpheus. Indeed, for Jackson, the implications of the comparison extend beyond characterization to an adumbration of the entire tragedy of Tristan: 'he is at once the seer and the interpreter, like Orpheus, the singer and the mover. And like Orpheus he must lose his love and perish as the result of his gift.'[2] But Orpheus isn't the only figure Gottfried's audience could have recalled; even more than this classical counterpart, Tristan would have been compared to the most famous of biblical harpers, David.

When God withdrew his favour from Saul, the king of Israel was at times afflicted by an evil spirit. To bear these attacks more easily, Saul's counsellors advised him to seek a man skilful in playing the harp. One counsellor recommended David, whom he describes as a skilful player, a man of great strength and a man fit for war, prudent in his works, and a comely person. So David was sent for, and entered Saul's service. And Saul loved him exceedingly, and made him his armour-bearer (1 Samuel 16:18–23).

The resemblance between Tristan and David is evident: both are young, both seemingly from low station yet destined for kingship; King Mark comes to love Tristan exceedingly, and by presiding over his investiture as a knight, makes Tristan his armour-bearer. Indeed, David's attributes, his great valour, prudent words, readiness in combat, and comely appearance, would qualify him as the forerunner and model of thirteenth-century knighthood. Consider the benediction Mark addresses to Tristan at the end of his investiture:

> 'sich,' sprach er, 'neve Tristan,
> sît dir nu swert gesegnet ist
> und sît du ritter worden bist,
> nu bedenke ritterlîchen prîs
> und ouch dich selben, wer du sîs;
> dîn geburt und dîn edelkeit
> sî dînen ougen vür geleit:
> wis diemüete und wis unbetrogen,
> wis wârhaft und wis wolgezogen;
> den armen den wis iemer guot,
> den rîchen iemer hochgemuot;
> ziere unde werde dînen lîp,
> êre unde minne elliu wîp;
> wis milte unde getriuwe
> und iemer dar an niuwe!
> wan ûf mîn êre nim ich daz,
> daz golt noch zobel gestuont nie bas
> dem spere unde dem schilte
> dan triuwe unde milte.'

'Nephew Tristan,' he said, 'now that your sword has been consecrated and you have become a knight, think of the glory of knighthood, and also of yourself and who you are. Let your birth and nobility be always in your mind. Be modest and without deceit: be truthful and well-bred. Always be good to the poor; to the mighty always be proud. Cultivate and attend to your appearance. Honour and love all women. Be generous and loyal, and never tire of it. For on my honour I think gold and sable never sat better on spear and shield than loyalty and generosity.' (5020–38)

From this passage and the harp-playing, we sense that had David been alive in thirteenth-century Cornwall or Parmenie, he certainly would have been Tristan. And if we need further evidence, consider that shortly after David enters Saul's service, he slays Goliath: soon after his entrance into knighthood, Tristan returns to Parmenie to revenge his father's death, but then rejoins Mark in Cornwall, where he engages the huge Morold, Gumrun's champion, in single combat and beheads him. About to enter the lists, Tristan himself makes us recall his biblical predecessor when he says,

> ja ist der dinge vil geschehen;
> man hât des winder gesehen,
> daz unrehtiu hôchvart
> mit kleiner kraft genidert wart:
> daz möhte ouch vil wol noch ergân,
> der ez getörste bestân.

Many things do happen: one has so often seen lawless arrogance brought low by puny strength, and it might very well happen again, if someone dared to do it. (6219–24)

The question we must ask is why Gottfried wished us to see so much of David in Tristan. Certainly Tristan's stature is enhanced by the comparison, but more important, the tragedy of Tristan's life is foreshadowed. Of all the virtues a knight should possess, King Mark has set one above the rest: 'Be loyal, and never tire of it.' Here is the real basis of Gottfried's analogy: for the stories of David and Tristan both are tragedies of broken loyalties, impossible allegiances, and the division which sunders the closest bonds of parenthood and family. In a sense, David is son to many fathers – to Jesse, to Saul, and to Samuel – and the demands they make on David cannot be reconciled. For although he can leave Jesse to follow Saul, David cannot follow Saul and remain loyal to Samuel. The tension increases with David's friendship with Jonathan; Saul's house, which is Israel, becomes divided from within, and eventually falls.

Saul's downfall, of course, results from his disobedience to God; David's more significantly for *Tristan*, from excessive passion for Bathsheba. David's terrible attempts to convince Uriah to sleep with his wife, whom David had already impregnated, mark the beginning of his sorrows. Only later, when David has himself become father to many sons, and one, Absalom, rises against him, do we know the enormity of anguish David must have felt, seeing so much of himself in his son.

Tristan too is son to many fathers: to Rivalin, whose desire for the fame of chivalry brought him to Cornwall, where his passion for Blanchfleur led first to her impregnation, then to her willing abduction, and finally to both their deaths, his in battle, hers as she gives birth to Tristan. He is son as well to Rual li Foitenant, the man who keeps faith, who remains loyal to the charge of Rivalin and raises Tristan as his son and king. And finally he is son to Mark, who sponsors Tristan in knighthood, and whose wife-to-be Tristan woos and loves.[3] In King Mark's house, Tristan tries to hold the passion of Rivalin and the loyalty of Rual in a desperate balance, but the conflict caused by the demands of knighthood, his love for Isolde, and his loyalty to Mark cannot be resolved. This house too is divided; it cannot stand.

Tristan's similarity to David, therefore, goes beyond characterization; in the greatness of his emotions and the depth of his sorrows, the history of David embodied the profound mingling of joy and grief which Gottfried saw as the essential meaning of Tristan's life. As Gottfried says in his prologue,

> Wan swâ man noch hoeret lesen
> ir triuwe, ir triuwen reinekeit,
> ir herzeliep, ir herzeleit,
>   Deist aller edelen herzen brôt,
> hie mite so lebet ir beider tôt.
> Wir lesen ir leben, wir lesen ir tôt,
> unde ist uns daz süeze alse brôt.

For still whenever one hears the recital of Tristan and Isolde's troth, their pure loyalty, their hearts' joy, their hearts' sorrow, this is bread to all noble hearts. With this their death lives on here. We read their life, we read their death, and to us that is sweet as bread.   (230–35a)

But the resemblance between the two heroes goes beyond theme as well; ultimately it is an element of moral structure.[4] The entire outline of Tristan's career has been foreshadowed. As he plays the harp, Tristan's life is being set to a pattern, and if we do not as yet know its accidents, that is to say, the particular events that will make up Tristan's life, we do know its ethical direction and final outcome. Nor is *Tristan* unique in this aspect: in many medieval texts, a figure's personality seems to recapitulate his destiny. By examining how this phenomenon works, what its sources are, and how medieval poets develop and extend its possibilities, we shall understand an important aspect of the medieval idea of character.

First a name should be given to this extended resemblance between Tristan and David, a resemblance that points not only to shared physical qualities, but to the similar contour of their fates as well. I will call this technique literary typology, and in order to explain and justify what I mean by this conjunction of terms, a digression into the history of the interpretation of the Bible is necessary.

The word typology, of course, is familiar as part of that allegorical process which for Christians revealed the true significance of the Old and New Testaments. The theoretical aspects of typology, and its relation to allegory in general, perhaps received their clearest and fullest articulation in the *Summa* of Thomas Aquinas, but for a discussion of the bearing typology might have had on literature, the remarks of Dante, which in fact follow what Thomas had to say, seem a more appropriate starting point.[5]

In the *Convivio*, Dante tells us that there are two kinds of allegory: the allegory of poets and the allegory of theologians. In the allegory of poets, one story is used to tell another: like a nut within its shell, the true kernel, that is, the moral significance of the story, is hidden beneath a fiction, a beautiful lie. Thus, to use Dante's example, the story of Orpheus taming the wild beasts with his harp is a fiction that serves only to conceal the truth that 'the wise man with the instrument of his voice will make cruel hearts humble, and make those who do not live in science and art do his will.'[6] In this kind of allegory, literal sense is sacrificed to ultimate meaning. So long as the inner meaning is revealed, any violence or distortion practised on the fictional casing is justified.

The allegory of theologians, however, is different, and to demonstrate the difference, Dante asks Can Grande della Scala to consider the opening of Psalm 114: 'When Israel went out of Egypt, and the house of Jacob from a barbarous people: Judea was made his sanctuary, Israel his dominion.' If we look to the letter alone, Dante says, we read of the departure of the children of Israel from Egypt in the time of Moses; if, however, we look to the allegorical sense, we see man's redemption wrought by Christ. Furthermore, there is a moral sense: the conversion of the soul from the grief of sin to a state of grace, and a final encompassing sense, the anagogical: the departure of the holy soul from the slavery of this life of corruption to the liberty of eternal glory.[7]

The allegory Dante is talking about here is theologica, not poetical. The difference is that the Psalm does not deal in fiction, but in history: there really was an Exodus from Egypt. The allegory of the Psalm, therefore, exists in facts, in events, not in words. Or, to take another example: the Bible says that Abraham had two sons, one by a bondwoman, Hagar, and one by a free woman, Sarah. This is something that is not a mere fable, a poetic fiction like the story of Orpheus; this was an actual fact. It is this historical event that enables Paul to see Abraham's two children, Ishmael and Isaac, as representatives of the Old and New Testaments respectively.[8] This distinction between word and deed, between word and fact, lies not only at the heart of the allegory of theologians, but at the heart of Christian typology as well.

For Dante, as for any medieval Christian, all doctrine concerned either things or signs. Signs are used to signify something: words, for instance, by their very nature are signs that point to things, and derive their meaning from them. A thing is something that normally doesn't signify something else, like wood, stone, or cattle. The wood Moses threw into the bitter waters to dispel their bitterness, however, is not a thing in this sense, nor is the stone Jacob placed beneath his head when he dreamt of the angels ascending and descending the ladder. These are things that were thought to be signs of other things. The wood Moses cast into the water was seen as a sign that pointed to the cross Jesus bore, and the stone beneath Jacob's head was said to represent the human nature of Christ. These things that point to other things are to be used, and the things they point to, that is, the substance of Christian revelation, should be enjoyed. To mistake a mediating figure for its ultimate significance, to fail to see that Moses' wood was also a symbol for Christ's cross, was considered a sin.[9]

The system that determined the final meaning of these things, which could be substances like Jacob's stone or historical events like the crossing of the Red Sea, was given the name typology. Typology, therefore, is the use of symbols to make sense out of history. Already in the Old Testament, certain events, such as the Exodus, began to assume paradigmatic significance for the nation of Israel. Psalms and Isaiah, Hosea and Jeremiah all hark back to the Exodus, and seek to remind the Jewish people what happened then, the better to understand what they must do now. Christians extended this idea to cover the relationship between the Old and New Testaments.[10] The events of the Old Testament both were and meant; they happened, and they had a meaning. This meaning, however, could only be revealed in retrospect, that is, in the fullness of time with the coming of Christ. Typology therefore sought to show how singular events from the past found their true meaning in the life of Christ.

Typology is a system that establishes correspondences between events in history. The allegory of theologians takes this one step further and seeks meaning in a series of such events: it is a theory of history. We can perhaps understand this concept by means of an analogy. When words are arranged in systematic patterns of meaning, they form sentences. No sentence, however, is complete until it reaches its end-point, its period, which retrospectively gives meaning to what has come before. Allegory is to history roughly what syntax is to a sentence: a master pattern that orders and reveals the significance of many seemingly random events. Allegory arranges the events of the Bible as words are arranged in a sentence: each word or event not only has meaning in itself, but assumes additional meaning in the position it occupies relative to its neighbour, that is, in its context. It is with the context of history that allegory is concerned: it sees history from God's perspective. This linguistic analogy can be carried even further because God is the Logos: in the beginning was the Word. The Middle Ages took this statement to mean that God was the author of two books – the Bible and the created world – and it is the nature of God's writing in either that words or things or events both exist in themselves and point beyond themselves to an ultimate signification. Allegory will determine the pattern of the words and events, will reveal the overarching design of the history recorded in the Old Testament by viewing that history from its end-point, which for any Christian was the coming of Christ.

By establishing the relation of typology to allegory, we can see how Gottfried appropriates both concepts in the *Tristan*. David becomes the typological forerunner not of Christ, whom he does prefigure in exegetical tradition, but of Tristan. But in so far as the pattern of Tristan's life recalls the events of David's, Gottfried has adopted the methods of allegory. This then is what I mean by literary typology: not the facile personifications one finds in so many medieval poems, but a method that converts a theory of history into narrative structure, and rechannels a system of foreshadowings and prefiguration into the formation of living character.[11]

In general, therefore, character in medieval works can be of two sorts. In works that employ what Dante calls the allegory of poets, exemplary figures verge toward personification. If in antiquity a man was identified by his ruling passion, in the Middle Ages the disposition itself came to be depicted. The classical paradigm was 'Cato ille virtutum viva imago / Cato the living embodiment of virtue': medieval counterparts range from Prudentia and Ira in Prudentius's *Psychomachia* to Raison and Danger in the *Roman de la Rose*.[12] The idea behind such abstractions seems classical: certainly the concern is for the universal rather than the particular, yet few writers of Athens or Rome would have divorced generic attributes from the men who act in accordance with them.

Even those less rarefied characters, the kings, knights, maidens, prelates, and the like who haunt medieval narratives, obey the same impulse toward the typical. The writers of poetic handbooks, Matthew of Vendôme, Geoffrey of

Vinsauf, John of Garland, for example, knew the classical conception of character from Cicero, Quintilian, Priscian, and Horace, among others; the precepts of these authors, however, were applied in a peculiarly medieval way. [13] As Faral says, even more than their ancient authorities, medieval commentators lost sight of individuals in order to consider the moral and psychological categories to which they belonged. [14] Matthew, for instance, explains that a prelate's attributes should be 'constancy of faith, desire for virtue, purity of devotion and grace of piety'; a king's should be the rigour of justice ('rigor justitiae'). [15] The particular is of no concern whatever; Matthew even recommends that the poet learn his model character sketches by heart so that he would be less likely to indulge his personal fantasies. [16] The antique preoccupation with 'convenientia' was transformed into a prescriptive set of rules: characters drawn from them will carry conviction only when we judge how well they conform to these rules, or better, refashion them.

Recently, Wesley Trimpi has shown the extent to which rhetorical exercises and instruction throughout the Middle Ages assured the transmission of ancient literary theory. [17] Oratorical distinctions between thesis and hypothesis, the determination of the status of a cause, and the claims of equity against the letter of the law all affected the quality of medieval literature. But even when writers adopted or were influenced by these rhetorical ideas and structures, and produced a fiction more sophisticated than most of the personification allegories, the characters remained abstract in a way few figures in antiquity are. Various men in Andreas Capellanus's *De arte honeste amandi*, for instance, try to persuade women from stations above or below their own to love them. In every case the characters are unknown and unnamed, since Andreas means his dialogues to have a validity beyond particular circumstances. [18] The figures exist to demonstrate a thesis; compared to the characters of Andreas's main source, Ovid's *Ars Amatoria*, who are vibrant because they are willy-nilly made the spokesmen of the narrator's often outrageous views, Andreas's figures are ciphers. The same is true of the characters whose actions form the basis of some of the 'questioni d'amore' in Boccaccio's *Filocolo*. These figures, as Branca says, are also 'senza nome e senza paese'; they too are elements of a general proposition that will be argued, in true rhetorical fashion, 'in utramque partem.' [19]

Such figures are, to use Auerbach's term, all foreground; naked expositions, as it were, of simply what they are. [20] The only chance for complication arises, as we shall see, when such characters appear in a story told by a different character. But in a text structured by literary typology, characters will necessarily possess depth, a sense of implication and complexity. They become like the mysterious 'vilain' in Chrétien's *Yvain*. When asked what kind of man he is ('Quiex hom ies tu?'), he responds: 'Tex con tu voiz; / si ne sui autres nule foiz / Such as you see; for I am not at all otherwise' (329–30), but by saying it this way (compare Exodus 3:14), he immediately becomes more than he says.[21] The reader asks at once why this rustic lout, who knows nothing of 'aventure,' echoes the words God spoke in the wilderness. From this moment, we wonder what the relation of this monster to Calogrenant and Yvain will be. In biblical exegesis, typology establishes a connection between two persons separated in time yet within temporality.[22] In typological fiction, however, the correspondence often is not between figures who appear in the same work, but an implied likeness, not so much by the way a character is depicted, as by what he says or does, between one character within the poem and another outside it. David never appears in the *Tristan*: only when Tristan plays the harp do we begin to sense a resemblance between him and the son of Jesse. Yet once an implicit correspondence between this king of Parmenie and the king of Israel is admitted, we wonder whether their destinies might be similar as well. Character begins to implicate plot; by plucking his harp, Tristan plays the prelude to his own tragedy.

In the tenth canto of the *Inferno*, the canto of Farinata, we find an even clearer anatomy of how these techniques could aid in fashioning a typological secular literature. In the *Divine Comedy*, characters are typological, but Dante's meeting them allegorical. Farinata is shaped figurally; he is, as we shall see, a Florentine Aeneas. But this resemblance, even as it fixes Farinata's identity forever, becomes a motive in the allegory of Dante's life: this encounter in hell prefigures Dante's future meeting with Cacciaguida in heaven. Even more than in *Tristan*, the method by which character has been drawn parallels the design by which the narrative unfolds.

As Singleton, Freccero, and others have shown, the mediation of language and desire is perhaps the most pervasive theme of the *Divine Comedy*. Since each affirms what it lacks, the movement of language is analogous to the movement of desire: both are means to an end. We desire the apple because we do not have it, even as the word 'apple' is not the apple itself, but a sign that points to it. In Dante's poem, God is the end-point, the thing signified: He is the peace that satisfies all desires, the eternal Word all temporal language is derived from and refers to. In the fifth canto of the *Inferno*, Paolo and Francesca were brought to satisfy their physical desires by reading a book; neither understood that the words they read and the desire they felt ought to have been signs that mediated between themselves and God.[23]

With this in mind, we can consider the canto of Farinata. It begins with Dante asking Virgil to speak, 'parlami e sodisfammi a' miei disiri / speak to me and satisfy my desires' (6).[24] A few lines later Virgil responds that when they come to the uncovered sepulchres, Dante's question 'satisfatto sarà tosto / will soon be satisfied' (17). At the end of the canto, Virgil asks Dante why he is so lost in thought. 'E io li sodisfeci al suo dimando,' Dante replies, 'and I satisfied his question.' Dante structures this canto paratactically: Dante and Virgil in conversation; the interruption by Farinata; the interruption by Cavalcante; the return to Farinata; Dante and Virgil in conversation. What distinguishes Dante from other writers, however, is the careful balance of parts which gives a sense of symmetry. Each section is related to the others by theme: satisfaction is a term more usually applied to desires than to communication, but in the *Divine Comedy*, the two are inseparable.

Farinata and Cavalcante are burned in the circle of the heretics. Heresy is peculiarly medieval; it is the only sin in the *Divine Comedy* that is not found in Aristotle's and Cicero's classifications of vices, and it is unique among sins in that it is entirely intellectual. Unlike Gluttony, Avarice, or Envy, Heresy does not arise from the attraction of some external object; the error originates in man's rational soul. Now two people speaking and understanding one another is an intellectual act as well, or at least the understanding is intellectual, yet this is exactly what does not happen when Dante speaks to Farinata and to Cavalcante. The heretics are burned by fire, a symbol of the mind; their real punishment, however, is the complete failure of understanding.[25]

Thus the emphasis of the canto is on language, the means to understanding. Farinata is elaborate in his dignified speech about Florence, the supercilious grandeur of his bearing – 'non mutò aspetto, / né mosse collo, né piegò sua costa / he changed not his aspect, nor moved his neck, nor bent his side' – gives evidence that here indeed is the great-souled man.[26] Dante's curt answer, however, for the moment leaves him speechless, so that Cavalcante's chin can inch its way above the edge of his sepulchre and say,

> ... Se per questo cieco
> carcere vai per altezza d'ingegno,
> mio figlio ov' è? e perché non è teco?

If you go through this blind prison by the height of genius, where is my son, and why is he not with you? (58–60)

Dante's answer has provoked one of the most extended critical debates in the *Commedia*:

> ... Da me stesso non vegno:
> colui ch'attende là per qui mi mena,
> forse cui Guido vostro ebbe a disdegno.

I come not of myself. He who waits there leads me through here, whom perhaps your Guido held in disdain. (61-3)

'Cui' can mean 'to whom' or 'for whom': does it refer to Virgil or to Beatrice? I agree with Singleton that Virgil is the person referred to, a conclusion strengthed by the fact that Farinata and Cavalcante have been drawn typologically.[27]

In the third book of the *Aeneid*, Andromache, pining away in Buthrotum, that dried-up image of Troy, sees the approaching Aeneas and directs to him a haunting question:

> 'uerane te facies, uerus mihi nuntius adfers,
> nate dea? uiuisne? aut, si lux alma recessit,
> Hector ubi est?

Are you a real form, a real messenger, coming to me, goddess-born? Do you live? Or, if sweet light has passed, where is Hector? (III, 310-12)

Andromache's spirit has died with her son at Troy: Cavalcante's question has been modelled on hers because, like Andromache, Cavalcante thinks amost exclusively of his family, of his son Guido, a poet of prominence in Florence and a friend of Dante's.[28] Such excessive concern for one's family and heritage on earth, a single-minded devotion which so blinds Cavalcante that he does not see the larger, heavenly family of God, is damnable to Dante. For the epicurean Cavalcante, life on earth still constitutes the highest good.

The same holds true for Farinata, for, if Cavalcante thinks only of his own, Farinata, like Aeneas, thinks almost exclusively of the state. Farinata is the great soul, the saviour of Florence, yet Farinata too is in hell. Dante here is reading Virgil allegorically: not only the family, but even Rome is a sign that points beyond itself to the city and empire of God. For Dante, this, in fact, is the way Virgil must be read. Perhaps Guido failed to realize this, or worse, realized, but would not. In any case, father Cavalcante completely misunderstands Dante's words, thinks his son is dead, and sinks down dispirited. There is no communication at all. Farinata, who himself had been a victim of misunderstanding, then explains to Dante that the damned lack the very means for understanding, knowledge of the present moment. The implications of not having a present moment, both for language and for existence, are too great to enumerate here. But the point is clear that such a state makes the possibilities for confusion boundless. It is both ironic and fitting that this great canto closes with Dante and Virgil communicating with each other.

Yet, for all they say, we sense that Dante and Virgil still speak to one another through a glass darkly. Not until we meet Cacciaguida in the fifteenth canto of the *Paradiso* does everything Farinata has said here become clear. Even as Farinata was made a latter-day 'pater Aeneas,' so it now becomes clear that he himself foreshadowed Cacciaguida, the truer father. 'Sub specie aeternitatis,' the statesman of Florence yields to the humble citizen of the City of God. But if Farinata does prefigure Cacciaguida, we realize that it is not typology so much as the allegory of exodus, the flight from the City of Man to the City of God, that requires Dante, once he had met Farinata, to meet Cacciaguida.[29] Like the Bible, the *Divine Comedy* is conclusive and self-referential, containing within itself a complete matrix of foreshadowing and fulfilment which mirrors both the overall design and individual accidents of the world's history. Unlike Ovid's heroes and villains, who exist primarily as metaphors for the poet's art, Tristan, Farinata, and Cacciaguida become metaphors for the narratives they appear in. They all reveal the power and depth of a figure whose character has been drawn typologically.

Both Dante and Aquinas, of course, came at the height of a time which, from the standpoint of literary interpretation, could well be called the age of allegory: theirs is the mature expression of ideas that were a thousand years in the making. Similarly, Gottfried's *Tristan* impresses us by the sophistication of its use of biblical techniques, from which his characters gain their cohesion and power. But if we wish to locate the wellspring of this power, the very proficiency of Dante's and Gottfried's art might make the search more difficult. To understand why Farinata and Tristan move us the way they do, we must divorce the idea of one figure foreshadowing another from these particular literary applications, and consider typology generally as an element of style. And as we do this, we should search for an answer to an equally important matter: why was typology so singularly a Jewish-Christian phenomenon; why did it not develop in classical Greece and Rome?

If typology and biblical allegory liken the movement of history to the movement of a sentence, they do so because of the peculiar nature of what they attempt to explain. In Genesis, God created by speaking; in John, God has become the Word Himself. That the children begotten by the Word, that is, the world and the destiny of men in it, should share the genetic make-up, as it were, of their parent is only natural.

For Christians, the history of the world was recorded in the Bible: in it, therefore, one would find not only the matter of salvation, but in the choice and arrangement of the words, the style of salvation as well. One of the most noticeable and influential features of biblical style, as Erich Auerbach has shown, is parataxis.[30] Parataxis is that rhetorical term which, simply put, means placing clauses side by side, often without connecting conjunctions. A familiar example would be, 'And God said, Let there be light. And there was light. And God saw that the light was good.' Here are three independent statements concerning the creation of light: no causal or temporal relation exists among them. We do not read, 'Because God said, let there be light, light was created,' or 'After God said, let there be light, there was light.' Each phrase simply is there, in direct discourse, unexplained yet fraught with questions of consequence. Or consider these two sentences: 'Troy fell; Rome rises from its ashes,' and 'Troy fell so that Rome might rise from its ashes.' The first statement is a recitation of two historical facts; the second is Virgil, and by extension, all classical style. For even as history has acquired a sense of mission and purpose, its language has been articulated by conjunctions with precisely defined shades of meaning and a sequence of verbs that reflects fine distinctions of time and mood. In the language of classical antiquity, relationships are articulated, but paradoxically, they are articulated at the loss of dramatic effect. Somehow, even more than spelling out the ways in which they are related, juxtaposing events seems to underscore their degree of interdependence. 'And God said, Let there be light. And there was light' is far more powerful than 'Because God said, let there be light' or 'After God said, let there be light, light was created.' And it is more powerful precisely because of what is not said, because of what has been left out. The dependence of the creation of light on God's speaking is absolute, as if beyond the power of any conjunction or any accumulation of conjunctions to express. The baldness of the statement brings the reader up short: in our minds we supply the connections; we say 'Because God said,' or 'When god created,' but ultimately we are left with a feeling of the inadequacy of our explanations, a feeling which only strengthens our conviction that in some mysterious, inexpressible way, light could not have been created had God not spoken.

The connection between typology and parataxis is not difficult to define, for at its heart, typology is paratactic. By juxtaposing correspondences rather than explaining them, typology allowed Christian thinkers to formulate as sophisticated a view of history as any Greek or Roman could offer, even though all history was reduced to absolute dependence on the design of God. Yet, as Auerbach notes, such a conception of history

was completely alien to the mentality of classical antiquity, it annihilated that mentality down to the very structure of its language, at least of its literary language, which – with all its ingenious and nicely shaded conjunctions, its wealth of devices for syntactic arrangement, its carefully elaborated system of tenses – became wholly superfluous as soon as a vertical connection, ascending from all that happens, converging in God alone became significant. Wherever the two conceptions met, there was of necessity a conflict and an attempt to compromise – between, on the one hand, a presentation which carefully interrelated the elements of history, which respected temporal and causal sequence, remained within the domain of earthly foreground, and, on the other, a fragmentary, discrete presentation, constantly seeking an interpretation from above.[31]

The compromise Auerbach speaks of is nowhere better seen than in St Augustine. In the *De Doctrina Christiana*, Augustine quotes Cicero's classification of style according to subject matter: 'Is igitur erit eloquens, qui poterit parva submisse, modica temperate, magna granditer dicere / He therefore will be eloquent who can speak of small things simply, of middling things in the intermediate style, and of great things in the grand manner.'[32] Under Christian dispensation, however, even the lowliest things, legal transactions or the deeds of fishermen, since they concerned Christ, were sublime and could be discussed in the high style; moreover, the highest mysteries of the faith often were expressed in the Bible in the simplest, most accessible words. But rather than reject the classical gradations of style, Augustine reformed the criteria for their use. Instead of subject matter, the style to be used now depended on the author's purpose: the low style was most suitable for teaching, the intermediate for condemning or praising, the grand manner for persuading (IV, 19). In his *Sermones*, Augustine instructs the faithful of Hippo; not surprisingly, the language in general is simple, the incidence of parataxis, given the careful balance and artful arrangement of the periods, quite high. The *De Civitate Dei*, on the other hand, is a work of salvation history: events are related not only chronologically but causally as Augustine sets his chronicle of the times to a figural pattern. The fall of Rome, for example, far from a catastrophe, was a pre-ordained element in the grand design of history, a fulfilment of Christ's revelation on earth. Augustine's language, therefore, 'preserves precise gradations of temporal, comparative, and concessive hypotaxes';[33] the relative lack of paratactic periods compared to other works Augustine wrote after his baptism is notable.

In the *Confessions*, however, Augustine's purpose is more complex: certainly he praises God and bitterly condemns his own sins, but the recounting of Augustine's life is less an autobiography than an exemplary history of the effects of God's persuasion on the restless soul. The style of the *Confessions* is extraordinarily artful, its periods balanced and graced with all the ornaments of rhetoric. Yet paratactic constructions abound, often precisely in those incidents, such as Alypius at the gladiatorial shows, or the moment of Augustine's conversion itself, which today we find most powerful and memorable. The conversion, of course, is the most famous incident of the *Confessions*; after hearing the story of St Anthony, Augustine rushes out into a garden:

ego sub quadam fici arbore straui me nescio quomodo et dimisi habenas lacrimis, et proruperunt flumina oculorum meorum, acceptabile sacrificium tuum (Ps. 50:19), et non quidem his uerbis, sed in hac sententia multa dixi tibi: et tu, domine, usquequo? (Ps. 6:4) usquequo, domine, irasceris in finem? ne memor fueris iniquitatum nostrarum antiquarum. (Ps. 78:5, 8). sentiebam enim eis me teneri. iactabam uoces miserabiles: 'quamdiu, quamdiu, cras et cras? Quare non modo? Quare non hac hora finis turpitudinis meae?'

Dicebam haec et flebam amarissima contritione cordis mei. et ecce audio uocem de uicina domo cum cantu dicentis et crebro repetentis quasi pueri an puellae, nescio: 'Tolle lege, tolle lege.' Statimque mutato uultu intentissimus cogitare coepi, utrumnam solerent pueri in aliquo genere ludendi cantitare tale aliquid, nec occurrebat omnino audisse me uspiam repressoque impetu lacrimarum surrexi nihil aliud interpretans diuinitus mihi iuberi, nisi ut aperirem codicem et legerem quod primum caput inuenissem.

I threw myself down under some fig tree – I don't know how – and let loose the reins of my tears, and a flood broke forth from my eyes, a sacrifice acceptable to you, and, not in these words, but with this sense, I spoke many things to you: 'And you, O Lord, how long? How long, O Lord; wilt thou be angry forever? Remember not our former iniquities.' For I still felt myself held back by them. I kept crying in misery, 'How long, how long, [will I say] tomorrow and tomorrow? Why not let this moment be the end of my foulness?' I was saying this and was weeping with the most bitter sorrow in my heart. And behold, I hear a voice from the next house, whether a boy's voice or a girl's, I don't know, singing and often repeating, 'Take it and read, take it and read.' And at once, with a changed expression, I began to think most intently, whether children were accustomed to chant words such as these in any kind of game, nor did I recall I had heard them anywhere at all, and, having quelled the onset of tears, I stood up thinking this could be nothing else but a divine command that I open the book and read the first passage I found.   (Book VIII, 12)[34]

The language is simple and unadorned, the cola and sentences short and independent: 'Ego sub ... fici arbore straui ... et dimisi ... et proruperunt ...' Augustine's model, it is clear, is biblical, specifically the Psalms. The parallel verses of Psalms 6 and 78 are skilfully juxtaposed; Augustine's own expostulations, 'quamdiu, quamdiu, cras et cras? quare non modo? quare non hac hora ...' then reproduce their rhythm, their common, almost colloquial diction, their elementary syntax. In the second paragraph, the biblical elocution 'et ecce ...' announces the extraordinary shift to the present tense: 'audio uocem ... dicentis ... Tolle lege, tolle lege.' The moment of grace is so vivid, so present to Augustine, it transcends tense; his language becomes a temporal image of God's timelessness, an instant of the *is* of eternity. And then there is the utter simplicity of the child's words: two commands, unconnected yet complete, whose fullness of meaning is beyond the power of syntax to express. Augustine himself seems to emphasize this fact. His complex reaction, first his trying to remember if he had ever heard these words, his face now showing perhaps a child's puzzlement; his consequent decision, the tears now staunched, that the chant could be nothing other than a divine directive; all is delineated in the carefully co-ordinated, hypotactic period that follows. But reason follows revelation, both in language and in the mind: for all his ratiocination, the conversion is effected only when Augustine reads the 'sermo humilis' of Paul. Augustine's crisis is a crisis of style as well as of the soul; this is why Melchior Verheijen calls his study of Augustine's Latin *Eloquentia Pedisequa*. Eloquence is the handmaiden of grace, and much of the *Confessions* chronicles Augustine's attempt to accommodate the classical and biblical styles.

Other stylistic features in the passage deserve mention. By recalling the language of Paul's rapture to the third heaven, Augustine invests his conversion with visionary fervour. Somehow Augustine had thrown himself down beneath a fig tree (itself allegorically significant: cf John 1:48 and Micah 4:4), 'nescio quomodo'; later, he hears the voices chanting ' "tolle lege," – quasi pueri an puellae, nescio.' One remembers how Paul was caught up, 'sive in corpore nescio, sive extra corpus, nescio, Deus scit / whether in the body, I know not, or out of the body, I know not, God knoweth' (2 Corinthians 12:3). Heaven descends to earth in the voice of children, and the simplicity of their words confounds the wise.

Even more significant than such linguistic subtleties, however, is the typological function of the entire scene itself. Augustine's moment of salvation must be read in conjunction with his moment of original sin. Earlier, in Book II, Augustine had discussed with great shame and self-reproach the bitter implications of his gratuitous theft of pears from an orchard. Now, in another garden, Augustine is called to take up a better life. The movement, as Burke and others have shown, is from Eden to Eden, from pear tree to fig tree, from Adam and the fall from grace to Christ, the second Adam, who comes to redeem the sins of man on the cross.[35] Augustine sees in the particulars of his life an image of the pattern of all history, and the progress of each is set to a biblical paradigm.[36] Augustine therefore structures the autobiographical section of the *Confessions* typologically: by a series of paratactic appositions, the conversion recalls the theft, even as both re-enact scenes from the Bible. A thousand years later, Dante would chart the course of his own life by the same co-ordinates: he too moves from a 'selva oscura' to the garden of a 'paradiso terrestre.' Augustine realized, as did Dante after him, that typology, when used in secular texts, offered the means whereby a character could be made the epitome of his history: an extended analogy between a figure and an earlier archetype would suggest a similarity between the events of the two narratives as well. But at a level even more fundamental than this, Augustine understood that typology at its heart is a reformulation of the style of the Bible itself. The genius of the paratactic style would enable both the characters and events of any work that used typology to embody the profoundest truths about man and his place in history in language that was universally accessible.

As a mode of thought in the Latin West, parataxis and typology therefore came to dominate the language and art of the early Middle Ages. How often Old Testament figures stand beside their New Testament counterparts, as in the fifth-century mosaics in Santa Maria Maggiore in Rome. The panels simply represent each scene without comment; the viewer supplies the intellectual space in which the connection between, for example, the sacrifice of Isaac and the passion of Jesus is articulated. One sees that the triumph of these most elementary means of syntactic and artistic structure was not due solely to what Norden calls 'Entartung,' the decline of culture in general and literary Latin in particular; the new style to some degree represents the triumph of Christianity as well.[37] Until the latter part of the fourth century, Greek was the predominant language of the liturgy and Christian discourse in Rome. Many of the early converts to Christianity in Italy, Africa, Spain, and Gaul, however, were from the lower classes: Christianity had to speak to them in their own language.[38] The simple style of the Bible would have been a natural point of contact: as the sacred writings were translated into Latin, their style would present few problems to their intended audience. Indeed, vulgar Latin, the Latin spoken by the masses, was itself a potent linguistic force. By late antiquity it had already exerted considerable influence on literary Latin;[39] not surprisingly it also influenced the early Latin writings of men in the Church. The two tendencies complemented each other: the result of their trend toward simpler language and syntax can perhaps best be seen in works like Gregory of Tour's *History of the Franks*, in which events are haphazardly related, juxtaposed rather than connected to one another by cause or logic. The language itself is elementary and emphatically paratactic.[40]

With the Carolingian reform, however, a more manneristic Latin began to develop, in which temporal distinctions and concessive hypotaxes were once again observed. But in doing so, this language lost all contact with a speaking public.[41] Indeed, during the centuries from the fall of the Empire to the age of Charlemagne, Latin ceased to be spoken at all by the people: the romance vernaculars had begun to emerge. Dag Norberg, for instance, after examining the writings of Caesarius of Arles, Gregory of Tours, Sidonius Apollinaris, the

Strasbourg Oaths, and the Council of Trent (813 AD), has argued that linguistic change had become so general in Gaul that a 'nouveau système linguistique,' discrete from Latin, was being spoken by the seventh century.[42]

Certainly the early literary artifacts we have in that developing language, *Roland* and the chansons de geste, are highly paratactic, both in their language and their structure. This perhaps is a reflection of their oral composition, but if we look at a later text, the *Roman d'Eneas*, the style and arrangement of thought is still paratactic, despite the near certainty that it was produced by a cleric, or someone taught by one, and would therefore show more direct syntactic evidence of its Latin past than would a chanson de geste.[43]

As the vernaculars continued to develop, of course, complex relationships were able to be expressed with greater preciseness, to the point where in the hands of men like Guinizelli, Cavalcanti, and Dante, thirteenth-century Italian could accommodate the most refined disquisitions on the nature and effect of love. But even when parataxis ceased to be an element of style, it remained an ingrained unit of organization and presentation of both characters and plots. One finds it everywhere in the literature of the Middle Ages: in the later Old French romances, in the Middle English *Pearl* and *Alliterative Morte Arthure*, in Dante and Boccaccio. In the hands of a master, a character drawn paratactically could be extraordinarily complex. Talbot Donaldson has shown how Chaucer, for instance, tells us less than we tell ourselves when he describes Criseyde:[44]

> She nas nat with the leste of hir stature,
> But alle hir lymes so wel answerynge
> Weren to wommanhod, that creature
> Was nevere lasse mannyssh in seemynge.
> And ek the pure wise of hire mevynge
> Shewed wel that men myght in hire gesse
> Honour, estat, and wommanly noblesse.

All we find out about Criseyde here is that she's extremely attractive to men. By saying that never did a woman look less like a man, that her every movement seemed to indicate honour, station, and womanly nobility, that indeed she wasn't 'the least of her stature,' Chaucer has invited each reader to make of Criseyde what he will. The fact that history has branded so charming a female a whore only adds to the tension. The parataxis of Chaucer's style certainly involves us as readers: each of us must measure and define the nature of the relationship that is implied between the extraordinary uncertainty and vagueness of Criseyde's description and her actual character.

This element of disjunctiveness, even in works whose narrative line is continuous, resembles the paratactic arrangement of the elegies in Ovid's *Amores*, although the penchant for juxtaposition is the godchild of the biblical rather than the classical style. Of course, not every text whose parts are unsubordinated therefore follows the form of Scriptures or makes use of literary typology. But the simple yet sublime language of the Bible was everywhere known, as were the allegorical principles by which it was organized: secular writers and artists in the Middle Ages would have looked to the Old and New Testaments for models of characterization, theme, and narrative structure. And to those who did, typology offered a device which showed how two or more paratactically juxtaposed personal or narrative events could be connected.

The digressive nature of medieval narratives, their episodic quality, the sense we have of jagged seams showing through, far from defects, therefore, could well be sought-after effects sanctioned by a sophisticated esthetic theory. Indeed, medieval literary works ultimately would follow Augustine's example and create their own internal typology. In Chrétien de Troyes's *Yvain*, for instance, no character resembles David or any other biblical figure the way Tristan does, yet here, in a fiction whose premises are fundamentally not religious, one character's actions clearly prefigure another's. This has caused some to think Chrétien's romance lacks proportion, is full of vain repetitions and is illogically constructed. I would suggest, however, that these are instead typological elements of a work in which character anticipates both structure and theme.

The *Chevalier au Lion* begins with Calogrenant, Yvain's cousin, who recounts an unsuccessful adventure he undertook seven years before. Coming across a road that bore off to the right, Calogrenant entered a thick forest, full of brambles and thorns, and discovered a castle. He was received there with much honour and courtesy by the lord of the palace and his daughter. The next day he departed and soon came upon wild bulls battling among themselves, making such a frightful din that Calogrenant drew back in fear. Suddenly he catches sight of a huge, rustic lout, of surpassing ugliness; his hair in tufts his ears as big and mossy as elephants.' Calogrenant challenges this monstrous creature: 'Va, car me di / se tu es buene chose ou non / Come, tell me whether you are a good thing or not' (328–9). The herdsman's answer startles us: he says 'il ert uns hom,' he was a man. As if in disbelief Calogrenant then asks, 'What kind of man,' and the 'vilain' answers: 'Such as you see, for I am not at all otherwise.' Calogrenant asks this man-creature for counsel of some adventure or marvellous thing. The 'vilain' says he knows nothing of adventures ('d'avanture ne sai je rien'); nevertheless, he directs Calogrenant to a seemingly enchanted garden, which is swept by storms and lightning when water from a basin is spilt on a rock that stands near a chapel there. Calogrenant spills the water, and barely survives the storm. A knight then appears, who complains that Calogrenant has driven him from his home and woods by rain and lightning. This knight, whose name we later learn is Esclados the Red, defeats Calogrenant, who has no choice but to return to Arthur's court, having gained little but shame. On hearing the story, Yvain, vexed by Key, vows to avenge his cousin's honour. He journeys to the same garden, meeting the same people Calogrenant met, but in jousting with Esclados, Yvain wounds him grievously. Esclados flees, Yvain pursues to gain a token of his victory, and eventually finds himself trapped within Esclados's castle. He is saved from certain destruction by Lunete, and after a short time, marries Laudine, Escaldos's widow. It is at this point that Yvain's adventures truly begin.

Calogrenant himself seems to feel his experience has a meaning beyond its mere events: before his recitation begins he warns his listeners that 'he will not speak of a dream, or a fable, or a lie / ne vuel pas parler de songe, / ne de fable, ne de mançonge' (171–2):

> ore antandez!
> Cuer et oroilles me randez!
> Car parole est tote perdue
> S'ele n'est de cuer antandue.

Now listen! Give me your hearts and ears, for a word is lost completely if it is not understood with the heart. (149–52)

In a very courtly way, Calogrenant is asking us to read his story for its hidden, allegorical significance, as well he ought, since Calogrenant's adventure becomes typological, foreshadowing both the actual and especially the moral events of Yvain's life.[45]

Chrétien's romances in general, and *Yvain* in particular, sing most of arms and the woman, or, more specifically, of the irreconcilable tension which results when absolute devotion to knighthood and chivalry comes into conflict with a knight's absolute commitment to honour and serve women.[46] This conflict appears to be inevitable, for by pursuing adventures in arms, a knight invariably is led to meet beautiful women, and pledge his troth to them. In a sense, Calogrenant experiences this, not so much when he meets the castellan's lovely daughter as when he tells the story of his adventure. Calogrenant reveals his shame only because Guinevere commands him to: loyalty to his queen battles and overcomes the shame he suffered as a knight. By extension we can say that Chrétien himself in writing *Yvain* followed the same pattern, except that here making poetry out of the deeds of knighthood takes the place of doing them. For *Yvain* has struck many, myself included, as among other things a re-reading of *Lancelot*, that romance of adultery Chrétien wrote, unwillingly it seems, at the command of Marie de Champagne.[47] But more important, the experiences of Calogrenant and Chrétien foreshadow the experiences of Yvain, who, to the fullest extent possible, becomes subject to the conflicting demands of loyalty to arms and loyalty to a woman.

Yvain's pursuit of knightly honour leads him to marry Laudine, a woman he has widowed by his own hand. Their love, of course, and their subsequent marriage, is totally problematic: Chrétien himself represents it in terms of arms, revenge, and death. By falling in love with Laudine, Yvain desires the creature who hates him most; being loved, Laudine, 'although unaware of it, has well avenged the death of her lord / Bien a vangiee, et si nel set, / la dame la mort son seignor' (1362–3). Courtly love certainly is a paradox for a knight: to win in love he must be defeated by the woman he loves, but even more than this, Chrétien suggests that the emotion itself is as much hate as it is affection. In a famous internal monologue, Yvain ponders what he feels:

> toz jorz amerai m'anemi,
> que je ne la doi pas hair
> se je ne vuel Amor trair ...
> Et moi doit ele ami clamer?
> Oil, voir, por ce que je l'aim.
> Et je m'anemie la claim,
> qu'ele me het si n'a pas tort;
> que ce, qu'ele amoit, li ai mort.
> Et donc sui je ses anemies?
> Nel sui, certes, mes ses amis,
> c'onques rien tant amer ne vox.

I shall always love my enemy, for I ought not hate her unless I want to betray Love ... And should she call me friend? Yes, truly, because I love her. And I call her my enemy because she hates me, nor is she wrong, since I killed the one she loved. Am I therefore her enemy? Not at all, but her friend, for I have never desired nor loved anyone so much. (1452–4; 1456–63)

Nor is Laudine's love for Yvain any less problematic, founded as it is on insecurity and resentment. Both Laudine's and Yvain's passions are divided; neither person's thoughts or actions, though all too human, seem exemplary.

All this was anticipated by Calogrenant: his innocent seeking of adventure led to not so innocent consequences. Only his lack of prowess as a knight kept him from experiencing the true contention between chivalry and love. Yvain, however does marry Laudine, but considering the circumstances of their meeting, the bases of their affection, the time – two weeks – they have known each other, it is hardly surprising that Gawain is able to lead Yvain away from Laudine to fight in tournaments, or that Yvain should forget to return to his wife one year later, his fervent vows to do so notwithstanding. When, however Yvain is reminded of his lapsed promise, he goes mad, and the rest of the romance chronicles Yvain's attempts to refashion himself into a new man, a man who can hold allegiance to arms and devotion to Laudine in precarious balance. As he gained his wife by arms, and lost her by arms, so by meeting a series of increasingly difficult challenges does Yvain hope to regain Laudine. Yvain seems capable only of knightly responses, yet he comes to know by his own experience that the path of chivalry which leads to the obligations of family and society is indeed a difficult one.

At the end of the romance, Gawain and Yvain, both in disguise, engage each other in battle so equal, that they cease only when both are at the point of exhaustion. In analysing the situation (5993–6107), Chrétien shows how each knight loves and hates the other at the same time. The passage balances exactly the earlier descriptions of Yvain's and Laudine's psychology in falling in love, and points to the fact that love and arms are most similar in the sometimes deadly division they cause.

The outcome of the battle is happy, as Gawain and Yvain discover each other, but as readers we are left with an uneasy feeling. Perhaps we remember that this battle has dimly been foreshadowed. Calogrenant came upon wild bulls in terrible combat:

> qui s'antreconbatoient tuit
> et demenoient si grant bruit
> et tel fierté et tel orguel,
> se le voir conter vos an vuel,
> que de peor me tres arriere,
> que nule beste n'est tant fiere
> ne plus orguelleuse de tor.

Who were fighting among themselves and making such a great noise and showing such ferocity and such pride, that, if the truth be told, I drew back in fear, for no beast is so fierce or more proud than the bull. (281–7)[48]

To liken Yvain and Gawain in combat to these bulls may seem audacious, even if we assume Chrétien wished to emphasize the beastliness of this knightly civil warfare; there is, however, a good precedent, for Chrétien's beasts are themselves modelled on a description from Virgil:

> ac uelut ...
> cum duo conuersis inimica in proelia tauri
> frontibus incurrunt, pauidi cessere magistri ...
> illi inter sese multa ui uulnera miscent
> cornuaque obnixi infigunt et sanguine largo
> colla armosque lauant, gemitu nemus omne remugit:
> non aliter Tros Aeneas et Daunius heros
> concurrunt clipeis, ingens fragor aethera complet.

Just as when two bulls crash their brows in hostile battle, the pale herdsmen withdraw ... the bulls wound each other with great force, they rip each other with opposing horns, and wash their necks and shoulders with flowing blood, and the whole wood roars with groans, so Trojan Aeneas and the Daunian hero [Turnus] crash their shields, the prodigious clamour fills the air. (*Aeneid* XII, 715–17; 720–4)

A simile in Virgil becomes typology in Chrétien, nor is the manly courage of Yvain and Gawain any less qualified than that of their Roman counterparts. For in *Yvain*, the bulls were shepherded by the loutish 'vilain,' a true peasant, who knows nothing of adventures, and yet is completely straightforward: he is what he appears to be. What are we to make of him and the creatures he tends if we compare them to Gawain and Yvain, brother knights who truly love each other, who are blindly committed to deadly combat, each as the champion of quarrelling sisters, each disguised as someone other than himself? Were we asked to judge between the simple directness of the peasant and the refined behaviour of the chivalrous knight, which would we commend? Were we to say to Gawain or Yvain: knight, know thyself, what would they answer? Chrétien certainly extols the virtues of love and chivalry, but not to the extent that he blinds himself to their shortcomings. The standards of measure are relative. The 'vilain's' words recall the words of God to Moses: 'I am what I am.' Indeed, throughout *Yvain* there are unmistakable allusions to Christ: to many, Yvain himself becomes a Christ-like figure.[49] I am not as sure of this as I am that Christian notions of love and valour underlie and colour Yvain's progress as a knight. But in the end, the entire enterprise of love and chivalry is seen in perspective. The 'vilain' and his bulls stand at once as a proleptic and final comment on the fierce and proud battle of two glorious knights, a battle that finally leads to the reconciliation of Yvain and Laudine. The very premises of 'aventure' have been opened to question.

A simile in Virgil becomes typology in Chrétien: in this transformation we begin to see both how the idea of character changed from classical antiquity to the Middle Ages, and how techniques for representing it changed accordingly. In the prologue of *Erec et Enide*, Chrétien says that from his confused and ill-proportioned source he has drawn 'une molt bele conjointure' (14). The precise structural principles Chrétien worked by to achieve this highly pleasing arrangement have been debated for a long time.[50] Most today agree with Frappier, who argues that the romances are triptychs: an introductory adventure results in the happy union of the hero and heroine; a crises then occurs in which a psychological drama is played out in conjunction with a conflict in the moral or social fabric; and finally there is a longer concluding section in which the hero gains in stature by meeting a series of progressively more difficult challenges, until one final mysterious, magnificent exploit leads to a happy denouement: the perfect reconciliation of the lovers.[51] The narrative line of *Yvain* certainly fits such a scheme, but besides establishing the order and nature of the parts, one would like to account for inherent connections among the parts as well. One notes the similarity between Yvain's fight with Esclados and his fight with Gawain, Lunete's aid to Yvain in Esclados's castle and Yvain's battle to save Lunete's life, the 'vilain' himself and the hermit who cares for the unaccommodated Yvain. Across the three divisions of his romance, Chrétien balances monologues, characters, and events according to the typological pattern of foreshadowing and fulfilment. Indeed, Chrétien's word 'conjointure' suggests the techniques we have been discussing. The digressions, the episodes, the repetitions in *Yvain* are not its chaff, but its fruit.

As much as it elucidates the breadth of Yvain's character, therefore, the adventure of Calogrenant is a device that predicts the structure of the narrative. Calogrenant, in fact, is less a knight than he is a context;[52] a precursor to Yvain as man-at-arms, a herald to Chrétien himself as story-teller. Indeed, there is a thematic dimension to Calogrenant as well, a dimension that ultimately permits us to see why Chrétien made of Calogrenant what he did.

After Arthur has heard of Calogrenant's exploits, he decides that he will himself journey to the wonderful fountain. Yvain is upset when he learns this, since he knows that the king will allow Key first chance to battle the mysterious knight of the wood, 'or perhaps my lord Gawain, should he ask' (675ff). Yvain therefore resolves to go before them, and not to return until he has revenged his cousin's disgrace. With this in mind he steals away from Carduel.

In Yvain's response to Calogrenant's adventure. Chrétien announces that, like *Tristan*, his romance is at its heart a story about broken allegiances and divided loyalties in families. As an individual, Yvain will learn that he need not so much avenge his cousin's dishonour as atone for his own disgrace, the forgotten promise to Laudine, his wife. Yet in Chrétien, a breach of faith between husband and wife usually points to the tearing of a larger social fabric. As knight, Yvain will find that his desire to usurp Gawain's prerogative to do battle is challenged and satisfied, for each man opposes the other as champion of sisters, the elder of whom has usurped the rights of the younger. Calogrenant's most telling characteristic, we see, is really his consanguinity. Calogrenant's disgrace implicates and forecasts that of his cousin Yvain with Laudine, even as it looks forward to division in Arthur's court as two of his best knights nearly destroy each other. Ultimately, in Calogrenant's kinship and the events it gives rise to, we can perhaps seen an adumbration of the final sundering of Arthur's kingdom, of Guinevere's adultery with Lancelot, of Mordred's battle with Arthur. As he reveals his character, his desire to seek adventure, his obedience to Guinevere, his relationship to Yvain, Calogrenant evokes the tragic complexion of the entire Arthurian cycle. It is true that Chrétien never writes of the fall of Arthur's kingdom, yet *Yvain*, with all its premonitions of broken marriages and civil warfare, does seem an adumbration of it. In Calogrenant we see an emblem of Chrétien's artistry, for he is a complete exemplification of the modes of literary typology.

Medieval writers, then, could use literary typology in many ways. In texts like *Tristan* and the *Divine Comedy*, a secular character repeats the experience of another character, usually biblical, thereby demonstrating the universality of his condition and providing a frame of reference in which to understand the full implications of the character's actions. In works like the *Confessions* and *Yvain*, an internal typology orders seemingly random, paratactically narrated events into a coherent structure. Because medieval literature was modelled on the style of the Bible, it would not demand precise correlations between qualities of character or events in the narrative. The characters in such a literature, like those in the Bible, could therefore assume a thematic dimension that would suggest the moral, if not the actual direction in which the plot unfolds. These characters, like Ovid's, become metaphors of their poet's art; unlike Ovid's, however, who are merely reflections of the poem's style, figures like Tristan and Yvain possess a background and the depth of implication. Such characters have been set in the context of history, and have gained that sense of reality only history can give.

These varying uses of literary typology point to two general conclusions. If, as I have argued, writers and artists in the Middle Ages frequently employed the principles of parataxis and typology not only for the purposes of characterization and theme, but as a feature of narrative structure as well, it should be clear that secular works could adopt biblical techniques without adopting biblical meanings. Perhaps one reason why critics like D.W. Robertson came to see all medieval literature urging either the practice of charity or the avoidance of cupidity was that they to some extent discerned typological designs in the works they read, and assumed that a good hortatory message must accompany such a style. The assumption, of course, does not follow, any more than it follows that by adopting a hypotactic syntax a piece's style will be classical. Writers are forever putting old techniques to new material. Literary typology at its heart is a way of giving shape to a story and the people who act it, which brings me to my second point. As a process, literary typology is essentially dramatic; ultimately I would suggest that it offered methods of organization and expression that the great Elizabethan playwrights used to give their characters their extraordinary range and power. Shakespeareans have frequently adopted Wölfflin's conception of 'multiple unity' to account for the sense we have that scenes are discrete and finished, yet integrally related to their play.[53] They have noted as well how characters often undergo development offstage, how we see what Mark Rose has called 'before and after' pictures. Lady Macbeth coldly inciting her husband to murder becomes all the more nightmare-like when next we see her, six scenes later, sleepwalking. Hamlet seems a different man after his sea voyage; so does Romeo after his journey to Mantua; so too Lear after he has come to Dover.[54] Both plot and character in Shakespeare, whose theatre owes so much to the morality plays of medieval England, bring to perfection in a different medium the techniques I have discussed here. This itself only adds to our sense of how important a phenomenon literary typology is for us to come to terms with in our understanding of the medieval idea of character.

4

Boccaccio's Characters and the Rhetorical 'Disputatio in utramque partem'

Throughout classical antiquity and the Middle Ages, poetry and rhetoric were never far apart: recently, Wesley Trimpi has demonstrated that the rhetorical disposition of experience in fact 'presupposes and transmits principles of construction analogous to those of poetic composition.'[1] That is, since poetry and rhetoric were equally concerned with questions of 'qualitas' and 'aequitas' in their interpretation of real or imaginary events, both arts developed similar techniques of organizing and presenting those events. By the time the Roman schools of declamation flourished in the first century AD, the procedures of rhetorical and literary exposition had become 'virtually indistinguishable':[2] as we have seen, many still call Ovid's *Heroides* 'suasoriae' in verse. Exercises in declamation often turned upon a fictional case which was made up of given circumstances to be interpreted in light of one or more fixed statutes; the orator was therefore obliged to appropriate many of the modes and techniques of literature in exemplifying his position. Fictional exercises of this sort were popular throughout late antiquity and were widely practised during the Middle Ages, thereby assuring the inherent influence of classical rhetoric in much medieval poetry.

One striking feature of declamatory instruction was the 'disputatio in utramque partem,' the arguing of an issue from both sides. This process, as Trimpi has shown, was first widely used by the Peripatetics, who, distrustful of perceptions received through the senses, thought that by such debate they could arrive at a sufficient degree of probability ('verisimile') to permit choice and action.[3] Cicero later would incorporate this technique into his rhetoric, since for him the orator's first responsibility was to distinguish the true from the false, and hold to the real while rejecting the illusory:

We do not assert that nothing is true, but that all true sensations are associated with false ones (*omnibus veris falsa quaedam adiuncta*) so closely resembling them that they contain no infallible mark to guide our judgment and assent. From this follows the corollary, that many sensations are probable, that is, though not amounting to a full perception, they are yet possessed of a certain distinctness and clearness (*visum quendam haberent insignem et inlustrem*), and so can serve to direct the conduct of the wise man.[4]

It is precisely in the discovery of this probable truth in any particular situation ('in quaque re veri simile esset inveniri') that the 'disputatio in utramque partem' is most effective.[5]

As a means of analysing the verisimilar, the 'disputatio in utramque partem' would naturally be congenial to literature. Cicero himself noted the resemblance between the peripatetic method of debate and the dialogue of tragedy and comedy;[6] Horace's advice about poetry in general seems to echo Cicero's words: 'atque ita mentitur, sic veris falsa remiscet, / primo ne medium medio ne discrepet imum / And thus he invents, thus he mixes false with true so that the middle is not discordant with the beginning, nor the end with the middle' (*Ars Poetica* 151–2). Beyond literature and rhetoric, however, what Cicero has described here is, as Trimpi says, 'virtually a process of "elenchus," not of the reason but of the imagination.' This 'logic of the imagination' is

deeply involved in the psychological procedures of mnemonic systems, of the handling of *topoi*, and of placing vivid representations (*visiones*) before the inner eye of the audience. And the fact that its psychological material is a *visum quendam insignem et inlustrem*, whose virtue is probability, relates its processes clearly to the literary functions of *imagines* and *exempla*.[7]

In the last chapter we saw how the exemplary figures of antiquity became one source for characterization during the Middle Ages; the rhetorical 'disputatio in utramque partem' is yet another.

Of course, the most obvious way arguing both sides of a question could influence a work would be seen in its structure. Andreas's *De arte honeste amandi*, for instance, makes frequent use of speaking 'in utramque partem,' not only in the 'variis indiciis amoris' (II, vii), but in its larger design as well. Andreas's third book, a Stesichorean palinode, reverses the thesis of the first two: Walter now is told he should reject earthly love and seek the love of God. The malevolent effects of cupidity are enumerated, as are the rebarbative qualities of womankind, in an effort to persuade Walter that the love he pursues is not as perfect as it might seem. After he has read the entire book, and has considered both points of view, Walter can 'judge more securely between the *regulae amoris* and the *lex caritatis*.'[8] By organizing his work according to rhetorical as well as philosophical methods, Andreas has fulfilled Horace's presciption for fiction: the *De Amore* is both 'dulce' and 'utile.'[9]

So too the form of the 'quistioni d'amore' in the fourth book of the Filocolo shows the influence of the 'disputatio in utramque partem.' While in Parthenope (Naples), delayed from his search for Biancofiore by a sea-storm, Florio enters with Parmenio a lovely garden at the invitation of a group diverting themselves there. The 'brigata' decides to spend the hottest hours of the day sitting by a shaded fountain where they will discuss questions of love. Each member proposes a question: Fiammetta, who has been chosen queen, then renders her judgment. The person who asked the question offers a counter-argument, an 'altera pars' similar to what one finds in declamation or progymnasmata.[10] Fiammetta then confirms her original answer by refuting the alternative interpretation.

Branca, Trimpi, and others have examined the essentially rhetorical nature of these 'quistioni,' persuasively defining what separates them from Andreas's vignettes on the one hand, and from the novelle of the *Decameron* on the other.[11] Because her thesis has been argued from both sides, Faimmetta's judgments appear to carry conviction. Graziosa's question, to cite one example, is typical: 'qual sia maggiore diletto all' amante, o vedere presenzialmente la sua donna, o, non vedendola, di lei amorosamente pensare – which is of greater delight to the lover, to see his lady before him, or, not seeing her, to think amorously of her?'[12] Fiammetta contends that thinking gives far more pleasure than seeing: all the senses take joy in contemplating something beloved, whereas the eyes alone rejoice in seeing. To Graziosa's objections that the more something pleasurable is seen, the more pleasure it gives, Fiammetta responds that one might see one's beloved and do no more, whereas in thinking of her, the mind can imagine a rendezvous in which sweet words and affections are exchanged and love is requited. This kind of thought will seem more real than imagined ('in quell'atto che il pensiero gli porge, in quello con la cosa amata essere gli pare'), and thus gives delight to all the faculties a human possesses.

Fiammetta's rebuttal ends the discussion, but is by no means the final answer to the question. A silent debate continues: one wonders, for instance, what Florio would say, if courtesy did not bid him keep silent? Contemplated answers arrived at in the quiet of a shaded garden sometimes may be hard to reconcile with the active passions of a less sheltered world. Biancofiore's absence causes Florio great distress, which no amount of thinking can lessen. Even within the *Filocolo* there are grounds to think no answer is so true that its status does not depend upon the 'qualitas,' that is, the character, of the person who gives it.

Certainly the narrator of the *Filostrato* would disagree with Fiammetta. He has heard a similar question debated at the court of love:

Uno giovane ferventemente ama una donna, della quale niun'altra cosa gli è conceduta dalla fortuna se non il poterla alcuna volta vedere, o talvolta di lei ragionare con alcuno, o seco stesso di lei dolcemente pensare. Quale gli è adunque di queste tre cose di più diletto?[13]

A youth fervently loves a lady, but fortune grants him nothing else except sometimes to see her, sometimes to talk of her with someone, or to think sweetly of her to himself. Now which of these three things gives him the greatest delight? (*Proemio*, 2–3)

At first, a victim of false appearances ('vinto dal falso parere'), the narrator says he maintained at great length that the delight of being able to think of the beloved was greater than that which either of the other two could offer. But now, 'amara esperienza' has taught the speaker to know better: his Filomena has left Naples and has gone to Sannio, and her absence has only made his heart grow miserable. The *Filostrato* itself is the result of the poet's attempt to express his grief at Filomena's departure.

Nor would the Fiammetta whose *Elegia* so many consider the first psychological novel agree. After Panfilo's perfidious desertion, the remaining seven books chronicle the agonies Fiammetta feels in his absence. Thinking of Panfilo only makes Fiammetta's distress greater. When, however, by a cruel trick of fortune, Fiammetta imagines she will soon see her Panfilo again, all her grief disappears. Plunged into deeper despair as the book ends, Fiammetta still says Panfilo's return even now would convert all her tears into tears of happiness.

Boccaccio's ambivalent characters make us realize that the virtue of presenting, or, in literature, of representing both sides of a question goes beyond the organizing and structuring of narratives. In his fiction, argument and counter-argument can both seem equally valid. Boccaccio's world is the world of the verisimilar, of the probably true; all phenomena in it have an equal right to be heard. The 'opere in volgare' have traditionally been thought to champion naturalism, as Aldo Scaglione has defined and explained that term.[14] Recently, however, Robert Hollander has argued that Boccaccio uniformly condemns carnal love in each of his vernacular works, from the *Caccia di Diana* to the *Corbaccio*.[15] Both elements, it seems to me, coexist in Boccaccio; like Andreas's *De Amore*, each of Boccaccio's books simultaneously propounds the virtues and the defects of love. Taken together, Boccaccio's corpus speaks 'in utramque partem' to one question: 'Qual sia questa cosa, ch'è Amore?' Yet neither individual works, nor the vernacular canon in its entirety, offers a final judgment. As the narrator says in the conclusion to the *Decameron*, his stories, 'chenti che elle si sieno, e nuocere e giovar possono, sì come possono tutto l'altre cose, avendo riguardo allo ascoltatore / whatever they themselves may be, can be harmful or useful, like all other things, depending upon the listener' (*Conclusione*, 8).[16] Boccaccio's fiction only proposes, the reader disposes.

The simultaneous presence of sometimes contradictory themes perhaps reminds us of *Tristan* or *Yvain*; the technique of speaking 'in utramque partem' can easily become the rhetorical equivalent of literary typology. Boccaccio himself stressed the resemblance of poetry to Sacred Scripture: each reveals the causes of things, the effects of virtues and vices and what we are to shun and pursue ('le raggioni delle cose, gli effetti delle virtu e de'vizi, e che fuggire dobbiamo e che seguire').[17] And, as Trimpi says, the rhetorical analysis of this topic 'de expetendo fugiendoque' again and again provided Boccaccio with his principle of exemplification.[18] Boccaccio spoke not as a preacher, labelling the good and the bad, but as a poet, showing them as they are in the world, mixed together. He is no less moral than his religious 'semblable,' only more philosophical.

Boccaccio's conception of character, like Dante's, is essentially classical, but it is grounded much more in rhetorical presuppositions than in the techniques of literary typology: a man's disposition is revealed in how he answers a general thesis. A character in Boccaccio, therefore, no longer recapitulates his plot, as he does in literary typology, so much as he is seen in reaction to it. Farinata remains magnificent whether in Florence or in hell, but the narrator of the *Filostrato*, like Criseida, thinks and acts differently in different situations. There is in Boccaccio an incipient sense that character is multiplex, subject to the processes of becoming. This is not to say Fiammetta grows or develops; rather there exists in her the potential to exemplify both the virtues and the vices of love. And as we read, we are left to decide what to embrace and what to shun.

A character skilfully fashioned 'in utramque partem' will possess a complexity of conflicting impulses that rivals Tristan's. In the second book of the *Filostrato*, for instance, Pandaro tells Criseida that she is indeed fortunate; her face so pleases a man, 'che se ne sface,' that he is undone by it (II, 37). Criseida's reaction upon hearing this is telling:

> Criseida alquanto arrossò vergognosa
> udendo ciò che Pandaro diceva,
> e risembrava mattutina rosa.
> Poi ta' parole a Pandaro moveva:
> Non ti far beffe di me, che gioiosa
> d'ogni tuo ben sarei. Poco doveva
> avere a far colui a cui io piacqui,
> che mai più non avvenne poi ch'io nacqui.

Criseida blushed somewhat with shame hearing what Pandaro said, and she looked like a morning rose. Then she answered Pandaro in these words: Do not mock me, who would be happy for every good thing that happened to you. The man I pleased must have had little to do for this has never happened since the day I was born. (II, 38)

Such an answer certainly seems to befit a woman of high integrity, whose 'onestà,' as Pandaro tells Troiolo, has made her contemptuous of matters of love (II, 23). Yet even here, with the first words she utters in the poem, Criseida's position seems somehow compromised. Her disdain for the fatuities of love brings to mind Troiolo's similar scoffing: Troiolo, however, now is the very man Criseida's beauty has so undone. Even as Troiolo has changed, so too, we infer, will Criseida. Indeed, in denying her ability to induce love, Criseida's blush explicitly recalls Troiolo's when he discloses his love to Pandaro:

> e dopo il trarre d'un sospiro amaro,
> e di rossor nel viso tutto accesso
> per vergogna ...

And after he drew a bitter sigh, and his face all turned to red for shame ... (II, 15)

Yet Criseida only half-blushes, 'alquanto arrossò.' Why somewhat? In contrast to Troiolo, Criseida's sense of 'vergogna' seems conspicuously qualified. From this moment, the more sceptical among us may begin to read Criseida's responses in light of her future actions.

Criseida's blush, the narrator tells us, makes her look like a 'mattutina rosa.' Although a commonplace, this image, with its overtones of freshness and beauty, is definitely a mark of homage.[19] Virtue as charming as Criseida's more than likely would have led the Filomena addressed in the *Proemio* to understand this description as praise of herself. For the narrator has told Filomena that 'quante volte la bellezza e' costumi, e qualunque altra cosa laudevole in donna, di Criseida scritta troverete, tante di voi esser parlato potrete intendere / as often as you find beauty and graceful manners and anything else praiseworthy in a lady written of Criseida, you can understand them to be said of you' (*Proemio*, 34). And Criseida's conduct here does seem unimpeachable. Yet again there is a nagging sense of inappositeness. Criseida (or Filomena) may be fresh as a rose at dawn, but when the says she has never been loved or admired, which is clearly what Pandaro and she mean by 'piacere,' since the day she was born, in her humility she seems to have forgotten her past. Criseida is a widow; it would be difficult to imagine her first husband to have been such a dullard that he was unattracted to someone so beautiful. Her experience in marriage is at odds with the virginal connotations of the image, 'mattutina rosa,' connotations again simultaneously implied and undercut when the narrator calls Criseida a 'perla orientale' (II, 108). Pearls were commonly associated with virginity, yet we are told Criseida resembles one at the very moment when Pandaro delivers to her Troiolo's importunate letter, a crucial development in her seduction.[20] Both lover and moralist will find much to appraise in Criseida.

Of course, in making Criseida a widow, Boccaccio may simply have wished to establish a further bond between his heroine and Troiolo: he too has had experience in love, which has given him the right, so he thinks, to speak of its folly: 'Io provai già per la mia gran follia / qual fosse questo maladetto foco / I once experienced by my own great folly what this accursed fire was' (I, 23).[21] But Boccaccio also drew Criseida with Dido in mind, another widow who thought she disdained love:

> ille meos, primus qui me sibi iunxit, amores
> abstulit; ille habeat secum seruetque sepulcro

He stole my love who first married me; let him keep it with him and guard it in the grave. (*Aeneid* IV, 28–9)

Criseida clearly echoes these sentiments when she chides Pandaro, telling him that any regard for her honour would compel him not to encourage but to restrain her if she were to fall into the folly ('se io / in tal follia giammai fossi caduta') of desiring Troiolo:

> Ben so che Troiolo è grande e valoroso,
> e ciascuna gran donna ne dovria
> esser contenta; ma poi che 'l mio sposo
> tolto mi fu, sempre la voglia mia
> da amore fu lontana, ed ho doglioso
> il core ancor della sua morte ria,
> ed avrò mentre che sarò in vita,
> tornandomi a memoria sua partita.

I know indeed that Troiolo is great and valorous, and each great lady would have to be happy with him, but since my husband was taken from me, my desire has always been far from love, and my heart is still heavy over his wrongful death, and always will be while I live, recalling his leavetaking. (II, 49)

The thought is virtuous, but Criseida's resolve to adhere to it will, we fear, be no greater than her Carthaginian counterpart's.

The parallel with Dido adds to the mosaic of Criseida's character and shows how Boccaccio fashioned her looking backward and forward at once. The severest moralist could hardly fault Criseida here; by any standard her words are straightforward and free from all hint of connivance. But because Criseida's demurral recalls Dido's, ideas as yet totally unwarranted, ideas of broken vows, of excessive, illicit passion, of desertion, of death, begin to insinuate themselves in our minds.[22] History reports that one woman who spoke the words Criseida speaks now changed her mind. Beneath Criseida's probity, then, there is an inescapable suggestion that she is changeable as well. And history, alas, will level at Criseida a charge far worse than fickleness. Through allusion and other means, Criseida first appears to us 'in utramque partem'; her words simultaneously redound to her credit and intimate a brazenness which, though unfounded at this point in the story, is justified in retrospect. Troiolo's love is from the beginning both the angelic lady he thinks she is and the 'Criseida villana' (VIII, 28) she will become.

With such a character, the most innocent action can seem full of the direst implications. On the first night they celebrated their love, Troiolo secretly entered Criseida's house and awaited her in a dark and remote spot. Criseida had heard him come, for she coughed so that he would hear her from where she was 'per che, acciò ch' ei la 'ntendesse / com' era posto, ella aveva tossito' (III, 26). Criseida's cough brings to mind the Lady of Malehaut's, which forecast the fatal love of Lancelot and Guinevere.[23] In the *Lancelot de Lac*, Malehaut, who herself had hiddenly fallen in love with Lancelot, overhears the knight's passionate declaration of love for Guinevere at their first clandestine meeting. When Guinevere asks, 'From where does this love of yours for me come?', Malehaut coughs, signalling not only the impossibility of keeping their love a secret, but the adulterous nature of the liaison as well. To those who knew the story, the romance between Troiolo and Criseida will seem similarly tainted. Yet Criseida is a widow, and Troiolo is unmarried: adultery between them is impossible. But the obsessive need for secrecy, which every character emphasizes, and the devious furtiveness of the assignations, inevitably lend to the lovers' movements a sense of shame, the feeling that the quality of their affection could not bear the light of day. In any event, Criseida's cough only confirms what we already knew merely by reading her story: all attempts to keep her love for Troiolo undetected are futile. At the very moment of their happiest union, there are clear presentiments of doom.

In truth, of course, Criseida herself coughs, not her hostess; Boccaccio complicates his heroine by putting in her mouth premonitions of her own moral downfall. But Criseida is far from unwitting; she knows her own mind, which is to say she can see both sides of a question. In Book II, Criseida debates the virtues and drawbacks of loving Troiolo through many stanzas. In Book IV, after the Trojans have agreed to exchange her for Antenor, Criseida similarly argues the merits of her plan to return to Troiolo by answering his objections to it. Troiolo then proposes what amounts to a counter-thesis – come away with me – but Criseida responds by confirming the wisdom of her original plan. Criseida's departure, therefore, is treated as a 'quistione d'amore' similar in structure to any of those in the *Filocolo*. But in these instances Boccaccio uses the 'disputatio in utramque partem' more as a mechanical device for exposition, an orderly means for reaching a decision, than as a device to present Criseida's character. Criseida is most interesting, as we have seen, when her attitudes, words, and actions move in opposing directions at once. Listening to Diomede in the Greek camp, Criseida desperately tries to reassume her widow's habit:

> Amor io non conobbi, poi morio
> colui al qual lealmente il servai,
> sì come a marito e signor mio,
> né greco né troian mai non curai
> in cotal atto, né m'è in disio
> curarne alcun, né mi sarà giammai.
> Che tu sie di real sangue disceso
> cred'io assai, ed hollo bene inteso.

Love I have not known since he died, to whom I loyally tendered it, as to my husband and my lord. In such a way I have never cared for either Greek or Trojan, nor do I want to care for any, nor will I. That you spring from royal blood I quite believe, and have well understood it. (VI, 29)

But Criseida's own words betray her: the provocative placing of Greek before Trojan, the ambiguously ironic phrasing 'in cotal atto' – it is quite true that Criseida has never loved Greek or Trojan as loyally as she says she loved her first husband – the fact that in swearing her allegiance to Troiolo she has said 'not commands, flatteries, or a husband will ever turn my desire from you / comandamenti, lusinghe o marito, / non torceran da te mai l'appetito' (IV, 146), and the startling non sequitur of the final couplet – if she isn't interested in Diomede, how has she found time to observe his bearing so closely that she can see the nobility of his blood in his every action? – all clearly point to her unfortunate disloyalty to Troiolo. Forgetting another Trojan husband, Criseida leaves the poem almost as she entered it, now, however, not with the merest suggestion of the possibility of change, but in the sorry process of it.

Indeed, as the story progresses, Boccaccio seems to chart the successive stages in Criseida's transformation from complex woman to simple harlot. Initially, Criseida's modesty contains just enough hint of sensuality to make her fascinating; by the time she yields to Diomede, Criseida's affirmations of fidelity are so much pretence. We see Criseida somewhere between these two extremes when she and Troiolo first sleep together, although her probity already seems a garment Criseida can shed at will more than an innate attribute. Entering her bed still clad in one last shift, Criseida asks Troiolo: 'Spogliomi io? Le nuove spose / son la notte primiera vergognose / Shall I undress? Newlyweds are shamefaced the first night' (III, 31). This bit of coquetry might well derive, as Branca notes, from 'romanzi bretani,' but Criseida's words are all her own. They are, of course, lies; Troiolo and Criseida are not married, and Criseida's representing them as such only serves to remind us once again of the more unfortunate implications of her resemblance to Dido. And when in the next stanza Criseida abandons both coyness and her shift with passion ('E la camiscia sua gittata via'), coquetry seems too nice a word for this kind of philandering. Criseida is far less a mystery here than a strumpet.

Yet even as Criseida herself becomes one-dimensional, we continue to see her 'in utramque partem.' Troiolo's love for Criseida never ceases, as his valedictory description of her makes clear. This remarkable speech, which occupies ten stanzas in the eighth book (92–102), presents the ideal Criseida, the almost miraculous embodiment of beauty and virtue Troiolo still loves in his mind. The portrait is all the more poignant in that Troiolo is virtually certain that Criseida has betrayed him. His great-hearted loyalty is the unkindest cut, the most devastating counter-argument against Criseida and what Chaucer called her 'slydynge corage.' By loving her so faithfully, Troiolo has become Criseida's antithesis, a final perspective which leaves no doubt about the truth of what she has become.

In many respects, Criseida is the most interesting and complete woman Boccaccio ever drew. Compared to her, Emilia, the young damsel Palemone and Arcita suffer so much for in the *Teseida*, is one-dimensional, flat, and lifeless. Throughout she is a 'giovanetta semplicetta e bella' (III, 9), a flower, the morning star: a figure rather like the Persephone Ovid painted in the *Fasti*. Emilia's feelings are never called into question: she causes love, but hardly feels its effects. In Boccaccio's epic, as in the *Aeneid* and *Thebaid*, women are peripheral; it is the men who hold centre stage.

Despite its name, however, the *Teseida* has no central hero. Theseus dominates the narrative, but more as a presence than as a participant. After the first two books, he withdraws from the action, appearing only to determine the direction of Palemone and Arcita's fate. The two Theban knights thereafter become the protagonists of the story, but they are a strange pair to cast as an epic's centrepiece. When we meet them they are defeated, perilously wounded, and soon to be cast into prison. Yet though not much by themselves, Theseus, Palemone, Arcita, and Emilia together do represent 'in utrasque partes' responses to the complex question the *Teseida* implicity poses: when war leads to love, will Mars ever live with Venus in harmony and peace? Boccaccio's answer is, in a sense, an elaborate gloss on the complete title of the poem itself: *Teseida delle nozze d'Emilia*, the *Theseid of the marriage of Emilia*.

In his dedicatory letter to Fiammetta, Boccaccio invites the readers of the *Teseida* to associate one of the lovers with himself:

che ciò che sotto il nome dell'uno de'due amanti e della giovane amata si conta essere stato, ricordandovi bene, e io a voi di me e voi a me di voi, se non mentiste, potreste conoscere essere stato detto e fatto in parte.

that in what is said to have happened under the name of one of the two lovers and under the name of the young beloved, remembering truly, you shall be able to recognize, if you have not lied, something of what I have said and have done for you, and something of what you have said and have done for me.[24]

Although Fiammetta herself might be counted on to understand ('ché so che ve ne avvedrete'), latter-day critics have by no means shared this lady's insight. For every commentator who, like Hauvette,[25] argues that Boccaccio most surely identified himself with Arcita, it seems there is a Whitfield[26] who will stand under Palemone's banner, or another who, with Torraca, denies all possibility of reading Boccaccio's personal experience not only in the *Teseida*, but in any of his other romances as well.[27]

Boccaccio himself, of course, has endlessly complicated the matter by making his knights so similar. Every admirable action undertaken by Arcita seems balanced by an equally magnanimous gesture on Palemone's part; Arcita's every misfortune finds its equivalent in Palemone.[28] Those who argue for either knight will take issue with this, pointing to Arcita's noble behaviour in the grove or at his death on the one hand, pointing to Palemone's prayer to Venus or to his noble humility in defeat on the other, but the very differences point to their essential sameness. Boccaccio seems to have been not so much interested in each knight's individuality as he was concerned with the similarity of their actions when in love; it is for the power to portray the equality of such crazed acts that the poet specifically seeks the aid of Cupid:

Ponga ne' versi miei la sua potenza
quale e' la pose ne' cuor de' Tebani
imprigionati, sì che differenza
non sia da essi alli loro atti insani ...

May he [Cupid] put his power in my verses as he put it into the hearts of the Theban prisoners, so that there be no difference between them in their crazed acts ... (III, 2)[29]

If this is so, we have been asked to differentiate the roundness of two gems, rather than their colour, the age of fraternal twins, rather than their sex; in short, an exceedingly arch question whose very answer will seem hopelessly one-sided. In the *Filostrato* Boccaccio used the rhetorical techniques of the 'quistione d'amore' to create a character; in the *Teseida* he begins to use them to interpret his audience.

It was not archness, however, that prompted Boccaccio to tangle his readers in his poetic allegory so much as it was his desire to communicate the connection between his artistic and his amatory intentions. In writing the *Teseida*, Boccaccio seems to have had two goals equally uppermost in mind: to recover his lady's love, and to write in 'volgar latino' an epic of arms. To gain the first, the narrator-Boccaccio, in the person of Palemone, demonstrates his love to the cruel but godlike Fiammetta; to accomplish the second, the poet-Boccaccio, as Arcita (and, on a different level, as Theseus), symbolically offers his services, through the intermediary of the Muses, to Mars. Just as the narrator and the poet are subsumed in the figure of Boccaccio, so the knights in the *Teseida* represent two aspects of a single literary love, which has two interrelated objects: the lady, and poetry. Palemone and Arcita are, in fact, two aspects of Boccaccio's fictional self.

There has never been any question that arms and the woman are the subjects of Boccaccio's song; the poet himself invokes their numinous presence at the outset:

> Siate presenti, o Marte rubicondo,
> nelle tue armi rigido e feroce,
> e tu, madre d'Amor, col tuo giocondo
> e lieto aspetto, e 'l tuo figliuol veloce
> co' dardi suoi possenti in ogni mondo:
> e sostenete e la mano e la voce
> di me che 'ntendo i vostri effetti dire
> con poco bene e pien d'assai martire.

Be present, or rubicund Mars, fierce and severe in your arms, and you, o mother of Amor, with your gay and cheerful looks, and your swift son, with his darts powerful in every realm, and sustain my hand and my voice, for I intend to speak of your effects with much anguish and very little benefit to myself. (I, 3)[30]

What has been doubted is whether Boccaccio successfully integrated the competing strains of epic and romance. Theseus battles the Amazons and Creon of Thebes in the first two books of the *Teseida*, a promising start, perhaps, for a poem dealing with the twelve feats of the king of Athens as Boccaccio listed them in the *Genealogia Deorum*.[31] But thereafter Palemone and Arcita occupy centre stage, and their story is the quest for Emilia's love. Not all the trappings of epic poetry, the similes, the cataloguing of armies, the battles, and the descriptions of temples, which so often appear in the romance, can counteract the feeling some have that the first two books were introductory, a gratuitous appendage to the essential matter of the poem.[32]

Boccaccio, however, carefully manipulated his plot so that the epic would present a situation familiar to the reader of courtly literature. After Theseus had conquered Creon, the two knights, Palemone and Arcita, were imprisoned, where they remained, in great sorrow and distress, cursing their misfortune and calling on death, for almost a year:

> E in istato cotanto dolente
> presso che l'anno avevan già compiuto,
> quando per Vener, nel suo ciel lucente,
> d'altri sospir dar lor fu proveduto;
> né prima fu cotal pensiero eletto,
> che al proposto seguitò l'effetto.

And they had been in such a state, sorrowing, almost a year, when it was foreseen by Venus in her bright heaven that they should sigh different sighs; nor was such counsel chosen more quickly than it was put into effect. (III, 4)

These other sighs, of course, are the sighs of courtly love; spring, the beautiful garden with its amorous birds, and Emilia all enter the poem with them. And subsequently Book III does indeed paint a conventional setting for love. Has Boccaccio, though, merely juxtaposed the courtly with the epic, or has there been some connection, some set of circumstances brought about by the martial elements of the story, which might have prompted such thoughts of romance?

Ever since Ovid, those in the snares of love have been likened to prisoners;[33] ever since the *Roman de la Rose*, however, the perilous latchkey that gains admittance but no exit from the prison of love had been Idleness. Both elements, the Idleness that is an essential prerequisite of courtly love, and the prison, are present in the *Teseida*, but in a curious fashion. Boccaccio has reversed the courtly equation of the *Roman*, taking what in Guillaume de Lorris's poem is metaphorical as his reality. Here the prison we find is real, and the idleness we see is shackled to the knights, not the casual result of nobility's leisure time. The length of time Palemone and Arcita were imprisoned, therefore, is not a merely gratuitous detail, but Boccaccio's rather subtle introduction of verisimilitude to courtly love, of epic to romance. The realistic detail is joined with a corresponding emotional reality: the physical idleness of imprisonment has served as psychological preparation for the knights' entrance into the lists of courtly love. Boccaccio has bridged the gap between the martial and the amatory by means of his characters.

There can be no question that the species of love Palemone and Arcita fall into is indeed courtly, for their actions, at first, correspond exactly to the definition of a different, higher love Raison gives at the beginning of Jean de Meung's continuation of the *Roman*:

> Amours sont de pleseurs manieres,
> Senz cele qui si t'a mué
> E de ton dreit sen remué ...
> Amitiez est nomee l'une;
> C'est bone volonté comune
> De genz entr'aus senz descordance,
> Selonc la Deu benivolence.
> E seit entr'aus comunité
> De touz leur biens en charité,
> Si que par nule entencion
> N'i puisse aveir excepcion.
> Ne seit l'uns d'aidier l'autre lenz,
> Come on fers, sages e celanz,
> E leiaus, car riens ne vaudrait
> Li sens ou leiauté faudrait.
> Que l'uns quanqu'il ose penser
> Puisse a son ami recenser
> Come a sei seul seurement,
> Senz soupeçon d'encusement.
> Teus meurs aveir deivent e seulent
> Qui parfaitement amer veulent.

There are many kinds of love besides the one that has afflicted you, removing you from your good sense ... Friendship is one kind. It is good will shared between two people without discord in accordance with the benevolence of God. And all their goods should be shared charitably between them so that there can be no thought of making any exception. Nor should one be slow to aid the other. They should alike be steady, wise, prompt, and loyal, for intelligence without loyalty is worthless. Whatever one may dare to think he can tell his friend as securely as to himself, without fear of disclosure. Such customs those who want to love perfectly must and are wont to have. (4680–2; 4685–702)[34]

In addition, a friend must be constant in good times and in bad, someone in whom one can confide both 'joie ou clamour' without shame; he must be one who keeps his tongue and who does as much as he can to succour his friend in distress (4716–36). If he finds he is unable to grant his friend's request, he

> ... de son deul la meitié porte,
> E de quanqu'il peut le conforte;
> E de son joie a sa partie,
> Se l'amour est a dreit partie.

bears half of his grief and does what he can to comfort him, and has his share of his friend's joy, if love is shared rightly. (4743–6)[35]

At least through Books III and IV, Boccaccio's knights follow these precepts rather literally: Palemone and Arcita remain friends who share their love and their pain, confide in one another and offer each other comfort in their mutual misfortune. Once Palemone escapes from prison, however, and meets the disguised Arcita in the 'boschetto,' rivalry, contention, and strife, in the name and in the place of love, again become the prime movers of the romance. Perhaps the major tragedy of the *Teseida*, certainly its most ironic comment on the nature of 'fin' amor,' is the fact that Palemone and Arcita's love for Emilia remains refined only so long as there is no possibility of attaining her. To be sure, except for occasional lapses, the two knights continue to act in high courtly fashion, but their love for Emilia undoes whatever love and friendship there has been between them. All is changed as Venus again yields to Mars: by arguing the virtues of both deities, the *Teseida* begins to demonstrate that they are inseparable in the division and rancour they cause.

Boccaccio emphasizes this point in his glosses on the temples of Mars, Venus, and Diana in Book VII. The evening before the knights are to joust for the right to marry Emilia, all three petition their patron deities. Arcita prays to Mars, the lover of Venus, for victory; Palemone prays to Venus, the lover of Adonis, not for victory but for Emilia; Emilia prays to Diana, 'deitate triforme,' for peace between the lovers or, failing that, to have the knight who loves her best. The situation has become, mutatis mutandis, rather like Ascalione's 'questione d'amore' in the *Filocolo* (IV, x): reduced to its essentials, the reader is again asked which of two noble suitors loves a beautiful and virtuous maiden with greater courtesy. All three prayers present positions on a specifically qualified question: the battle the next day is in effect a metaphorical equivalent of a debate argued 'in utramque partem'[36]

The paradox of their contention is that Palemone and Arcita act not in opposition but in accord. In commenting on the temple of Mars, Boccaccio says

... in ciascuno uomo sono due principali appetiti, de' quale l'uno si chiama appetito concupiscibile, per lo quale l'uomo disidera e si rallegra d'avere le cose che, secondo il suo giudicio, o ragionevole o corrotto ch'egli sia, sono dilettevoli e piacevoli; l'altro si chiama appetito irascibile, per lo quale l'uomo si turba o che gli sieno tolte o impedite le cose dilettevoli, o perché quelle avere non si possano.

In each man there are two principal appetites, one of which is called the concupiscible appetite, through which man desires or rejoices in having things which, according to his judgment, whether it is rational or corrupt, are delightful and pleasing. The other is called the irascible appetite, through which man becomes upset if delightful things are taken away from him, or his access to them is impeded, or because these things cannot be had.[37]

By praying to Venus and Mars respectively, Palemone and Arcita are clearly associated with the concupiscible and irascible appetites. These are not, however, discrete states of being; rather they are related powers of the sensitive soul. St Thomas Aquinas explains that the sensitive appetite, though one generic power, is nevertheless divided into two powers, the irascible and the concupiscible. In nature, corruptible things possess not only a natural inclination to acquire the suitable and to avoid the harmful, but also an inclination to resist anything that would hinder acquiring the suitable or would lead them to harm. In the sensitive soul, therefore, one finds two appetitive powers as well:

one – through which the soul is inclined absolutely to seek what is suitable, according to the senses, and to fly from what is hurtful, and this is called the concupiscible; and another, whereby an animal resists the attacks that hinder what is suitable, and inflict harm, and this is called the irascible.[38]

Boccaccio follows Aquinas's definitions faithfully, even when he says that the concupiscible appetite desires and rejoices in having things 'secondo il suo giudicio, o ragionevole o corrotto ch'egli sia,' whereas Aquinas had said 'secundum sensus.' In the third article of the same question, Aquinas proves that the irascible and the concupiscible appetites both obey reason. Boccaccio's comment has conflated the two points, and in so doing, has removed Palemone and Arcita from the kind of moral censure Robert Hollander levels at them. The first objection to the proposition that the irascible and concupiscible appetites obey reason holds that they are parts of sensuality and sensuality does not obey reason. To Augustine, in fact, sensuality was the serpent.[39] But, as Aquinas responds, sensuality is signified by the serpent in what is proper to it as a sensitive power. The irascible and concupiscible powers, however, 'denominate the sensitive appetite rather on the part of the act, to which they are led by reason,' as Aquinas has just demonstrated. Boccaccio's comment alone neither argues the virtues of the knights' behaviour nor excoriates their vices. Instead, the *Teseida* presents the acts of both appetites, which can be judged 'in bono' or 'in malo,' depending on the reader's own standards.

Aquinas also defines the relationship between the two appetites. Each counteracts the other: 'concupiscence, being roused, diminishes anger, and anger, being roused, very often diminishes concupiscence.' But in any case, 'the passions of the irascible appetite rise from the passions of the concupiscible appetite and terminate in them.' Arcita and Palemone quarrel from love; Arcita identifies himself with the anger of Mars, and dies, yielding Emilia to Palemone, who has identified himself with Venus. In many ways the destinies of the two knights in the *Teseida* are an allegory of the natures of the appetites they represent.

Those appetites are joined in the figure of the narrator. In his dedicatory letter to Fiammetta, this spokesman of Boccaccio has described how, though now spurned in love for his lady, he has consoled himself by remembering 'la piacevole imagine della vostra intera bellezza' / the pleasing image of your perfect beauty.' We can well imagine this resignation has succeeded a good measure of anger at Fiammetta's departure and subsequent betrayal, his chagrin at no longer being able to have her, all access to her now denied. Fiammetta herself in the *Elegia* shows just such anger at Panfilo's treachery. But the irascible appetite, now tempered by hope, has yielded to the concupiscible: the narrator still loves his lady and desires to return to her grace. Palemone and Arcita, then, are species of the narrator's sensitive appetites: together they form, 'in utramque partem,' a complete picture of his sensuality.

Yet Boccaccio is not only a lover; he is a poet as well. Palemone and Arcita are used to discuss single aspects of love; unlike Criseida, neither realizes nor embodies it contradictions. Nor is Love the sole reason for their existence; they also are the minions of Mars, character witnesses, as it were, who support Boccaccio's claim that the *Teseida* is the first epic written in the vernacular tongue of Latium.

Boccaccio points to this when he describes the deeds of the love crazed knights as 'atti insani' (III, 2; see above); once again two traditions are joined which together further unite the epic with the romance. Curtius has demonstrated that Plato's theory of the poet's divine frenzy was known in the Middle Ages, although in a form Plato himself might not have recognized.[40] Medieval poets knew of the phenomenon indirectly through Horace, Ovid, and Statius, all of whom at one point or another state that they were possessed by some divine inspiration. Among the authors Curtius cites as acknowledging the tradition are Fulgentius, an author Boccaccio definitely knew, 'ut insanus vates delirabam / I was babbling like a mad poet'; the Carolingian poet Modoin, 'Nonnulli adfirmant etiam insanire poetas, / Carmina dum statuunt mente carere sua / some even claim that poets go mad, lacking their senses when they are fashioning poems'; and the anonymous author of the *Ligurinus*,' solis licet insanire poetis / poets alone are permitted to go mad.'

Curtius has also followed the fortune of the Muses through western literature.[41] In Greece, the Muses were both consorts to the epic and the divine mistresses of all higher intellectual pursuits; for Virgil they were the patronesses of science and philosophy. Their appearance in the *Aeneid*, however, assured their continuation in the Middle Ages only as stylistic elements of the epic, for even in Imperial Rome, poets not writing epics began to mock the Muses of all knowledge. Horace parodies them, in Ovid, as we have seen, they become wanton, and Christian poets, not surprisingly, reject them entirely. Patristic writers later rendered this species of Muse harmless by interpreting them allegorically: they became representatives merely of the art of music and non-spiritual poetry. By the time they reached Boccaccio, therefore, although still used allegorically for the purposes of edification, only the epic poet continued to look to the Muses for inspiration. In the *Teseida* Boccaccio has joined these threads; he has asked the Muses to inspire his epic (I, 1), but the traditional effects of such inspiration appear not in the poet but as the knights' 'insanity' in love. Their love is purely literary, Boccaccio seems to say, and his literature is the epic of love.

Judged then by literary and artistic standards of the fourteenth century, Boccaccio has, I think, successfully wed the epic with the romance. Within the unified whole, however, Boccaccio continues his pursuit of the Muses' crown by aligning Arcita's irascible appetite with the epic elements of the *Teseida*. When Arcita prays to Mars rather than to Venus, the Theban knight associates himself with Theseus and his motivation for battle. But beyond the narrative, Boccaccio may, in the person of Arcita, seek aid from the God to sustain the poem, which, after all, concerns 'gli affanni ... di Marte':

> Poi che le Muse nude cominciaro
> nel cospetto degli uomini ad andare,

già fur di quelli i quai l'esercitaro
con bello stilo in onesto parlare,
e altri in amoroso l'operaro;
ma tu, o libro, primo a lor cantare
di Marte fai gli affanni sostenuti,
nel volgar lazio più mai non veduti.

Since the Muses began to walk unclothed in men's sight, there have been some who cultivated them with refined style in honourable speech, and others who practised amorous song; but you, o book, are first among their songs to sing the tribulations borne for Mars, never before seen in the vernacular of Latium.   (XII, 84)

Indeed, even as Arcita's prayers appear as personified votaries to Mars in the seventh book of the *Teseida*, so in the two sonnets that conclude the poem the Muses act as intermediaries between Boccaccio and poetic fame. The cult of Mars has been translated into the cult of poetry, an association perhaps already hinted at in the *Thebaid*. When Theseus finally returns to Athens, Statius writes

Iamque domos patrias Scithice post aspera gentis
Proelia laurigero ... curru

And now he returns in the laurel-bearing chariot to his native land after harsh battles with the Scythian people ...   (XII, 519–20)

In the *Teseida*, the conqueror's laurels have become the poet's.

If through a love similar to Arcita's Boccaccio gains poetic laurels for writing a kind of poem that never was written before, as lover he may yet hope to win Fiammetta by demonstrating an analogous happenstance in the fortunes of his other self, the noble and faithful Palemone. This knight of concupiscible appetite is Venus's disciple. That this goddess and her son are all-powerful in the realm of literature a love poet's poem will necessarily demonstrate; it is certainly the narrator's hope that she may be equally persuasive in his own affair.

Yet if Boccaccio hopes that his love and fortune may be similar to Palemone's, the agency which actually courts Fiammetta is poetry itself. As the concluding sonnets reveal, the Muses not only are the bearers of the poet's laurels but are messengers between the narrator and Fiammetta as well. Boccaccio's valediction establishes once again what has been clear throughout the *Teseida*: his desire for Fiammetta and his cult of epic poetry are interchangeable. The correspondence between life and literature is essentially Ovidian: Boccaccio implies that if he dies because of his lady's continued cruelty, his death will be a textual one, which shall gain both love and reward from the Muses.

And so the Muses shuttle message and response between lover and beloved in the concluding sonnets, and the ten ladies together (Fiammetta of course is included as one of the Muses) decide upon a title for the poem. The title they choose most perfectly celebrates the union of Boccaccio with his two loves: *Teseida delle nozze d'Emilia*. The poet in love has created the love poem which crowns the poet with epic laurels. Courtly love and epic poetry are thus joined by a framing idea that shares many of the characteristics of the 'disputatio in utramque partem.' Each knight represents one aspect of Boccaccio's artistic goal: together they define the character of the work. In both its subtlety of conception and methods of exposition, the *Teseida* is the spiritual heir of the *Amores*, even as its characters look forward to those of the *Decameron*.

As a general principle of characterization, therefore, portrayal 'in utramque partem' never seems to have been far from Boccaccio's mind. What is extraordinary about his characters, what differentiates them from those most often found in medieval literature, is their lack of tendentiousness. No longer are figures exemplars whose moral is the sole justification for their existence. An individual can now appear to be, like Criseida, a conjunction of good and bad qualities, or can, in concert with another figure, like Palemone with Arcita, be an exposition of different aspects of the human condition. In either case, characters in Boccaccio seem more presentations then representations; they exist more than they admonish or commend. They themselves do not decide a moral question so much as they provide the reader with the necessary arguments to arrive sufficiently close to the verisimilar, to the probably true. Boccaccio's characters may, as Todorov says, be comparable to adjectives, but the subject nouns they modify are not so much their narratives as the poet's art.[42]

Perhaps the most remarkable example of Boccaccio's commitment to seeing a character from more than one side is his treatment of Dido. In the earlier works, the *Filocolo*, *Comedia ninfe*, *Amorosa Visione*, and *Elegia di Madonna Fiammetta*, Dido is the woman we know from Virgil. But when Boccaccio compiled his *De mulieribus claris*, the Carthaginian queen's fate and character had been considerably altered. No longer a victim of her own mad passion, Dido now is an exemplar of chastity in widowhood, a woman who, when tricked into consenting to marry the king of the Musitani, kept such faith with the ashes of Sichaeus that she committed suicide. 'Per ut vultis, cives optimi, ad virum vado / O excellent citizens, just as you wish, I go to my husband,' she says as she falls into the flames of an altar her people thought she had built to placate the shade of her first husband.[43] Later, in the *Esposizioni sopra la Comedia di*

Dante, Boccaccio again defended Dido, saying that her history is told in two different ways ('la istoria della quale si racconta in due maniere').[44] Boccaccio first repeats the account he had given in the *De mulieribus,* then briefly recapitulates the Virgilian version of the story, and finally appends a chronological discussion in which he argues, based on dates given in Eusebius's *Chronicon,* that Dido lived and died before Aeneas came to Carthage.

This Dido ultimately derives from a tradition that goes back to Servius and Macrobius, but, as Padoan says, the ideological, religious, and sentimental qualities of such a figure always fascinated Boccaccio.[45] The point I wish to make is simply that Boccaccio was willing to fashion a story which presents another side of this heroine's presumed character in much the same way he says Dante invented the *integumenta* of the meeting of Paolo and Francesca.[46] Obviously Boccaccio did not countenance this second version merely to present Dido 'in utramque partem,' but the fact that an alternative account exists shows a general tendency in his thought.

In this respect, the Dido who appears 'in bono' and 'in malo' throughout Boccaccio's work has become a figure cut from the same cloth as Fiammetta. As Branca says, only a literary creation could accommodate the inconsistencies in her behaviour:

è impossibile accordare i tratti che delineano l'amata come persona di alti sensi, di onestà invitta fino alla passione fatale; e quelli che la rappresentano come una donna rotta a tutte le avventure amorose, avida di piacere, pronta ai tradimenti e alla più crudele civetteria.

It is impossible to reconcile the traits which delineate the beloved as a person of high character, of honour unconquered even by fatal passion, and those that depict her as a lady broken by her every love affair, avid for pleasure, readily inclined to betrayals and to the most merciless coquetry.[47]

The same woman who in the *Elegia di Madonna Fiammetta* castigates the licentiousness at Baiae, in the *Rime* gives vent to her unbridled lust at Baiae as she consummates her betrayal of Boccaccio there. In most of the 'opere in volgare' Fiammetta is the object of love, but in the *Elegia* she is its victim.[48] Seen whole, Fiammetta becomes the Beloved; like Ovid's Corinna, she is more generic than individual. By presenting her in love and out of it, inviting and disdainful, tender and angry, chaste and passionate, Boccaccio exhibits in her the essence and the *differentia* of 'l'amata,' a complete picture of the woman who is loved.

Artistic propriety would demand that the figure who desires such a woman should himself share her characteristics: Boccaccio's surrogates are similarly hard to reconcile.[49] In the *Filocolo*, Idalogos and Caleone have both been identified with Boccaccio, and they in turn are decidedly different from Boccaccio's other narrators. In the *Filostrato*, the narrator addresses his despairing letter to Filomena, not to Fiammetta. In the *Decameron*, the narrator is now a former lover, and the narrator of the *Corbaccio* is completely misogynistic. This final work in Italian certainly is, in Billanovich's words 'L'inevitabile, conclusivo Adversus Amorem.'[50] Taken together, Boccaccio's narrators are an anatomy of the Lover and the perfect counterpart to Fiammetta the Beloved: through them Boccaccio has chronicled the complete course of love as he would have known it in Ovid, from the *Amores* to the *Remedia Amoris*.

Earlier I suggested that Boccaccio's vernacular works in many ways could be seen as an extended exposition 'in utramque partem' on one question: what is love? No one, I think, will be surprised to find that the emotion itself differs little from the characters who express it. In 1958, Walter Pabst published a brief essay, *Venus als Heilige und Furie in Boccaccios Fiammetta-Dichtung*.[51] Concentrating on the *Elegia di Madonna Fiammetta*, Pabst argued that there are essentially two Venuses, one who appears as a saint, the other as Tesiphone, an avenging Fury. In two reviews, A.E. Quaglio objected, emphasizing the fact that both Venuses share the same iconography, and that Pabst failed to relate the Venus of the *Elegia* to Boccaccio's other works. Robert Hollander has recently attempted to do this. Pointing to Boccaccio's gloss to the temple of Venus in Book VII of the *Teseida*, in which the attributes and functions of each Venus are carefully delineated, Hollander contends that all of Boccaccio's works champion the holy Venus and decry the concupiscent. This I think is a misreading of the evidence: Hollander sees only bad where both good and bad exist. Troiolo, for instance, experiences a joy in love that cannot be denied, but when he offers Pandaro his choice of his sister Polyxena or his 'cognata' Helen (III, 18), love has induced a moral blindness that cannot be ignored. Both Venuses do share the same iconography, for Love itself is always seen 'in utramque partem.'

In fact, if we judge by the *Teseida*, love and literature are analogous for Boccaccio. When we turn to the *Decameron*, we find that the 'novelle' exhibit exactly the same ethical attributes Love possessed in Boccaccio's earlier poems. The narrator of the *Decameron* emphasizes this in his conclusion:

chi vorrà da quelle [novelle] malvagio consiglio o malvagia operazione trarre, elle nol vieteranno ad alcuno, se forse in sé l'hanno, e torte e tirate fieno ad averla: e chi utilità e frutto ne vorrà, elle nol negheranno, né sarà mai che altro che utili e oneste sien dette o tenute, se a que' tempi o a quelle persone si leggeranno per cui e pe' quali state sono raccontate.

Whoever will want to derive evil counsel or plan wicked deeds from them will not be prohibited from doing so by the tales, if by chance they contain such things in them and are twisted and distorted to reach this end; and whoever will want to derive something useful and profitable from them will not be prevented, nor will it ever happen that the stories are called or regarded as anything but useful and honourable, if they are read at those times or to those people for whom they have been told.   (*Conclusione*, 14)

The 'novelle' are morally neutral: like rhetorical exempla, they interpret their audience, or, more precisely, they are the means whereby the audience can come to interpret themselves, both as individuals and as members of society.[53] This, I take it, is at least partly what Boccaccio had in mind when he gave the *Decameron* the subtitle *Prencipe Galeotto*. Like love, literature is an act of mediation: just as Palemone and Arcita, as representatives of the irascible and concupiscible appetites, together constitute a portrait of sensuality, so the tales of the *Decameron* provide one hundred perspectives on the human condition. The exact difference between the mediation of the *Decameron* and that of Christian allegory in general, and the *Divine Comedy* in particular, is that God no longer is the Love that is the end of all love, the thing all things point to. The world of the *Decameron*, as many have noted, is human, subject to the vagaries of fortune and the deceptions of appearance, a world in which no truth is more than probably true. As Branca has said, the first tale contains elements of the infernal: Ser Cepperello is another Judas, the worst man who ever was born ('era il piggiore uomo che mai nascesse'). The last tale tends toward celestial: on Griselda's poor house there surely rained divine spirits from heaven ('nelle povere case piovono dal cielo de' divini spiriti ...'). But both these tales, and all those that intervene, are characterized, in Branca's phrase, by 'industria umana.'[54] The ring that is the emblem of the true religion cannot be told apart from its duplicates (1, 3): this is the world of the verisimilar.

Boccaccio's manipulation of his audience rivals Ovid's; by the mere fact of reading, we are made characters of the *Decameron*. As we have seen, in Ovid our responses are predetermined: the audience is gay and witty, like Ovid himself. With Boccaccio, however, our ethos depends upon the quality of our judgment as readers: we are good or bad according to how we take the stories. Our reactions are not prescribed so much as they are seen as alternative possibilities. As a group we are, willy-nilly, involved in the *Decameron's* process of perception, and we too are seen in perspective.

In this the actual audience of the *Decameron* becomes an analogue of its fictive audience, those 'delicate donne ... che amono / tender ladies in love,' who, cooped up in their rooms, sit 'quasi oziose ... volendo e non volendo in una medesima ora, seco rivolgendo diversi pensieri / almost in complete idleness, at the same time wishing and not wishing something, turning over in their minds diverse thoughts' (*Proemio*, 10).[55] These ladies and Boccaccio's readers both share what in a different context Mazzotta has called a condition of marginality, of simultaneously being in something and removed from it.[56] Because these women are in love yet restrained from it, they become potential means of understanding love by feeling its joys and sorrows at once ('volendo e non volendo in una medesima ora'). Similarly, as readers, we are in a marginal position with regard to the *Decameron*; because it deals with human desire and experience, we are a part of it, yet because it is a fiction, we stand apart from it. The *Decameron* becomes the means of understanding ourselves by delighting and counselling us as we will. The reader of Boccaccio's book finds he is much like Boethius's idea of man in a provident universe: he retains his autonomy and free will even though the possibilities, indeed the contours of his character have been foreseen.

In much the same way, the narrator has been in love but is no longer: because his recollections are distanced from his experience, he becomes an ideal figure to demonstrate how his stories should be interpreted. And, on another level, the 'novelle' themselves, so grounded in history – 'piacevoli e aspri casi d'amore e altri fortunati avvenimenti ... così ne' moderni tempi avvenuti come negli antichi' (*Proemio*, 14), the narrator calls them, 'pleasing and harsh affairs of love and other eventful incidents which occurred both in modern and ancient times' – are told in gardens, in places deliberately set off from time and history. We understand the chaos of the plague only by escaping it entirely; to survive Joyce's nightmare of history we awaken to Boccaccio's 'pastoral of literature.'[57]

In every case, whether Boccaccio's subject is love, history, literature, or his audience, his exposition finds an analogue either in a rhetorical demonstration 'in utramque partem' or in an even more intricate conjunction of attitudes and viewpoints. The plague is juxtaposed with the garden, vices are mixed with virtues, the 'aspri' appears with the 'piacevoli' in what Aristotle would call an enthymeme that leads to an understanding of the multifarious events of human nature. And this is only natural since the technique of presenting an issue 'in utramque partem' is itself a process of mediation the orator used to lead his audience to firm conclusions. It would almost inevitably become one mode of presentation in a book that calls itself *Prencipe Galeotto*.

But if the 'novelle' reveal their genetic ancestry in what Jolles has called the simple form of the case ('Kasus'), Boccaccio's use of rhetorical techniques, however expected, is more than mere annexation.[58] Ultimately the strict formalism of rhetorical debate could not accommodate the expanding complexity of Boccaccio's fiction. Binary oppositions developed according to the rigid rules of disputation cannot account for the different stages of love in which

Boccaccio's narrators find themselves throughout his works, much less for the diversity of styles of conduct in the *Decameron*. By the time he composed his masterpiece, the 'disputatio in utramque partem' had become less important to Boccaccio as a principle for literary characterization than as a habit of mind which encouraged him to see his characters in increasingly greater perspective. Unlike the earlier figures, the characters of the *Decameron* resist being reduced to a rhetorical principle; by making his readers an integral part of the process of perception, Boccaccio in fact transcended the techniques of debate. Characters in stories now can show more or less insight, as can their tellers; many attitudes and points of observation can now be considered in determining the verisimilar. The characters of the *Decameron* in effect become metaphors of perspective.

In the famous introduction to the fourth day, Boccaccio makes this clear when he answers in his own voice criticisms that had been levelled at the first part of the *Decameron*. In typical fashion, Boccaccio explains the nature of his work by telling part of a story concerning Filippo Balducci and his son. Filippo, it seems, was a happily married man of the world, but when his wife died, he took his two-year-old son and withdrew from mundane affairs, devoting himself to the service of God. He raised his son in complete ignorance of worldly things. One day, when the youth was eighteen, he accompanied his father to Florence. Seeing women for the first time in his life, he asked his father what they were. 'Mala cosa,' his father replied. But his son persisted and asked what they were called. 'Papere,' 'goslings,' his father answered. 'Padre mio, io vi priego che voi facciate che io abbia una di quelle papere / Oh, father, I pray you arrange for me to have one of those goslings,' the boy then said (IV, *Introduzione*, 24). And Filippo realizes that he cannot win, knowing that 'Nature had more power than his wits / più aver di forza la natura che il suo ingegno' (IV, *Introduzione*, 29).

As a defence of the *Decameron*'s 'naturalism,' this little parable is well known and has received much comment;[59] at the same time, however, we should be aware that Filippo and his son exemplify Boccaccio's dynamics of meaning as well. Their story, in fact, is a conglomeration of actual and potential opposites. Although Filippo's life in the world stands in contrast to his life removed from it, his judgment that women are evil things is one-sided. We suspect that his opinion, besides being hollow lip-service to the traditional misogyny of monasticism, is a biased overreaction to his wife's death. Perhaps he, like Dido, felt betrayed, not only by his spouse, but by womankind itself. At any rate, Filippo speaks as if in ignorance of his past: his wife was a good woman ('buona donna'), he loved her deeply, and they lived together in complete happiness, trying more than anything else to please each other ('e insieme in riposta vita si stavano, a niuna altra cosa tanto studio ponendo quanto in piacere interamente l'uno all'altro,' IV, *Introduzione*, 12). Filippo is portrayed from two points of view, but because we see him whole while he sees himself only partially, our judgment differs from his. Knowing what Filippo chooses not to remember exposes the half-truth of his contention.

Filippo's son, on the other hand, will grow to be the mirror image of his father. Although his life has been entirely sheltered, we see him at the moment he enters the world, and immediately his inclinations are at odds with his experience. As yet his desire is little more than a child's for something that has caught his eye, but his attraction to women seems probable and true because we see it in the innocent light of his previously sequestered existence. Unlike his father, Filippo's son is an uncomplicated character who is seen from only one point of view. Rather than an object he is an agent of perspective, whose simple passion qualifies his father's abstinence. The reader gains a fuller perception of both qualities from the way Boccaccio's characters have been portrayed.

Nor can language deceive when the multiplicity of human affairs is acknowledged. Filippo calls the women goslings 'in order not to awaken some desire to the less than useful in the concupiscible appetite of the young man / per non destare nel concupiscibile appetito del giovane alcuno inchinevole desiderio men che utile' (IV, *Introduzione*, 23). But despite Filippo's verbal misrepresentations, his son's desire remains unchanged. And because his feelings are so natural, they temper and qualify the unspoken implications of Filippo's comparison. Who can believe that his son's inclinations are bestial, or that they are directed toward an object more fickle than useful? The story of Filippo Balducci and his son forwards its defence of natural passion by bringing it into contact with the qualities of continence. The untold part of the tale would, to preserve no more than symmetry, require the youth to fall in love, marry some good woman, and live prosperously the rest of his life. For Boccaccio, neither monkishness nor licentiousness can offer the satisfaction of a wedding.[60]

Characters in the *Decameron*, therefore, are either complex or simple, objects or agents of perspective, fashioned from a number of points of view or from only one. Many indeed are simple figures of the kind Wayne Booth has analysed in *The Rhetoric of Fiction*.[61] But although a character may be uncomplicated, his context never is. Each tale has a teller who prefaces his story with more or less pertinent remarks. These frame characters for the most part are simple and unindividuated, though Angelo Lipari would assign to each member of the 'brigata' an abstract, allegorical quality.[62] In addition, the narrator usually gives a brief account of the group's reaction to each tale. In theory, therefore, the characters of any tale can bespeak one point of view, the teller another, the response of the fictive audience a third, and our response a fourth. Individual portraiture, be it of Andreuccio, Frate Alberto, or Fiammetta, though always artful, does not interest the Boccaccio of the *Decameron* as much as do differing views of what someone says or does.

Any discussion of the *Decameron* certainly should heed Cesare di Michelis's warning not to substitute one system of contraries for another.[63] The variety of the *Decameron* is its most salient characteristic, and critics, especially since Branca, have explicated its designs and patterns in the light of relevant precepts from ancient and medieval rhetorical and literary theory. The first novella of ser Ciappelletto seems to me a clear example of structural and thematic exposition from a multiplicity of perspectives; but to argue this is not merely to repeat Branca's demonstration that stylistically the tale is antiphrastic and topically an instance of the 'mundus inversus.'[64] So too the last novella of Griselda seems to me more complicated than an exemplum of the 'mondo dover essere,' of the world as it should be. Branca comments on the contrasting 'registri' and 'stili' of the *Decameron*: since Boccaccio's human comedy proceeds from vices to virtues, from a world upside down to a world as it ought to be, all the while remaining in the world as it is, each 'register' commands its own appropriate mode of language. Parallel incidents in different stories, 'topoi' of literary tradition, are depicted now with salty precision, now with refinement and decorum; women are exalted, but one for her animal charms, another for her spiritual nobility.[65] But Boccaccio does not only set in contrast the similar actions and behaviour of different men and women, he understands that the acts and behaviour of any particular man are themselves equally liable to be seen from more than one standpoint.

In his prefatory remarks to the novella of ser Ciappelletto, Panfilo describes the human predicament in a way which, while manifestly Christian, nevertheless recalls the peripatetic's scepticism about the truthfulness of sensory perception;

Manifesta cosa è che, sì come le cose temporali tutte sono transitorie e mortali, cosi in sé e fuor di sé esser piene di noia, d'angoscia e di fatica e a infiniti pericoli sogiacere; alle quali senza niuno fallo né potremmo noi, che viviamo mescolati in esse e che siamo parte d'esse, durare né ripararci, se spezial grazia di Dio forza e avvedimento non ci prestasse.

It is a manifest thing that, just as all temporal things are transitory and mortal, so in themselves and to others they are full of worries and anguish and toil and subject to infinite dangers, which we, who live mixed among them, and who are part of them, would without exception neither be able to endure nor defend ourselves from, if special grace from God did not lend us strength and foresight. (I, 1, 3)

We live mixed ('mescolati') among unstable things; ser Ciappelletto's outrageous portrait of himself, a case in which extreme unction amounts to self-anointment, clearly bears witness to the necessity of possessing a rule whereby the probably true can be detected. The first story of the *Decameron*, as Panfilo says, expressly deals with the judgment of men ('non il giudicio di Dio, ma quel degli uomini,' I, 1, 6); and Cicero, we remember, had advocated the use of the 'disputatio in utramque partem' precisely because ours is a world in which true sensations are joined with false ones ('omnibus veri falsa quaedam adiuncta'). Boccaccio will similarly demonstrate that understanding is a matter of perspective by viewing each of his characters from a number of points of view.

The friar who hears ser Ciappelletto's confession has always been a difficult figure; many readers find him at best overly gullible, and at worst an unmitigated fool.[66] The narrator, however, asks his readers a pointed question: 'e chi sarebbe colui che nol credesse, veggendo uno uomo in caso di morte dir così? / And who is there who would not have believed him, seeing a man on the point of death talk in such a manner?' (I, 1, 74). The friar hears a saint because he lacks the ground to take a second sounding: what man's perception is so sure that were he with the friar he would have discerned the truth? Any reader will find Ciappelletto's goodness incredible, but the reader, we must remember, is better placed. We know ser Ciappelletto is a scoundrel; for us, therefore, his false confession reveals not so much the friar's naivety as his capacity for belief. Ser Ciappelletto's lie becomes the instrument that proves the holy man's sanctity. The usurer may think his confessor a fool, but we see him in a different light. The friar is exactly what he seems to be, a man of faith, a holy fool.

The friar, of course, is not the only person who hears ser Ciappelletto confess. The two Florentine money-lenders who have housed Musciatto's emissary to Burgundy have hidden themselves behind a screen; their barely contained laughter furnishes a second perspective on what Ciappelletto says:

e fra sé talora dicevano: 'Che uomo è costui, il quale né vecchiezza né infermità né paura di morte, alla qual si vede vicino, né ancora di Dio, dinanzi al giudizio del quale di qui a picciola ora s'aspetta di dovere essere, dalla sua malvagità l'hanno potuto rimuovere, né far che egli così non voglia morire come egli è vivuto?'

and among themselves they then said, 'What kind of man is this, whom neither old age, nor sickness, nor fear of death which he sees is near, nor even fear of God, before whose judgment he shortly must expect to be, has been able to turn from his wickedness, or make him not want to die any differently from the way he has lived?' (I, 1, 79)

Ser Ciappelletto's countrymen know he lies, but their knowledge gains them little benefit. Getto and others have noted the purely mercantile spirit that rules the hearts of these men, their tendency to see all aspects of life as provisions of a contract.[67] Their concern for the things of this world may allow them to see ser Ciappelletto more completely than his confessor does, but just as with the friar, ser Ciappelletto becomes a mirror which allows the reader to discern the nature of their hearts.

Together the friar and the Florentine money-lenders prove Boccaccio's contention that literature interprets its readers as much as they interpret it. Two men hear the same thing: one man's response gives an indication of his virtue, another man's response discloses his faults. In this Boccaccio's fiction is quite moral, although the moral itself is highly problematical. The novella of ser Ciappelletto is concerned with man's judgment, yet the 'due fratelli,' not the friar, see things more nearly the way they are. Is worldly perspicacity purchased only at the expense of spiritual innocence? It would seem so, for when the story ends, the Florentines and the audience alone know the 'truth.' But in Boccaccio worldly truth is only the apparent truth. The holy friar convinces his chapter house that Ciappelletto was a saint and hopes that God will work many miracles through him ('sperando per lui Domenedio dovere molti miracoli dimostrare,' 1, 1, 83). The Burgundian townspeople implicitly believe the friar's commendation of ser Ciappelletto's piety and elevate him into something like their patron saint. Moreover, they affirm that God has worked many miracles through him, and continues to work them every day for any person who devoutly commends himself to ser Ciappelletto ('e affermano molti miracoli Idio aver mostrati per lui e mostrare tutto giorno a chi divotamente si raccomanda a lui,' 1, 1, 88). Can any of this be true? When we are done reading the tale, all we can say with certainty is perhaps. Those willing to believe it associate themselves with the friar and the legendary, hagiographic elements of the story.[68] Those who smile and shake their heads, thinking that the Burgundians have found a perfect saint for themselves, someone depraved enough to match their own depravity, associate themselves with the sceptical and ironic elements.[69] On earth there are saints and cynics; the truth each sees is coloured by his own lights.

The cause of the reader's perplexity is Panfilo. The friar and the Florentine money-lenders are simple characters, mere agents of perspective. They ought to help us define ser Ciappelletto, but Panfilo simultaneously sanctions and qualifies the evidence of each. The friar establishes the effects of ser Ciappelletto as saint. No one can doubt the validity of the prayers addressed to God in the name of this rogue. Panfilo himself has said that even though the intercessor is himself corrupt, the efficacy of his office is not impaired if the supplicant's prayers are pure:

nondimeno Esso ... più alla purità del pregator riguardando che alla sua ignoranza o allo essilio del pregato, così come se quegli fosse nel suo conspetto beato, esaudisce coloro che il priegano.

nevertheless He ... attending more to the purity of the petitioner than to his ignorance or to the damnation of the intercessor, listens to those who pray to him just as if the advocate were blessed in his sight. (I, 1, 5)

But the tone of his account of the pious Burgundians is tinged with scepticism. To pray to a Saint Ciappelletto makes a man a devout fool.

Similarly, his Florentine hosts establish ser Cepperello's character as scoundrel, yet for all their testimony, is this terrible man beyond doubt suffering the torments of the damned in hell? Reason says he is, but Panfilo is unwilling to dismiss from consideration the possibility that the rogue repented at the eleventh hour and was saved. Man's judgment is an uncertain thing, even when it sees things in perspective. Some visions may be better informed than others, but all can be no more than probably true. Boccaccio captures the complexity of life in this world by seeing the figures who move in it from a number of points of view.

Ser Ciappelletto, of course, is at the centre of all these complications. He is a curious character: a man so ethically repugnant ought to elicit our disgust, yet not a few readers find his mocking bravado irresistible. The audience's divided reaction to him in fact recapitulates the ambiguous nature of the novella itself, nor is this an accident. Wherever he appears, ser Ciappelletto is by intention an exemplification of depravity but in effect an agent or principle of mediation. Thematically, he is a prince among galeottos; by balancing his perversity with the good that comes from it, Boccaccio makes ser Ciappelletto an emblem of his fiction. Like a mirror, he will show anyone who can see the good man his goodness and the evil man the shape of his wickedness.

To meet ser Cepperello evidently is to meet confusion itself. The man was often a visitor to the merchant Musciatto Franzesi's house in Paris, but, as the narrator continues,

per ciò che piccolo di persona era e molto assettatuzzo, non sappiendo li franceschi che si volesse dire Cepperello, credendo che 'cappello,' cioè 'ghirlanda' secondo il lor volgare a dir venisse, per ciò che piccolo era come dicemmo, non Ciappello ma Ciappelletto il chiamovono: e per Ciappelletto era consciuto per tutto, là dove pochi per ser Cepperello conoscieno.

because he was short and dressed very finely, the French – who did not know what Cepperello meant, but took it to mean 'chaplet,' that is 'garland' in their tongue, – called him, since, as I have said, he was short, not Ciappello but Ciappelletto, and he was known as ser Ciappelletto by everyone there where few knew him as ser Cepperello. (I, 1, 9)

How extraordinary that so scanty a description of the man's physical appearance provokes so many conflicting assumptions about him. Cepperello is short and elegantly attired; from this the French anticipate his conversion and canonization, changing his name and supplying him a metaphorical halo. But Boccaccio carefully distances us from the fanciful etymologies of the French, who obviously judge Cepperello by external appearance alone. In light of Panfilo's introductory remarks, this by itself should make us suspicious, and the confused logic of Boccaccio's serpentine sentence, with its deliberate repetitions and alternation of names, including one possible sobriquet that no one ever used, only strengthens our scepticism. We are almost encouraged to suspect that this is a man who will not be what he seems. From the start, the French view of ser Cepperello differs from ours.

Cepperello's initial appearance, therefore, is less a description of him than of two contrary reactions to him, one enunciated, the other implied. In truth, however, at this point only the severest support of sumptuary laws could possibly object to him. In so far as his looks are concerned, ser Cepperello is unremarkable, but the moral portrait which immediately follows changes everything. The Cepperello we now see is a total perversion of human order and virtue, a false man alien to the world of men, an encyclopedia of vices.[70] The enormity of his moral corruption dwarfs the smallness of his physical stature.[71] From this moment, ser Cepperello stands fixed in our minds, for suddenly we view him from God's perspective, seeing his heart as clearly as his face.

Under such light, the rogue is strangely diminished. Petronio has noted that Cepperello is unlike Boccaccio's other figures. Most characters in the *Decameron* are dynamic, fashioned out of an accumulation of suggestions gathered from the events they participate in. Ser Cepperello, however, is static: his portrait consists of a series of qualities which precede his actions and are isolated from them.[72] The Cepperello we see is constrained and one-dimensional: even his confession, as Mazzotta has said, is an unreal production, a species of usury, a verbal lie quite in keeping with the kind of man he is.[73] For us, Cepperello can be nothing more than an exemplary figure who exhibits all the attributes of man's evil.

Yet we must remember that our view of ser Cepperello is privileged. There are two Cepperellos to match his two names, and the other, the ser Ciappelletto, is vibrant and dynamic. This figure, however, is most alive not so much when he perpetrates his lie as when he becomes its victim. The devil's fiction has had the effect of making him a true intermediary before God. To the friar ser

Ciappelletto is the embodiment of man's highest capacity for good, a man worthy to intercede before God on man's behalf. To the townspeople who have called on him and continue to call upon him ('chiamaronlo e chiamono'), ser Ciappelletto is the soul who brings their words to the ears of God. By engaging in a spiritual commerce the worldly Cepperello could never have conceived of, this Ciappelletto lives on as the medium of other people's piety.

In short, the essential point about ser Ciappelletto is that he is many things to many people: an emissary for Musciatto, a well-dressed man of affairs to the French, a rogue to the Florentine money-lenders, a moral exemplar to the friar, a saint to the Burgundians, an abomination and yet a mirror to us. The merchant of Prato never changes: to us who see him best he is an archetype, an unmoving embodiment of earthly corruption, a human equivalent of the plague. But in his dealing with others, ser Ciappelletto is open to interpretation and becomes a figure of mediation; according to how others see him, so we see them. In the greatest of all the many reversals of the novella, as fictional character, ser Ciappelletto is morally neutral.

Ser Ciappelletto stands first: he is a paradigm for reading the characters of the *Decameron*, just as his novella is a paradigm for reading the entire book. Because Panfilo's tale concerns the judgment of men, Cepperello himself will not claim our attention for long: our opinion of him is fixed soon after we meet him and does not change. Rather we are interested in the different aspects of him different people see. Some perspectives reveal more truly the nature of the object seen, others reveal more truly the nature of those who see. Each point of view is verisimilar, a part of the probably true. Together they form an image of nothing less than the multifariousness of life itself.

All the tales of the first day recall Panfilo's in one way or another, and so refine even further our perception of it. No tale, however, more surely puts it in perspective than Dioneo's final novella of Griselda. The beginning and the end of the *Decameron*, as Petrarch knew, contain much of its import: both 'novelle' argue for the necessity of recognizing the complexity of things.

For many readers, Griselda perfectly balances ser Ciappelletto: Boccaccio's comedy progresses, however circuitously, from the worst of men to the best of women. For Branca, in fact, the story of Gualtieri and his wife allowed Boccaccio to pass in final review the great themes of the *Decameron*. Fortune, Love, and Intelligence all reappear, but their operations now elicit man's best qualities, his munificence, his liberality.[74] Yet Griselda and Gualtieri are not without their detractors: is she really the embodiment of the virtues of patiences or is she a masochist, a 'pathological case, verging on the monstrous?'[75] And is Gualtieri what he says he is, a husband who truly wished to teach Griselda how to be a wife, and his subjects how to keep one ('volendoti insegnar d'esser moglie e a loro di saperla tenere,' x, 10, 61), or is he a bestial tyrant? Vociferous support can be found for either point of view, which leads one to suspect that aspects of both might be present. Neither Griselda nor her husband is as simple as we wish or expect each would be. The literal complications of being human prevent both from becoming the moral abstractions Petrarch later would make them.

Griselda herself, for instance, is not merely another name for Patience: throughout the novella, Boccaccio reminds us that she is a sentient, intelligent woman. When Gualtieri's attendant demands Griselda's daughter, clearly implying Gualtieri has ordered him to murder the infant, she gives him the child, 'even though she felt great pain in her heart / come che gran noia nel cuor sentisse' (x, 10, 31). Later, when Gualtieri tells his wife he will leave her to marry another, her soul filled with grievous despair ('forte in sé medesima si dolea,' x, 10, 41). When Griselda hears that her husband has in fact chosen his new wife, 'not without the greatest of efforts, beyond the power of a woman's nature, did she suppress her tears / non senza grandissima fatica, oltre all natura delle femine, ritenne le lagrime' (x, 10, 44). Finally, when Gualtieri asks Griselda to array their castle for his nuptials, she agrees, 'although these words were all a knife in her heart / come che queste parole fossero tutte coltella al cuor di Griselda' (x, 10, 51). Griselda's deep joy on recovering her children only confirms her humanity; we feel she is so happy now because she suffered so much before. As we finish the story we know only her devotion to Gualtieri could have overcome the pain and grief he caused her.

Unfortunately, Griselda's human qualities are at odds with those she represents allegorically. Were Griselda a true saint, a 'sancta' Patientia standing with Cecilia, Perpetua, and the others, the pain of her martyrdom would be lost in the fervency of her desire to bear witness to the glory of God. Earthly concerns would cease to matter; knotty questions, such as whether a mother's concern for the safety of her children takes precedence over a wife's promise to her husband, would be moot. But Griselda suffers for a human being; her pain never has any higher purpose than to prove her promise of obedience to Gualtieri. The agony we know she feels becomes pointless, the gratification of a cruel whim on the one hand, absurd allegiance to a vow rendered void by Gualtieri's excesses on the other. And this causes Bergin and many others to think Griselda in her own way a 'monster' equal to her husband. Griselda is problematic precisely because she behaves like a saint but lives in the world. Her acts are heavenly in their simplicity, but her motivations are earthly in their complexity; whether she is virtuous or blameworthy depends on the point of view from which we see her.

Gualtieri, as we might expect, is Griselda's opposite. As removed as she seems from the complications of flesh and mire, so he seems involved in them. He too acts as though he were both a figure in a saint's life and a man in the world, but his conduct is much harder to countenance. At the end of the tale, Gualtieri claims that all Griselda's ordeals were part of a plan and purpose he knew from the beginning: 'Let all know that what I have done was done for a predetermined purpose / conoscano che ciò che io faceva a anteveduto fine operava ...' (x, 10, 61). Were this a saint's life, Gualtieri's actions would be nearly what he says they are, significant only in so far as they provide Griselda with the opportunity to give evidence of her devotion to God. Gualtieri ought to be merely an agent of perspective, a simple character whose motives are correspondingly simple. Instead the 'marchese' 's motives are inscrutable, which makes his presumption insufferable. As Mazzota has shown, Gualtieri does nothing less here than cast himself as God, with the ironic result that he becomes an inverted image of God.[76] He violates the well-known allegory which saw in marriage an analogy of the prelapsarian condition of man and woman in the Garden of Eden.[77] Gualtieri makes a hell of what should be a heaven; he becomes an exemplification of primordial corruption. Furthermore, Griselda's suffering intentionally recalls Job's at many points, and it does Gualtieri's reputation no credit to recall that Job's tormentor was Satan.[78] By allusion and implication, therefore, Gualtieri seems bad beyond redemption.

In Job, however, Satan is morally neutral: he is not so much the father of lies as the means by which the goodness of God's servant was proved. As we have seen, ser Ciappelletto, Satan's advocate on earth, also became a neutral intermediary: the agency of his mediation was his confession, a verbal construction itself by nature referential, which was open to all interpretation, depending upon the person who gave it. Can Gualtieri, Satan's surrogate in the trials of Griselda, similarly justify his actions by claiming they proved his wife's patience? Reason says no, but Griselda's behaviour does border on the saintly, and, as Panfilo said in the first story of the *Decameron*, there are things in heaven men on earth cannot understand. Petrarch certainly saw the 'marchese' of Saluzzo this way. Even Gualtieri, therefore, for all his indefensible harshness, is problematical. There is no man on earth, it seems, who is so bad that someone else might not see some good in him.

In reality, therefore, Griselda, a saint and a woman, is the mirror image of her husband, who is a devil and a man. She is 'in bono' what Gualtieri is 'in malo,' and both show each other for what they are. But distinctions such as good and bad are not clear-cut; Gualtieri's testings prove Griselda is saintly, yet her suffering makes him a beast. These contrary implications are not reconciled; rather they exist in an uneasy marriage. And yet, despite the inconsistencies in the protagonists, the tone and spirit of their story might still persuade us that Gualtieri and Griselda are characters in a saint's life were it not for the ironical comments of Dioneo. It is his cold eye that casts everything into doubt.

Since he means his account to have significance for the everyday world, an often meaningless world of disease and destruction, to which he will soon return, Dioneo constantly draws his audience's attention to Gualtieri. Before he begins the tale, Dioneo says:

Mansuete mie donne, per quel che mi paia, questo dì d'oggi è stato dato a re e a soldani e a così fatta gente; e per ciò, acciò che io troppo da voi non mi scosti, vo' ragionar d'un marchese ...

My dear ladies, this day has been devoted, so far as I can tell, to kings and sultans and people of that sort; and therefore, so as not to stray too far from you, I want to tell you of a marquis ... (x, 10, 3)

In his typically nihilistic way, Dioneo then immediately advises no one to imitate Gualtieri. Later, when his tale is done, Dioneo adds a further comment:

Che si potrà dir qui? se non che anche nelle povere case piovono dal cielo de' divini spiriti, come nelle reali di quegli che sarien più degni di guardar porci che d'avere sopra uomini signoria. Chi avrebbe, altri che Griselda, potuto col viso non solamente asciutto ma lieto sofferir le rigide e mai più non udite pruove da Gualtieri fatte? Al quale non sarebbe forse stato male investito d'essersi abbattuto a una che quando, fuor di casa, l'avesse fuori in camiscia cacciata, s'avesse sì a un altro fatto scuotere il pilliccione che riuscito ne fosse una bella roba.

What can one say here, except that celestial spirits rain down from heaven on the houses of the poor, as well as on the royal palaces of those who were better suited to watch swine than to rule men? Who but Griselda could have suffered not only without a tear but happily the cruel and unheard of tests Gualtieri devised? For perhaps it would have served him right if he had run into a woman who, when driven from the house in her shift, would have found someone else to shake her skin-coat for her, so that she might gain a pretty new dress in the process. (x, 10, 69–72)

Dioneo allows neither Gualtieri nor Griselda any moral stature. His distaste for her is obvious in the sour criticism of his conclusion; Gualtieri's actions, which perhaps are not at too great a distance from the experience and knowledge of his listeners, have been characterized as 'matta bestialità',' as senseless cruelty. The woman is a mindless victim, while the marquis becomes a jaundiced reminder of a fallen world.

Dioneo's perspective, therefore, like Panfilo's before him, deliberately muddies the water. It shows that Griselda and Gualtieri between them may provide a context in which to view marriage, love, fortune, and intelligence, but that the picture of these things which emerges is not clear. Like ser Ciappelletto, Griselda shows that seeing things from more than one point of view does not render the truth less partial or complicated. Sometimes the truth will remain dark, just out of man's sight; sometimes it will remain a mystery, in Donne's words, 'like the sun, dazzling, yet plain to all eyes.'

To some, then, Griselda is the soul of patience, to others she is an object of scorn. Both interpretations are encouraged for both contain a grain of truth. And this multiplex quality of Griselda's character, like that of ser Ciappelletto before her, is of central importance. 'L'uomo, il personaggio,' as Padoan says, man and character are always at the heart of the *Decameron*; in many respects Boccaccio's masterpiece is a vast enterprise in the interpretation of man and his actions.[79] In the earlier works, the rhetorical debate 'in utramque partem' furnished Boccaccio a principle for the exposition of character,[80] but in the *Decameron* the techniques of dispute are enlisted as only one way of establishing a variety of perspectives. In their very partiality, Boccaccio's characters become paradigms of discernment, spokesmen for one of the *Decameron*'s most insistent truths – that truth in this book is always verisimilar.

5

The Cast of Character:
Chaucer and the Conventions of Originality

Despite their complexity, characters in Ovid and Boccaccio do not dominate their narratives: we do not meet in their works, or in the works of any other medieval author, a figure like the Wife of Bath, whose sense of self dwarfs any tale she may tell or be a part of. Indeed, in Chaucer we seem to find a poet whose first concern was the presentation of character, so vivid are the figures he created. Dryden's enthusiasm, to cite a famous instance, is highest when he speaks of the Canterbury pilgrims, whom Chaucer managed to make universal and particular at once:

[Chaucer] must have been a man of a most wonderful comprehensive nature, because ... he has taken into the compass of his Canterbury Tales the various manners and humours ... of the whole English nation, in his age. Not a single character has escaped him. All his pilgrims are severally distinguished from each other; and not only in their inclinations, but in their very physiognomies and persons ... The matter and manner of their tales, and of their telling, are so suited to their different educations, humours, and callings, that each of them would be improper in any other mouth. Even the grave and serious characters are distinguished by their several sorts of gravity: their discourses are such as belong to their age, their calling, and their breeding; such as are becoming of them, and of them only. Some of his persons are vicious, and some virtuous; some are un-learned ... and some are learned. Even the ribaldry of the low characters is different; the Reeve, the Miller and the Cook, are several men, and distinguished from each other as the mincing Lady-Prioress and the broad-speaking, gap-toothed Wife of Bath. But enough of this ... ' Tis sufficient to say ... that here is God's plenty.[1]

Later Dryden calls the General Prologue Chaucer's 'Characters'; the words of this English Theophrastus truly are cousin to the people who speak them.

In his comments, Dryden clearly assumes that the rag and bone shop in which the Wife and the Pardoner were fitted stood next to a school of rhetoric.[2] The particular excellence of the pilgrims lies in their ability to comprehend the precepts of Aristotle and Horace without sacrificing their particularity. And although Chaucer's characters are hardly classical, it nevertheless is precisely that aspect of traditionality Dryden gives voice to, the appositeness not only to story-matter to speaker, but of the very style of the telling as well ('genera dicendi'), that distinguishes the Canterbury pilgrims from the *Decameron's* 'brigata' and most other personages in medieval literature.[3] Chaucer still is a long way from Henry James: a man's actions hardly depend upon his inner disposition; yet for each author, character is a matter of style. In both, a man's soul is mirrored in what he says and in how he says it.

Chaucer's canon, in fact, is conspicuous for the way its characters are conventional and original at once. The works utilize all the techniques I have examined in the previous chapters, often with greater success than their models. As we shall see, aspects of rhetorical debate 'in utramque partem' helped shape the characters of both the narrator and the Black Knight in the *Book of the Duchess*; in the *Parliament of Fowles*, the several species of birds characterize themselves in an outright debate over the various kinds of love.[4] In the *Troilus*, the contradictions inherent in Boccaccio's Criseida have been underscored yet somehow made more mysterious and fascinating. The narrator's affection for his heroine constantly colours his knowledge of her betrayal of Troilus: even more than in the *Filostrato*, Criseida is seen backwards and forwards at once.[5] And how often in the *Canterbury Tales* do the pilgrims debate one another. With bourgeois politesse the Wife, Clerk, Merchant, and Franklyn offer singular perspectives on marriage, experience, authority, perception, and all the other issues that subtend the 'marriage-group.' With a meanness that is vulgar, the Reeve quarrels with the Miller, the Summoner with the Friar, but now tales that are meant to disparage an antagonist redound to the discredit of their tellers. How far removed are these verbal brawls from the refinement of courtly debate, from the formal 'demande d'amour' that ends the first section of the 'Knight's Tale.'

If the characters of the *Book of the Duchess* seem drab compared to the Pardoner or the Prioress, they nevertheless share much in common with them. Even in this, Chaucer's earliest sustained work, the commonplaces of convention are manipulated to create surprisingly sophisticated characters. The Black Knight certainly stands as much a surrogate for bereavement as for John of Gaunt, and all he says can claim a fine lineage in medieval allegories of love and consolation.[6] Yet the eulogy for his lost 'fers' (queen), with his passionate commendation of her virtue and beauty, his profession of steadfast devotion, his bewailing of Fortune's duplicity, all move the reader more deeply than their conventionality would have allowed us to expect. And so too his interlocutor, the poet-dreamer, is a product of literary tradition, though he is something rather less than the sum of his expected parts. This 'mased' reader who ought to put us in mind of his French cousins, the narrators of Machaut's Judgment poems and Froissart's *Paradys d'Amour*, clearly lacks their sophistication: very few readers, I suspect, would desire to identify themselves with this 'poetical I.'7 Yet so unlikely a pair as this to perform a vital service for each other: the Black Knight and the poet enter into conversation, and as they speak, they change. Together they illustrate the intricate balance that marks the process of consolation.

The dreamer and Black Knight are characters ideally suited to sympathize with one another, but the actual nexus between them is hard to define precisely. It seems more associative than logical, for their condition is such that similarities underscore differences. Both men live in the margins of life because they have been frustrated in love, or, in the narrator's case, something whose effects resemble those of love. Both think they will die; the poet, however, from lack of sleep, the Black Knight because the lady he has loved more than life has died. The narrator, no matter his malady, certainly has not yet loved fully, the Black Knight can no longer live in the fullness of love. In terms of experience and depth of emotion, the poet is the Black Knight's shadow: how can we respond to the one, whose greatest desire is to go to sleep, in the same way we respond to the other, whose anger at life is an expression of his abiding love of a woman no longer alive? By equating their responses, Chaucer allows us to experience the difference between his Knight and his narrator. We feel the density of the Black Knight's grief because we measure it against the vagueness and insubstantiality of the poet's. Not surprisingly, the anger of sorrow moves us in a way the sorrow of self-pity never can.

On another level, the level of metonymic analogy, the narrator is like the Knight as sleep is like death. The poet begins his poem amazed that he isn't dead: 'I have gret wonder, be this lyght / How that I lyve, for day ne nyght / I may nat slepe ...' Later when he overhears the Knight's verses of complaint, they strike the poet as

> the moste pitee, the moste rowthe,
> That ever I herde; for, by my trowthe,
> Hit was gret wonder that Nature
> Myght suffre any creature
> To have such sorwe, and be not ded.   (465–9)

By making the dreamer desire sleep as much as the Black Knight desires death, Chaucer lightens the mood of his poem even as he prepares to underwrite its gravity. Compared to the Black Knight, the narrator's perplexed gloom is humorously ironic, for his sorrow seems far in excess of its ingenuously mysterious cause. With his decided uncertainty why he cannot sleep, and his firm conviction that maybe it is a sickness he has suffered these eight years – 'Myselven can not telle why / The sothe; but trewely, as I gesse, / I holde it be a sicknesse ...' (34–6) – the narrator nearly becomes the first pixillated character in English literature. In Froissart's *Paradys d'Amour*, Chaucer's immediate source for the opening of the poem, the speaker immediately explains that love has caused his wakefulness:

> Et pas ne les puis deslyer,
> Car ne voeil la belle oublyer
> Pour quele amour en ce traveil
> Je suis entres et tant je veil.

And I can't unbind them [the agonies being unable to sleep has caused him] because I do not want to forget the beautiful lady for whose love I have entered into this torment and am awake so much.   (9–12)[8]

But in the *Book of the Duchess*, the poet, rather than experiencing the travails of love, exhibits all the heartbreak of insomnia, something quite different indeed. Even as the poet's presence valorizes the high seriousness of the Black Knight's lament, so the presence of the Black Knight allows us to smile at the poet. The *Book of the Duchess* is the first instance of Chaucer's dialectic between 'ernest and game,' nor could a more appropriate setting for the juxtaposition of matters of consequence and good humour be found.[9] How often does consolation begin when the bereaved first manages to laugh?

In so far as the Black Knight and the dreamer embody different kinds of grief, they resemble the figures Boccaccio represents 'in utramque partem.' Indeed, Machaut's *Judgement dou Roy de Navaree* and *Jugement dou Roy de Behaingne*, the poems which, as Lowes says, suggested the central situation of the *Book of the Duchess*, together debate a typical 'demande d'amour': who has suffered the greater loss, a knight whose lady has betrayed him or a lady whose lover has died?[10] Each poem argues one side of the question; by incorporating elements of both into a single poem, Chaucer's characters would inevitably remain essentially partisan figures. And for the greater part of the poem the Black Knight and the dreamer are equally single-minded advocates of the primacy of their own grief. But because the narrator's discomfort cannot equitably be compared to the despair of fulfilled love cut short by death, the nature of the question has changed. No longer are we witnesses of a debate and judgment, but observers of a dialogue that leads to consolation. Chaucer's characters, however, retain qualities proper to both genres, and herein lies the source of their complexity. In their self-absorption the Black Knight and dreamer resemble their French progenitors who argue positions in Machaut's poems of debate, but in so far as they sympathize with one another they represent an anatomy of solace even as they provide the perspectives that are necessary to understand it.

The poet's celebrated dullness, for instance, is really a form of his self-concern, as we see in his reading of the tale of Ceyx and Alcyone.[11] The young Chaucer may as yet lack Ovid's narrative sophistication, but even here he is able to tell the story in such a way that it exemplifies its speaker's character. In the *Metamorphoses*, we have seen that the sea-storm which drowns Ceyx was a narrative ecphrasis that also metaphorically characterizes Alcyone's love: the tempest is so mean because for Alcyone anything that harmed Ceyx would have to be so, and it is described at such length because her love is equally vast. In Chaucer's telling, however, one hundred hexameters of 'Sturm und Drang' have been reduced to a couplet and a half of octosyllabics, so that we may all the more quickly gaze with wonder on the God of Sleep. As if a dream, all interest in the nature and operation of love has vanished; the poet sits ravished before the extraordinary prospect of a remedy for his insomnia. So powerful is the narrator's desire for sleep, it changes the way the story is told. No longer is Alcyone's prayer to Juno the brief, halting petition of someone afraid to offend:

> utque foret sospes coniunx suus utque rediret
> optabat, nullamque sibi praeferret

She prayed that her husband would be kept safe, and would return, and would prefer no one to her.   (XI, 580–1)

Alcyone now is so emboldened by love that she specifies in direct discourse the means whereby the truth should be revealed to her:

lady swete,

Send me grace to slepe, and mete	dream
In my slep som certeyn sweven	dream
Wherthourgh that I may knowen even	
Whether my lord be quyk or ded. (117–21)	

The idea of Alcyone's request for a dream comes from Machaut, who says the queen was so distraught in love she was unable to sleep (*La Fonteinne Amoureuse*, 553–4). But Alchioinne's prayer is unspecific: all she says to Juno is 'Je te pri, / Riche deesse, oy mon dolent depri / I pray you, noble goddess, hear my sorrowful supplication' (559–60).[12] Chaucer in fact fails to mention Alcyone's sleepless nights, but the narrator's sympathy with the queen of Trachis is so complete that her words reflect his desires.

Similarly, Juno is no longer the irritated goddess who summarily sends Iris to Morpheus so that she may cease to be vexed by Alcyone's vain prayers. Now she seems eager to explain to her messenger exactly how Morpheus should creep into Ceyx's body and appear to Alcyone in a dream, taking care to talk just as the king was wont to (135–50). Juno's instructions again marvellously reflect the narrator's fixity on dreams and sleep; no detail is so trifling that it does not receive serious, elaborate consideration.[13] Even startling connotations are overlooked in the poet's enthusiasm for this God of Slumber. Morpheus's cave is 'derk / As helle-pit overal aboute' (170–1). But rather than a sign for caution, this darkness becomes an inducement to see which of the cave's inhabitants could triumph in a sleeping contest: 'They had good leyser for to route[snore], / To envye who myghte slepe best' (172–3). And, as has often been noted, Ceyx and Alcyone's final transformation is ignored. By this point the narrator's obsession with Morpheus prevents him from noting anything more than the fact that Alcyone died three days after Ceyx appeared to her in a dream.

Thematically, of course, the story of Ceyx and Alcyone is the mirror image of the Black Knight's experience; it enables us to comprehend the dimensions of his sorrow by giving us something to compare it to. The narrator's dullness, however, which is to say his inability to respond to anything beyond his own needs, interferes with his perception. He misunderstands the significance of Ceyx and Alcyone, just as he will misunderstand the Black Knight's 'ten vers or twelve / of a compleynte.' To the narrator, such complaint is simply a text, a stylish example of a common poetic form, words divorced from experience.[14] The narrator's misapprehension of the Black Knight's lament is consistent and in character; the poet finds a man standing alone reciting doleful verse, and can only imagine himself alone in his cell, making similar moan these past eight years. He misunderstands what the Black Knight says in the only way his experience allows.

As he listens to the Knight, the dreamer in fact comes to exemplify what the nobleman repeatedly tells him: he 'wost [knows] ful lytel' what he means. Here is a real irony in Chaucer's characterization: he has transformed Machaut's subtleties of persuasive logic into the dreamer's uncomprehending obtuseness without loss of forensic effectiveness. An unshakeable inability to understand what an opponent has said is sometimes even more unanswerable than the finest counter-argument buttressed by the most rigorous logic. The Black Knight's continual elaborations make us realize that, as debater, the dreamer is formidable, even if, or better, precisely because he has no idea of the issue being discussed. Only at the final moment of truth, when the Knight declares 'She ys ded!' and the dreamer responds, 'Be God, hyt ys routhe,' does the poet finally see with eyes not his own. Yet even here the narrator appears unaware of the significance of his act. For this instant of commiseration is still a dream, an unactualized exchange of affection. When he awakens, he is sure of only one thing: no one, not Joseph, not Macrobius, could understand his dream (276–90). That the poet can construe neither Ovid's, nor the Black Knight's, nor his own poetry is one of the gentle ironies that make the *Book of the Duchess* so effective a poem of consolation.

For all his defects, however, the poet, like ser Ciappelletto, does not impare the efficacy of his profession.[15] Poetry, whether Ovid's, the Black Knight's, or the poet's, has real value as an instrument of consolation. The poet hardly changes because he hardly talks, but the Black Knight, prodded by the poet's unpenetrating questions, must continue to talk and in talking is comforted. The Knight's first words about his duchess show how personally he had taken her death:

> Y wreche, that deth hath mad al naked
> Of al the blysse that ever was maked,
> Yworthe worste of alle wyghtes,   (have) become
> That hate my dayes and my nyghtes!
> My lyf, my lustes, be me loothe,   pleasures are to me
> For al welfare and I be wroothe.   angry with each other
> The pure deth ys so ful my foo
> That I wolde deye, hyt wolde not soo;
> For whan I folwe hyt, hit wol flee;
> I wolde have hym, hyt nyl nat me.   (577–86)

In the space of ten lines, 'I,' 'me,' 'my' appear twelve times. But as he speaks, the Knight's concern for himself gives place to the goodness of the woman he has loved, until finally he comes to terms with the significance of her death. The Knight's progress as he returns to life is all the more discernible because we see it against the poet's immovable thick-headedness. Ultimately the Black Knight wins the argument he has been waging against himself by losing himself, by forgetting the pity he felt for himself when Blanche died and remembering her virtue. As with his duchess, the Knight finds favour by yielding, by asking 'mercy,' now of a different lady, Dame Nature, a mercy she is most willing to grant.

For all the qualities they share with the figures of personification allegory and the poetry of consolation, the Black Knight and the narrator are the linear descendants of the characters of poetic disputation. In his maturer fiction, Chaucer continued to play with the conventions of debate in even more subtle ways. Throughout the *Canterbury Tales*, direct confrontations often provide dramatic opportunities for characters to reveal their dispositions. The Knight, for instance, speaks of contention in love in his version of Boccaccio's *Teseida*; readers who remembered the *Altercatio Phyllidis et Florae*, or the *Concilium Romarici Montis*, or any of the similar 'Streitgedichte' that argue the relative merits of knights and clerks as lovers, might well have expected his tale to be answered by the Clerk.[16] Harry Bailly, of course, doesn't read much of anything; his choice for the next teller is the Monk. But suddenly the drunken Miller interrupts: he will not be denied his say now. And when his tale is done, we realize that the old debate has indeed been joined. The Miller responds directly to the Knight as sexual love exposes some of the absurdities of courtly love and the earthiness of fabliau challenges the sublimation of romance.[17] It is therefore highly appropriate that the protagonist of the 'Miller's Tale' who demonstrates the folly of the two Theban knights is that 'hende' clerk Nicholas. In Chaucer random chance or seemingly unpremeditated changes in plan on closer inspection often reveal the ironic contours of literary design.

Chaucer continually meets our expectation in the most unexpected ways; so many of his characters unwittingly obey the laws of one convention by seeming to disobey the laws of another. It is equally fitting that the threadbare Clerk we observe journeying to Canterbury has lost none of his traditional inclination to dispute the question of superiority in love. Instead of the Knight, however, our student confronts a far more surprising and formidable opponent in the Wife of Bath. Indeed, the Clerk must argue against the Wife, since she has shown that women should assume 'maistrye' not only over knights (the 'Wife of Bath's Tale'), but over clerks like Janekyn as well. She decides the venerable literary quarrel in one fell swoop! And so, when in his high-spirited Envoy the Clerk directs his tale of Griselda against Alice, what once was a rather facetious question of love has widened into a serious debate about marriage.[18] In joining the dispute, Chaucer's clerk acts in the lively mettlesome way clerks were supposed to behave.[18]

The irony of Chaucer's exposition of character often involves this kind of submerged conventionality, the juxtaposition of expectations of how people should act we have from books, and how we in fact see them behave in the *Canterbury Tales*.[20] Despite the Wife's assertion to the contrary, experience does not oppose authority, it validates it. For all their spontaneity, characters in Chaucer never cease to be literary. Poetic justice requires that the Reeve interrupt the Miller before he can tell his tale. Their altercation over sexual misconduct and harlotry becomes a low analogue of Palamon and Arcita's rivalry over Emilye.[21] Even as the Miller 'quites' the Knight, his quarrel with the Reeve makes him a copy of a character in the Knight's tale. The 'Knight's Tale' has established one of the paradigms of the *Canterbury Tales* – contention is part of love and life – and that paradigm remains intact, however much the Knight's courtly version of it is debunked. Through the different eyes of the Knight, Miller, and Reeve, Chaucer introduces the ideas of order, love, mortality, strife, and perception that bind together his collection of tales. As in the *Decameron*, these questions will be seen from many perspectives, and our comprehension of each grows as we measure the pilgrims' partial or complete misunderstanding of them.[22]

Techniques adopted from rhetorical debate, of course, are only one fruitful source Chaucer tapped in drawing his characters. The Pardoner, for instance, owes much of his extraordinary power to his conscious denial of the processes of literary typology. He is something more and less than the man Hugh of St Victor pictures standing perplexed before the Book of Creation:

The whole sensible world is like a book written by the hand of God, which is to say created by divine power, and the individual creatures are like so many characters ['figurae'], characters not arbitrarily devised by human will but instituted by divine will to manifest the wisdom of the invisible things of God. Consider the case of an illiterate man who looks at an open book and sees the characters but does not recognize them as letters; such is the case of the stupid and brutish man who cannot see what is contained within God's creatures. He sees the outer appearances; he does not grasp their inner meaning.[23]

As I have argued elsewhere, the Pardoner is not stupid; his training as a preacher would have ensured his knowing how to read a text spiritually. The allegorical exposition of the particular passage of the day was a common feature in medieval sermons.[24] Rather, the Pardoner refuses to allow any meaning informed by the Holy Spirit: to him all meaning is literal, fleshly meaning. Thus when he introduces figures such as a dove or an Old Man, figures that seem to call for an allegorical interpretation, we find his dove has nothing to do with the Holy Spirit, but rather is a barnyard purveyor, and the Old Man's too solid flesh blurs whatever symbolic significance he seems to demand. The Pardoner is not a spiritual man, and the very manner of the fiction he tells reveals his lack of faith.

Chaucer was also as capable as Ovid of extending an element of character into narrative incident; perhaps the clearest example of this is Alceste in the *Legend of Good Women*. This lady's personality, of course, is the amplification of a pun, which Chaucer's models, the French marguerite poems, had all playfully elaborated. Marguerite means both daisy and pearl, and the prologues of Chaucer's calendar of Cupid's saints artfully reflect each aspect.

In the first part of the poem, the narrator, in the manner of the *Romance of the Rose*, literally worships the daisy, leaving, as the F-version has it, both his books and his devotion to it 'alle reverence.' This extraordinary flower, however, has assumed characteristics nature had never given it: she is 'of alle floures flour, / Fulfilled of al vertu and honour, / And evere ilyke faire, and fressh of hewe' (F 53–5). The daisy has become very much a courtly heroine to whom the narrator does homage as though she were the Virgin Mary. We sense that if in the poet's eyes his lady is a daisy, in his heart she is a pearl.

The maiden who accompanies the God of Love in the narrator's dream is also daisy and pearl, an association Chaucer's description of her nicely conveys:

> a whit corowne she beer
> With flourouns smale, and I shal nat lye;   little flowers
> For al the world, ryght as a dayesye
> Ycorouned ys with white leves lyte,
> So were the flowrouns of hire coroune white.
> For of o perle fyn, oriental,   one fine pearl
> Hire white coroune was maked al.   (F 216–22)

In Alceste, however, pearl-like qualities predominate, to such an extent that they direct the course the narrative subsequently takes. In the F-version, after the balade has been sung, the dreamer sees nineteen ladies in royal habit who attend Alceste and who are followed by a procession of so many women 'trewe of love' that the poet thinks a third of all the women who ever lived must have been there. Seeing the poet's daisy, they all stop and kneel, saying 'Heel and honour / To trouthe of womanhede ... (F 296ff). They then all sit, 'Ne nat a word was spoken in the place / The mountaunce [amount of time it took to walk] of a furlong wey of space' (F 306–7).

The words and actions of these ladies are iconographical and derive ultimately from Apocalypse 7, where John describes those who were marked with the seal of the living God. First one hundred forty-four thousand are drawn from the twelve tribes of Israel;

And after I saw a great multitude, which no man could number, of all nations, and tribes, and peoples, and tongues: standing ... on the sight of God ... they all cried with a loud voice, saying: Salvation to our God ['Salus Deo nostro'] ... and all the angels ... fell down before the throne upon their faces, and adored God ... And when [the angel] had opened the seventh seal, there was silence in heaven, as it were a half an hour. (Apocalypse 7:9–11; 8:1)

In the G-version Chaucer eliminated the rather blatant parody of the salutation to God, but the other details remain unchanged, as well they should, since both the poet and John are witnesses to a day of judgment. When he sees the narrator, the God of Love becomes an angry God of Doom, while Alceste assumes the role of the Virgin Mary interceding for her not too repentant sinner. With his characteristic wit, Chaucer plays on the humour of this development: Alceste must deliver a very lengthy reminder to the God of Love to the effect that Amor and charity are not really incompatible. And Alceste's mercy being what it is, we wonder how the poet would have fared had he actually been guilty of something. My point, however, is that the transition from springtime and flowers to the court of Love is the transition from daisy to pearl, from one aspect of the marguerite to the other. Pearls, as the Middle English poem of that title should remind us, would have commonly brought to mind John's vision of the rewards of heaven for those who were chaste on earth. The twelve gates of the Heavenly city are 'twelve pearls, and every several gate was of one several pearl' (Apocalypse 21:21). Yet once Chaucer had associated the marguerite with a vision of paradise, he would have quite naturally remembered that John's heaven is a heaven of judgment as well. Thus in the first part of both prologues the poet literally worships a pun, but in the second, the setting and action of the vision are a very Ovidian extension of the other side of Alceste's extraordinarily literary character. As in Ovid and Boccaccio, the poet's experience is identical with the conventions of his books.

From these examples we see that the quality which distinguishes Chaucer's characters generally is the wit with which they are constructed. Their prototypes often seem stick-figures by comparison, an unintegrated mass of tired traditions. The Man of Law and the Clerk are good cases in point: more extended analyses of both reveal the cast of Chaucer's pilgrims, and, in the case of the Clerk, how Chaucer could make his teller an extension of the style of the tale he tells.

One of the more puzzling aspects of the Introduction to the 'Man of Law's Tale' is the catalogue of Chaucer's works that appears there. Why does the Man of Law, rather than Chaucer, speak these lines? The list would seem better placed were it part of the prologue to 'Sir Thopas,' or following the Host's interruption of that tale; preceding the tale of Constance it seems odd and jarring.[25] Certainly we hope, no matter the position, that had Chaucer listed his works his description of them would have been more accurate than the Lawyer's. In the case of the *Legend of Good Women*, at least, the Man of Law gets many of the tales and even the covering name of the poem wrong; apparently he has heard about Chaucer's collection, but one doubts he has actually read it. This inference makes all the more surprising the polite malice that informs the lawyer's recitation. Why does the Man of Law enumerate

Chaucer's works only to denigrate them? By answering these questions we define the literary quality of his character.

The Introduction to the 'Man of Law's Tale' begins with Harry Bailly's astronomical calculations; after he has determined that it already is ten o'clock, the Host cannot forbear urging that the pilgrims lose no more time. In that blend of proverbial philosophy and earthiness which is peculiarly his own, Harry warns that time 'wasteth nyght and day,' and can never be recovered:

> Wel kan Senec and many a philosophre
> Biwaillen tyme moore than gold in cofre;
> For 'los of catel may recovered be,
> But los of tyme shendeth us,' quod he.   ruins
> It wol nat come agayn, withouten drede,   doubt
> Namoore than wole Malkynes maydenhede,
> Whan she hath lost it in hir wantownesse.
> Lat us nat mowlen thus in ydelnesse. (B¹ 25–32)

Then, using words a lawyer would understand, Harry asks the Man of Law to abide by his agreement and tell a tale. The Man of Law consents by restating in a legal proverb that balances exactly the precept from Seneca the terms of the 'forward' between pilgrims and Host:

> For swich lawe as a man yeveth another wight,
> He sholde hymselven usen it, by right;
> Thus wole oure text. (43–5)[26]

The catalogue of Chaucer's works then follows immediately.

The Man of Law is a fine legal tactician. In keeping with the Host's injunction, the list of 'thrifty' tales becomes an elaborate rhetorical figure that seems to resemble 'occupatio.' The Man of Law would not waste the pilgrims' time repeating a story Chaucer has already told: 'What sholde I tellen hem, syn they been tolde?' (56); instead he lists these stories, and some Chaucer has not told, just as a prosecutor might list the arguments of the defence, only to reject them. For our Lawyer will not waste time, and so many are the stories he will not tell, we begin to find ourselves in the Man of Law's debt for all he has spared us.

Yet the Man of Law's seeming concern for the pilgrims' time hardly hides his low opinion of Chaucer's works. The 'occupatio' only seems to confer objectivity; in truth it is a device that drapes some rather captious commentary. The Man of Law can manipulate language with some subtlety, and a second look shows certain method in his disparagement. Contrary to what the lawyer claims, Chaucer did not write the story of Deianire, nor did he write of

Hermione, Hero and Leander, Helen, Penelope, nor of Laodamia. These unwritten tales are often interpreted as evidence of a more complete plan for the *Legend of Good Women*.[27] One notes, however, that all but one (Alcestis) of the additional stories the Man of Law credits to Chaucer come from Ovid's *Heroides*; our justice in assize seems to have made a more thorough study of Ovid's 'Epistles,' as he calls them, than of Chaucer. In fact, an implicit comparison between Ovid and Chaucer runs throughout the Man of Law's speech. There are as many references to the works of the Roman poet as there are to Chaucer's and the Man of Law leaves little doubt that, were one asked to judge between them, the English poet had better plead 'nolo contendere.' Perhaps the lawyer's ultimate innuendo is that, unlike himself, Chaucer is a waste of time, since all but one or two of his stories have already been told, as any reader of Ovid would know.

In his desire to denigrate Chaucer, however, the Man of Law, ironically enough, himself becomes the object of satire. The Lawyer has complained that Chaucer has told all the stories of 'loveres'; yet from his own mouth come the names of six or seven legendary women about whom Chaucer has written nothing. The Man of Law clearly hasn't got his facts straight, a considerable shortcoming, one would think, in a lawyer. Moreover, as he exposes Chaucer's deficiencies, the Man of Law actually does his 'auctor' a poetic service. Chaucer always jokes about how his writing really isn't very good, a traditional expression of modesty often employed by medieval poets. Now the lawyer speaks these words, so effectively that no one could possibly charge Chaucer with the sin of poetic pride.

Yet if the Man of Law is unaware of the full implications his words are made to have, he nevertheless knows that form and style can sometimes persuade without the benefit of fact and substance. Having mentioned the tales from Chaucer that he will not rehearse, the Man of Law finally directly compares himself to the poet:

> But of my tale how shal I doon this day?
> Me were looth be likned, doutelees,
> To Muses that men clepe Pierides –
> *Metamorphosios* woot what I mene;   knows
> But nathelees, I recche noght a bene   care, bean
> Though I come after hym with hawebake. baked hawthorn berries
> I speke in prose, and lat him rymes make. (90–6)

All at once his confession of inadequacy has been transformed into something like an 'argumentum ad hominem' against Chaucer, which first proudly displays with high style the colours of rhetoric to allude to classical learning, but then seems to give the impression of humility by abruptly switching to colloquial, vernacular expression.[28] The comparison to Ovid is completed by implication; beside the Roman the 'lewed' (unlearned) English poet seems shrill as a magpie. Chaucer's worth receives only the most indirect acknowledgment: unlike some other poets he doesn't tell wicked stories of forbidden sexual lust (77–89). The Man of Law, we see, is really an accomplished rhetorician; his language means both more and less than it says.

The motive for all this, however, remains a puzzle: why does the Man of Law single out Chaucer as the object of his attack? Long ago Manly suggested that the portrait of the Lawyer was Chaucer's way of revenging himself on Thomas Pynchbek, who in 1388, as chief baron of the Exchequer, signed a writ to arrest the poet for a small debt.[29] Ultimately, of course, such an identification is unverifiable and beside the point; however much Chaucer may have begrudged some particular lawyer, the Man of the Law's character depends more on literary tradition than on personal animosity.

Even in classical times, poets seem to have resented lawyers, if not for their actual wealth, then for the way they debased language to acquire it. Admittedly the mood is light in Horace's epistle to Torquatus (1.5), in which the poet in straitened circumstances ('contracta ... in paupertate,' 20) invites the rich lawyer to dinner. Horace must urge Torquatus to give up for a day the struggle for riches ('certamina divitiarum'): leave your affairs, he tells him as the poem ends, and elude your waiting client by slipping through the back door of the hall. As Gordon Williams says, the Epistle succeeds because Horace is able to 'build a contrast of two real personalities: the distinguished lawyer, with his ancient lineage and grand way of life, and the simple, quiet-living poor poet, with his philosophical meditations.'[30] Ultimately, however, the antagonism between the two professions is not so muted. In the darkest part of Virgil's Hades, Rhadamanthus presides over the punishment of the most wicked souls, among whom are those who deceived their clients ('fraus innexa clienti,' Aeneid VI, 609); lawyers are the only profession Virgil includes in this his severest censure of earthly conduct. And Ovid, who studied law because his father thought poetry a 'worthless pursuit' ('studium quid inutile temptas?' he asks his son, 'even Homer left no wealth,' Tristia IV, x, 21–2), held lawyers in contempt throughout his life. In Amores I, xv, Ovid answers the charges of 'Livor edax,' who claimed his profession was trivial. What if he does not pursue the dusty prizes of a soldier's life,

> nec me uerbosas leges ediscere nec me
> ingrato uocem prostituisse foro

nor memorize verbose laws nor prostitute my voice before the thankless forum? (5–6)

Poetry will nevertheless gain Ovid immortality. The idea that the men who haunt the courts of law sell their words for money became a standard complaint in medieval satires of lawyers and judges.[31]

In the *Ars Amatoria*, lawyers are special objects of scorn. Love may be found anywhere, our preceptor of Amor tells us, even, mirabile dictu, at the halls of justice:

> et fora conueniunt (quis credere possit?) amori,
> flammaque in arguto saepe reperta foro

And who would believe it, even law-courts are fit places to find love; flames of love often are found in the shrill forum.   (1, 79–80)

The counsellor himself may be seized in love; when this happens Venus sits in her temple and laughs with Ovid at the spectacle of this man for once tongue-tied ('desunt sua uerba') unable to defend himself, who practises defending others (83–9).

Ovid's opinion of legal eloquence is instructive since he certainly knew that the orator sought to surpass the poet's ability to use language. Quintilian perhaps best formulates the rhetorician's attitude toward poetry when he speaks of 'conversio,' that is, of paraphrasing the Greek and Latin poets into prose:

But paraphrase from the Latin (as well as from the Greek) will be of much assistance, while I think we shall agree that this is specially valuable with regard to poetry; indeed, it is said that the paraphrase of poetry was the sole form of exercise employed by Sulplicus. For the lofty inspiration of verse serves to elevate the orator's style and the bold license of poetic language does not forestall the power of using the language of ordinary prose. Nay, we may add the vigour of oratory to the thought expressed by the poet, make good his omissions, and prune his diffuseness. But I would not have paraphrase restrict itself to the bare interpretation of the original: its duty is rather to rival and vie with the original in the expression of the same thoughts (*sed circa eosdem sensus certamen atque aemulationem.*)[32]

Already in Quintilian the 'robur' of oratory triumphs over poetry's undisciplined flights of fancy; in the Middle Ages, as poetry increasingly became only one element of rhetoric, jurists trained in the arts of oratory eventually began to wonder how poets could ever have been their competitors. By the fourteenth century, a lawyer could dismiss a poet almost out of hand, as Boccaccio describes in the fourteenth book of his *Genealogy of the Gods*:

It is [lawyers'] practice, especially during a lull in their duties, to leave bench and court, and join an informal gathering of friends; if, in the course of the conversation, anyone happens to mention poets, they always praise them highly of course, as men of great learning and eloquence. But at length with honey they mingle poison – not deadly, to be sure. They say that poets can hardly be called wise to have spent their whole time following a profession that, after years of labor, yields never a cent. This explains, they add, why poets are always stark poor; they never make brilliant showing with dress, money, nor servants; from which they argue that, because poets are not rich, their profession is good for nothing.[33]

Such reasoning, Boccaccio continues, mendacious though it is, is nevertheless insidious, since people are inclined to believe it because 'we are all somewhat given to love of money, and foolishly take wealth to be the greatest thing in the world.' Lawyers therefore will not only dare to pass sentence on Boccaccio himself, but 'by implication to condemn poets themselves, together with their works and their poverty, as a supreme and detestable evil.'[34] Boccaccio, of course, will not allow this to pass unchallenged; he eloquently defends the nobility of poetry, and adds a long essay praising the virtues of poverty. It is no accident that the Man of Law chastises the evils of poverty in the prologue to his tale of Constance.

Thus there seems to have existed a traditional animus between lawyers, who use language for their own profit, making 'gold out of the tears of the wretched by the transmuting power of their own verbosity,' and poets, whose language moves the minds of men to ponder the eternal.[35] The lawyer applies the wrong standard of measure to poetry, for material considerations cannot appraise the value of the creations of the mind and spirit. Chaucer himself intimates that his Sergeant of Law shares this rivalry with poets:

In termes hadde he caas and doomes alle	In negotiating, cases, decisions
That from the tyme of kyng William were falle.	
Thereto he koude endite, and make a thyng,	
Ther koude no wight pynche at his writyng;	protest
And every statut koude he pleyn by rote.	knew he fully by heart

(A 323–7)

The Man of Law can 'endite,' and 'make a thyng,' that is, write opinions which, as Donaldson says, are not directed toward settling matters of right and wrong so much as toward making himself rich.[36] Chaucer, however, commonly uses these words to describe the making of poetry: 'endite' and 'make' literally mean to compose verse, and 'thyng,' as the OED tells us (s.v. thing, 13), could refer as much to an individual work of literature or art as to a deed of law.[37] When the lawyer snipes at Chaucer, therefore, he is only casting aspersion on a traditional adversary.

Indeed, the *Legend of Good Women*, the very poem the Man of Law cites most frequently as evidence in his character assassination, shows how inseparable the lawyer's behaviour is from literary convention. Certainly the verbal echoes, as well as the parallel lists of Chaucer's works, prompt a comparison of the two poems. Alceste, for instance, tells the God of Love that a king shouldn't be cruel, for, as the F-version has it, his people are 'his tresour, and his gold in cofre. / This is the sentence of the philosphre ...' (380–1). As we have seen, Harry Bailly uses the same rhyme in his speech against idleness, the starting point for one of the Man of Law's innuendoes against Chaucer. Most striking, however, are Chaucer's words in the *Legend of Good Women* concerning his belatedness and small stature as a poet:

> For wel I wot that folk han here-beforn
> Of makyng ropen, and lad awey the corn;   composing poetry, reaped
> And I come after, glenynge here and there,
> And am ful glad if I may fynde an ere
> Of any goodly word that they han left.
> And if it happe me rehersen eft   again
> That they han in here freshe songes said,   their
> I hope that they wole nat ben evele apayd ... displeased
> (G 61–8)

The Man of Law obviously is 'evele apayd' that Chaucer has rehearsed Ovid's *Heroides*. With unspeakable effrontery, the Lawyer appropriates Chaucer's own words as he steals a march on him and on poets in general: 'I recche nought a bene / Though I come after hym with hawebake. / I speke in prose, and let hym rymes make.'

In his fine article on the royal stanza in early English literature, Martin Stevens has elucidated the crux this last line poses.[38] The rhyme-royal tale of Constance definitely falls under the meanings 'prose' had in Middle English; we can now be more certain that Chaucer meant the Man of Law to tell this tale. And, as Stevens and others have argued, the telling is awful.[39] All the devices Chaucer the poet uses are trotted out in display: disclaimers regarding his skill as story-teller (42, 874, 881), assurances he will not linger over his matter (701, 983, 990, 1011), all to no effect. 'The narrator is a priceless example of ineptitude,' as Stevens says, and his tale is 'a brilliant satire of dullness.'[40]

Chaucer willingly allows the Man of Law to engage him in a not so friendly rivalry because by showing how bad a 'maker' the Man of Law is, Chaucer proves himself a superior poet.

For all his deft manipulation of convention, however, Chaucer's subtlest means of presenting a character lies in his celebrated ability to suit a teller to a tale. We discern qualities of many, though not all, the Canterbury pilgrims from the tale a character chooses to tell and from the way he tells it. There are some tales, such as the Clerk's, which allow us to see Chaucer in the process of this adaptation. By studying the changes Chaucer made in his source, we can better understand the art that makes this poet's men and women unique figures in medieval literature.

Not many Canterbury Tales disturb Chaucer's readers as much as the Clerk's Long ago, Lounsbury, a spokesman for many, said the Tale's 'central idea' was 'too revolting for any skill in description to make it palatable.'[41] Yet the suffering Griselda and the contemptible Walter must have had some appeal, for the fourteenth century's greatest poets, Boccaccio, Petrarch, and Chaucer, were each sufficiently attracted to try to describe their marital travails. The tale, in fact, has been repeatedly retold since Boccaccio ended the Decameron with it, but no telling, certainly not Baccaccio's or Petrarch's, has evoked as vitriolic a response as has Chaucer's.[42] Readers of some versions even praise the tale. One suspects, then, that the way the tale is told, perhaps more than its 'central idea,' accounts for the reader's reaction to it.

In Chaucer, the trials of Griselda and Walter are told by the Clerk, and it is his telling, I think, that has divided the critics so passionately. The Clerk, of course, recites a story he learned from 'Fraunceys Petrak.' Since the texts of Petrarch's letter, and an anonymous French redaction Chaucer used, have been established by Severs, we not only can consider the merits of the narratives of Chaucer's direct sources, but can appraise closely the making of the 'Clerk's Tale' as well. In doing this, the religious premises of Petrarch's recounting emerge, setting his telling entirely apart from its predecessor in Boccaccio. And when one examines the changes Chaucer made in his version, a design that combines secular and religious details begins to appear, a design that ultimately affords us a glimpse of Chaucer fitting a character to his tale.

The earliest extant literary accounts of Griselda and Walter are found in the Decameron and the Epistolae Seniles; the tone and purpose of Petrarch's story, however, differ markedly from Boccaccio's. Gone are Dioneo's cynicism and irony; in their place, the decorous and stylized words of Griselda and Walter have properly dignified the tale for its conversion into a religious exemplum. The moral Petrarch appends explicitly states that the intent of his tale is religious:

I thought to repeat this story now in a different style not so much that women today should imitate the patience of this wife, which seems to me hardly imitable, but that I may at least move my readers to imitate the constancy of Griselda; that since she was so faithful to her husband, we may venture to be so steadfast to our Lord, who, as James the Apostle says, may not be tempted with evil and would tempt no man. Yet he allows us to be vexed with many and sobering scourges, not that He may know our spirit, which He knew before we were begotten, but that our frailties might be made known to us through known and familiar signs. I would definitely include on a list of constant men whomsoever he was who suffered without murmur for his God what this rustic wife suffered for her mortal husband.[43]

This is a far cry from the lesson we have seen Dioneo draw from his story. Where he emphasizes Gualtieri's 'matta bestialità,' Petrarch enjoins us to consider Griselda, for in her lies the moral and spiritual centre of the story. The lines in the epilogue 'not so much that women today should imitate the patience of this wife, which seems to me hardly imitable,' stress the religious function of the tale and remove its events, as Elizabeth Salter says, 'from the danger of too close a secular application.'[44] We should not imitate the patience Griselda exhibits under torment; it is the constancy of her faith that is to be commended. As faithful as she was to Walter, a mortal man, so should we be to God.

In its secular setting, however, the tale becomes difficult. Walter's unanswerable testing of Griselda is no doubt hard to reconcile with conjugal, not to mention spiritual, love. But Petrarch hints throughout his story that not only does divine purpose inform Walter's action, though he himself may be unconscious of it, but that Griselda's actions imitate Christ's. Walter's first speech, for instance, contains overt religious references, and has none of the prying cynicism and harshness of the speech in Boccaccio:

Whatever good there is in man proceeds from God alone. I entrust my station and the fate of my marriage to Him, hoping for his accustomed mercy.[45]

And throughout the tale, whenever possible, Petrarch deflects our growing abhorrence away from Walter and on to some other character. When Walter's henchman comes to take Griselda's daughter, Petrarch says:

Report of this man was suspicious, his face suspect; suspect also the hour of his coming and suspect his speech.

In short, a real villain, and as such a surrogate for our censure of Walter. In Boccaccio, the man is little more than a cipher; he is simply said to come looking 'very sorrowful.'

In Petrarch's version, Walter is clearly an agent; when he is criticized, the criticism is muted. Before he marries Griselda, Walter is faulted for being 'most careless of the future,' 'incuriossimus futurorum erat.' When he finally is done testing Griselda, Walter justifies his actions by saying his subjects must know that he is 'curiosum atque experientem.' He means, I take it, 'caring, and active in proving it'; by this point, however, we are likely to understand the words as 'meddlesome (if not worse), and an expert taskmaster at it.' Considering the repugnance with which Augustine viewed 'mala curiositas' in the *Confessions,* some circuitous disparagement is being levelled at Walter.[46] As incurious before as he is curious now, in either case he earns little praise.

As for Griselda, consider (in Latin) the geographical prooemium Petrarch added when he translated the tale:

Est ad Ytalie latus occiduum Vesullus ex Apenini iugis mons unus altissimus, qui, vertice nubila superans, liquido sese ingerit etheri, mons suapte nobilis natura, Padi ortu nobilissimus, qui eius e latere fonte lapsus exiguo, orientem contra solem fertur, mirisque mox tumidus incrementis brevi spacio decurso, non tantum maximorum unus amnium sed fluviorum a Virgilio rex dictus, Liguriam gurgite violentus intersecat; dehinc Emiliam atque Flaminian Veneciamque disterminans multis ad ultimum et ingentibus hostijs in Adriaticum mare descendit.

There stands in Italy, toward the Western side, Mount Viso, one of the highest of the Apennines, whose summit, surpassing the clouds, thrusts itself up into the pure ether. This mount, noble in its own right, is most noble as the source of the Po, which, issuing in a little spring from is side, flows eastward toward the rising sun. Descending in its course, it soon swells with great tributaries, so much that it is not only one of the greatest rivers, but is called the king of rivers by Virgil; it cuts Liguria violently with raging waters; then, bounding Emilia, Ferrara, and Venice, it finally empties through many mouths into the Adriatic Sea.

Certainly the order and harmony of the natural world established here may be contrasted with the disorder and chaos in the human sphere that follows, but beyond that, Petrarch in effect recounts the moral of his entire story in a paragraph. Issuing in a small spring from the side of a noble mountain, the Po grows to be the 'king of rivers.' This action charts exactly Griselda's miraculous course from poorest peasant to renowned marquise of Saluces, allowing for even the rough periods and agitation ('gurgite violentus') she had to endure.[47] It recapitulates as well as important and relevant theme from the Epistle of James: 'Let the lowly brother boast in his exaltation, and the rich in his humiliation' (1:9–10), and again, 'Has not God chosen those who are poor in the world to be rich in faith? Is it not the rich who oppress you ... ?' (2:5–6). As we have seen,

Petrarch quotes James in his epilogue: God does not tempt us but allows us to be tested. Petrarch has knit up what Chaucer would call the 'sentence,' the moral significance of his tale with considerable art.

The small spring that becomes the mighty Po is 'fonte ... exiguo.' 'Fons,' even in classical Latin, could mean 'well'; Chaucer translated it thus, catching at the same time the further denotation of 'source.' When Walter comes to marry Griselda, he meets her just as she is returning carrying water from a distant well ('e longinquo fonte'), a detail Petrarch added to Boccaccio. We remember the fledgling Po and are meant, I think, to associate the two. 'Exiguus,' of course, denotes 'poor,' 'scanty,' as well as 'small': in medieval Latin, it also carried moral overtones of 'humility.'[48] It is a fine word to describe Griselda.

Moreover, the very act of the Po issuing ('lapsus,' itself a word overflowing with Christian connotation) from the side ('latere') of the most noble Mount Viso, recalls not only the blood and water that issued from Christ's side ('latus') at the Crucifixion, but the river of life ('fluvium aquae vivae') John saw coming from the throne of God and the Lamb in Apocalypse (22:1). At the very beginning of Petrarch's tale, we are reminded of Christ's suffering, so that Griselda's trials, and her rewards, might be seen in their proper perspective, as an 'imitatio Christi.'

In the Griselda legend, then, Petrarch found a worthy but slightly flawed story whose 'sentence' was almost consonant with Christian ethics. When the story's 'sentence' was translated into its Christian 'moralitas,' and Griselda's constant love for Walter became a model for man's faith in God, the spirit of the story became like that of the Book of Job (5:17–18):

Happy is the man whom God corrects: therefore despise not the chastening of the Almighty. For he makes sore and binds up, he wounds and his hands make whole.

Within the allegory Walter's impossible testings remain, but are unregarded in the purer light of Griselda's virtuous suffering.

In his dedicatory letter to Boccaccio, Petrarch said that he had greatly admired the story of Griselda all his life; one wonders why he waited so long to tell it. Yet the emotions Petrarch's tale enshrines strongly resemble those celebrated in the *Canzoniere*. The same steadfastness of purpose, the same single-mindedness of desire, the same intensity of devotion that distinguishes Petrarch's love for Laura are present in this tale; here, however, the end is Christian. In many ways, his tale of Griselda is Petrarch's final gloss on the *Canzoniere*.

When we turn to Chaucer's rendering, however, many problems confront us, The 'Clerk's Tale,' it seems, is constantly pulled in two directions, one human, the other divine, which makes many feel that the 'human sympathies so powerfully evoked by the sight of unmerited suffering form, ultimately, a barrier to total acceptance of the work in its original (religious) function.'[49] Now Chaucer followed Petrarch's narrative nearly to the letter, neither deleting any of the scenes nor changing the sequence Petrarch had given them. That Chaucer translated Petrarch's moral as well indicates that he knew the spirit of Petrarch's version as well as the letter. Yet in the 'Clerk's Tale' there are introduced at once realistic, sentimental, and religious attitudes that now direct our attention to the moral purpose of the story and now distract us from it. And although it was Chaucer who made these additions, it is the Clerk he makes responsible for them.

Before the Clerk begins his recital, he tells us that Petrarch wrote a 'prohemye' to his tale which, to the Clerk's judgment, is a long and impertinent thing:

> But forth to tellen of this worthy man
> That taughte me this tale, as I bigan,
> I seye that first with heigh stile he enditeth,
> Er he the body of his tale writeth,
> A prohemye, in the which discryveth he   prologue
> Pemond, and of Saluces the contree,
> And speketh of Apennyn, the hilles hye,
> That been the boundes of West Lumbardye,
> And of Mount Vesulus in special,
> Where as the Poo out of a welle smal   spring
> Taketh his firste spryngyng and his sours,
> That estward ay encresseth in his cours
> To Emele-ward, to Ferrare, and Venyse;
> The which a long thyng were to devyse.
> And trewely, as to my juggement,
> Me thynketh it a thyng impertinent,   irrelevant
> Save that he wole conveyen his matere ...   introduce
> (E 39–55)

The Clerk is making us here of the figure 'occupatio': he tells us all the superfluous facts and then dismisses them as unimportant. As a man who 'noght o word spak moore than was neede' (A 304), we might expect the Clerk to edit his material in such a way. Yet in using this figure, our student explains in nineteen lines of poetry why he is not repeating fifteen lines of prose; rehearsing nearly everything Petrarch says, the Clerk adds to the verbiage rather than reduces it. Furthermore, the Clerk's use of the 'occupatio' is premature, to say the last; not knowing at this point what Petrarch's 'mateere' is, we are cajoled into accepting the Clerk's arbitrary judgment as authoritative. Yet considering the prooemium, one wonders just how it is impertinent. Impertinent perhaps to the narrative matter of the tale, the prooemium is beyond doubt germane to the tale's 'sentence.'

The lines under consideration serve a double purpose: they identify the Clerk as the narrator of our tale, and they make it clear that, since clerks were practised exegetes as well as rhetoricians, our narrator might not balk at emending his text where he sees fit. Yet when he fails to see Petrarch's meaning, the Clerk's rhetoric miscarries; in his effort to speak to the point, the Clerk misses it, and the judgment and the perception of our narrator are unavoidably called into question.

In interpreting his 'mateere,' the Clerk enters his narration at three points to register complaint against Walter: first at verse 460,

> But as for me, I seye that yvele it sit   it befits badly
> To assaye a wyf whan that it is no nede,
> And putten hire in angwyssh and in drede.

Again at verse 621,

> O nedelees was she tempted in assay!   tested
> But wedded men ne knowe no mesure,
> Whan that they fynde a pacient creature.

And again at verse 696,

> But now of wommen wolde I axen fayn
> If thise assayes myghte nat suffise?
> What koude a sturdy housbounde moore devyse
> To preeve hir wyfhod and hir stedefastnesse,
> And he continuynge evere in sturdinesse?   cruelty

Surely the Clerk's moral righteousness prompts these rhetorical asides. Yet the effect of these lines is unsettling. Whatever his intention, by questioning Walter's behaviour the Clerk demonstrates his failure to understand that the very nature of Griselda's forbearance puts Walter's actions beyond objection. What Petrarch commends Griselda for not saying, for not even thinking, the Clerk here says time and again.[50] Furthermore, the Clerk has chosen the wrong subject to comment on. By directing his complaints against Walter, the Clerk evokes sympathy for Griselda's plight. We are reminded of Walter's cruelty, of his needlessly tempting his poor wife, whose virtue was already proved. It is Griselda's constant faithfulness, though, and not the circumstances that prove it, that Petrarch commends to us and that warrants our consideration; Griselda deserves our attention and our praise, not our sympathy. By commenting on Walter's actions, the Clerk has not only unjustifiably involved us with the tale's chaff, but seems himself to have lost sight of its wheat, Griselda's constancy. Our commentator has confused us rather than enlightened us.

Distracting too are Griselda's only disrespectful words to Walter, coming on her expulsion from his castle:

> O goode God! how gentil and how kynde
> Ye semed by youre speche and youre visage
> The day that maked was oure mariage!   (E 852–4)

Although tempered somewhat by the following stanza, the effect of these lines is nonetheless disconcerting when we remember the consequences of our lady's constancy:

> 'I have,' quod she, 'seyd thus, and evere shal:
> I wol no thyng, ne nyl no thyng, certayn,   want, not want
> But as yow list. *Naught greveth me at al,*
> *Though that my doughter and my sone be slayn,* –
> *At youre comandement, this is to seyn.*
> I have noght had no part of children tweyne
> But first siknesse, and after, wo and peyne.'   (E 645–51)

Compare this passage with Griselda's speech in Petrarch:

Griselda replied: 'I have said, and I say again, that I can want nothing nor not want anything except what you wish; nor do I truthfully have any claim to these children past the bearing of them ...'

Dignified, constant to itself and beyond criticism in Petrarch, Griselda's reaffirmation in the 'Clerk's Tale' seems to underline the tension between her suffering and her saintliness. The Latin 'neque vero in hijs filijs quicquam habeo preter laborem' seems decidedly flat besides the description of Griselda's morning sickness and her birth pangs, but this is just the point. A saint's life is marked by the absence of details which express merely human suffering; this tale is not.

Furthermore, the additional sentence changes the entire tenor of the passage, for by the Clerk's rendering Griselda's constancy has seemingly been made to justify Walter's murders, while in Petrarch's tale, her constancy justifies only itself. Knowing that Walter has not murdered his children makes Griselda's speech ironic for the reader of the Clerk's tale, and praiseworthy for Petrarch's. The Clerk has made Griselda at once a symbol of ever-constant fortitude proved by the greatest duress, and a mother who suffers undeserved cruelty, and the one can only work at cross-purposes to the other. Indeed, when Griselda later expresses her disapprobation of Walter (E 852ff, discussed above), this single inconsistency not only makes her functioning as a symbol impossible, but also makes her a mother who is morally accountable for her children's deaths. To 'grucche' (complain) at Walter's 'lust' now and not when her children were to be slain seems mistimed, at best. And as we might expect, Griselda's unfortunate demurral is the Clerk's addition.

Griselda's swooning is similarly the Clerk's invention. The four lines in Petrarch which describe Griselda's joy at her reunion with her children are heartfelt and direct:

When Griselda hears this she rushes inanimate with joy and out of her senses with piety and most joyful tears to the embraces of her children, and tires them with kisses and weeps softly with a loving sigh.

This is all Petrarch says. The Clerk, on the other hand, waxes ecstatic through five stanzas (E 1097–1113), so ecstatic that Griselda swoons twice. Robert Jordan is right in claiming that this scene engages our deepest sympathy, for as the Clerk himself says, 'O which a pitous thyng it was to se / Hir swownyng, and hire humble voys to heere' (E 1086–7). Pity in fact colours the entire passage, as the Clerk uses the word again and again (E 1080, 1082, 1086, 1104). Yet whereas Griselda is happy in Petrarch because she never despaired, because her faith and constancy precluded despair, the Clerk makes us feel that Griselda has suffered, even to the point of despair, and that her joy is so overwhelming because it springs from the depths of her long-anguished soul. In Petrarch, Griselda does not even speak; her joy is unalloyed, and the single sigh that escapes her mouth bespeaks her joy, which is beyond words. Griselda cries out in the 'Clerk's Tale,' however, and again her words are confused and unsettling:

> O tendre, O deere, o yonge children myne!
> Youre woful mooder wende stedfastly
> That crueel houndes or som foul vermyne
> Hadde eten yow ... (E 1093–6)

Can any mother who steadfastly believes that cruel hounds or foul vermin had eaten her children be praised for the constancy of her thought? Yet Petrarch's moral, which follows posthaste, asks us to commend Griselda's constancy. In an utterly human situation, Griselda speaks not as a parent, but as a personification of devotion, and again her words seem out of place. One moment a saintly martyr to Walter's demands, an anguished mother for the Clerk's pity the next, Griselda is caught between the conflicting demands of two incompatible worlds.

These instances which unintentionally distract our attention from the tale's religious import are at the same time set in sharper contrast by additions that support a religious reading. As a man who 'hadde geten hym yet no benefice, / Ne was so worldly for to have office' (A 291–2), the Clerk would embrace the religious intent of Petrarch's tale. In pious zeal the Clerk in fact outreaches Petrarch; God's name is invoked much more frequently, and the Clerk adds many descriptive details that have religious associations. Thus when Griselda's child is taken from her, she submits,

> And *as a lamb* she sitteth meke and stille,
> And leet this cruel sergeant doon his wille.   (E 538–9)

Even before Griselda is mentioned, we are reminded of the Nativity:

> But hye God somtyme senden kan
> His grace into a litel oxes stalle ...   (E 206–7)

This image is repeated, first when Walter comes to marry Griselda (E 290–2), and then to contrast her humble origins with her queenly deportment (E 396–9). Besides depicting the lowliness of Griselda's birth, these lines spiritualize the peasant girl by associating her with Christ and with the Nativity. They convey the religious purpose of the tale, as indeed does the Clerk's passage which likens Griselda's humbleness to Job's:

> Men speke of Job, and moost for his humblesse,
> As clerkes, whan hem list, konne wel endite,   wish, compose
> Namely of men, but as in soothfastnesse,   especially, truth
> Though clerkes preise wommen but a lite,
> Ther kan no man in humblesse hym acquite
> As womman kan, ne kan been half so trewe
> As wommen been, but it be falle of newe.   happened recently
> (E 932–8)

Similarly, Walter's nobles bid him marry for 'hye Goddes sake,' lest, 'as God forbede,' he should die without an heir (E 135–7), and Walter is said to live 'In Goddes pees' for a while with Griselda (E 432); when he reclaims Griselda, Walter again invokes God's mercy:

> 'Grisilde,' quod ne, *'by God, that for us deyde,*
> Thou art my wyf, ne noon other I have,
> Ne nevere hadde, *as God my soule save!'* (E 1062–4)

Walter's references to God at this point and throughout the tale have usually been explained as helping to justify his behaviour. As long as Walter can be identified as God's surrogate, his actions must be given our sanction, as they prove Griselda. The fact is, however, that Walter has been so vividly and adversely portrayed that, as Elizabeth Salter says, 'we are inclined – indeed encouraged – to believe in his heartlessness rather than in his inscrutability.'[52] Indeed, as we have seen, the Clerk's own moral interjections and sentimental embellishments do the most to confuse matters. By the time Griselda is likened to Job, Walter is so much a man and a symbol of cruelty that the reader is likely to complete the comparison and identify Walter with Satan, rather than with, say, the rich man who in the Epistle of St James rejoices in his humiliation. One is never tempted to such speculation in Petrarch; in the 'Clerk's Tale,' however, it is hard to avoid.

One sees, then, that it is the Clerk's rendering of his tale that has upset Chaucer's readers so. One wishes the Clerk had followed Harry Bailly's advice and had spoken

> ... so pleyn at this tyme, we yow preye,
> That we may understonde what ye seye (E 19–20)

Yet we realize from his injudicious apostrophes and from his confusing appeals to the reader's sympathy that the Clerk himself does not fully understand the tale he tells. In fact, behind Harry Bailly's request for plain speech lies a revealing question concerning the place of rhetoric in religious writing that was much debated in Chaucer's time. Sermons in the fourteenth century, especially those given by friars, tended to be prolix and would often neglect their thought for the sake of rhetorical colouring; there arose in opposition a call for simple writing which everyone could understand. The chief spokesman of this movement in England was Wyclif; in his Latin *Sermones* he argues generally that eloquence of rhetorical ornament has no necessary place in theological wisdom. When it was a question of instructing common people in matters of salvation, however, Wyclif insisted that plain, direct speech should be used, and 'heroic declamation' be avoided:

Sed non dubium quia plana locucia de pertinentibus ad salutem sit huiusmodi, ideo illa est eligenda declamatione eroyca postposita.[53]

So strongly did Wyclif feel, he instituted his order of poor preachers, many of whom were 'symple men' who wandered about England proclaiming the Gospel in clear sermons Wyclif had written for them.[54] Even if Hary Bailly could smell a Loller in the wind, he may have at least preferred their brevity to the interminable rambles of the orthodox.

As we have seen, the Clerk chooses or is made to ignore this advice, and introduces his tale (written, we must note, in rhyme-royal stanzas) with a rhetorical flourish that completely misses the mark. Thus it is fitting that when the Clerk does speak plainly, and that is in his Envoy, he is as much the butt of his satire and wit as is the Wife of Bath.

The Envoy has long been recognized as a mock encomium of the Wife, yet even Alice may smile when she hears the Clerk's counsel:

> O noble wyves, ful of heigh prudence,
> Lat noon humylitee youre tonge naille,
> Ne lat no clerk have cause or diligence
> To write of yow a storie of swich mervaille
> As of Grisildis pacient and kynde,
> Lest Chichevache yow swelwe in hire entraille!   (E 1183–8)

The Wife needn't loosen her tongue at all, for in his humility the Clerk has done the Wife's protesting for her. Walter, a man who would not be governed by his wife, is by the Clerk's own depiction despicable and abhorrent; in short, a monster. And Walter becomes a monster only after he assumes 'maistrye' over Griselda. A case in point, our Good Wife might say, of what happens, even to good men, when they and not their wives govern. The Clerk has once more failed to see his 'auctor's' purpose, for Petrarch's tale deals not so much with marriage or with marital relations as with transcendent virtue. Yet the Envoy epitomizes those addition which all along have secularized Petrarch's tale, and thus it is a nice irony in the marriage debate that the Clerk's tale offers a more persuasive argument in behalf of the Wife of Bath than any experience she has related.

One wonders what purpose Chaucer had when he introduced such ambiguity into his tale. Changes within the body of the tale seem consistent with the character who speaks the prologue and the Envoy; in this, the 'Clerk's Tale' may provide a glimpse into Chaucer's method of forming a character.

Manuscript evidence suggests that the tale of Griselda may have been written before Chaucer assigned it to any particular teller.[55] Chaucer recognized, I am sure, that his additions to the tale made it more complex, if only by pulling the religious exemplum in an unexpected, human direction. In fact, the way Chaucer complicated Petrarch's fiction seems to me typical of him. Griselda becomes problematic when, as in Boccaccio, the unbending patience of a martyr is joined with a mother's distress over the consequences of her actions. This juxtaposition of absolute and temporal perspectives is perhaps the only thing Griselda shares with another Chaucerian heroine, Criseyde. Here, as many have noted, the unchangeable facts of history, which, alas, have branded Criseyde unfaithful and a whore, are hard to reconcile with our memory of a lovely woman's charm and mytery. In both stories, difficulties arise when the intentions Chaucer's characters give voice to are unimpeachable, but their subsequent actions all too fallibly human. Chaucer's fiction is most ambiguous and disturbing when men and women are most naturally themselves.

In the *Troilus*, Chaucer managed to accommodate history and human nature in the figure of the narrator. When he decided to assign the story of Griselda to the Clerk, Chaucer, quite ironically, considering the Clerk's opinion of Griselda, again joined the conflicting traits of spiritual devotion and worldliness, and thereby created the character of his teller. In the Prologue, therefore, the Clerk is the meek, formal rhetorician of reverent bearing, a man who would compare Griselda to Job, and describe her with images of the Nativity. In the Envoy, on the other hand, an exuberant and witty human being appears, a young man who would object to Walter's cruelty, and who would use his tale as a secular rejoinder. The very sort of man who, in registering his moral indignation in the body of the tale, would cast the reprobation in the form of a 'demande d'amour':

> But now of wommen wolde I axen fayn
> If thise assayes myghte nat suffise?

The clash between these two contradicting traits produces a curious kind of double vision: the Clerk is both worldly and spiritual; he is neither worldly nor spiritual. Or in the more exact description of his portrait in the General Prologue:

> ... he hadde geten hym yet no benefice,
> Ne was so worldly for to have office. (A 291–2)

He is nearly, in fact, a walking litotes:

> And he nas nat right fat, I undertake,
> But looked holwe, and therto soberly. (A 288–9)

The Clerk, in sum, is 'in transitu'; a young and eager man, in orders, who may become a preacher of note; a man who reveres learning and eloquence, sometimes at the expense of substance, who in time we hope will learn that clarity of expression is a virtue. Beneath a modest yet severe front he hides desire enough to engage and experience the world. A complex man, our Clerk, whose plain speech and high style we may gladly hope to teach and understand.

The 'Clerk's Tale,' then, characterizes its teller, yet whatever uneasiness or uncertainty we feel reading the story is intimately connected with the Clerk himself. The basic ambiguity in the Clerk's character recapitulates the basic ambiguity in the tale he tells. In this, the 'Clerk's Tale' might provide a paradigm for understanding Chaucer's increasingly sophisticated conception of character in the *Canterbury Tales*. H. Marshall Leicester has recently argued that in the *Tales* 'language creates people';[56] what a person says does not reflect already existing qualities, but becomes those qualities. Character in the *Tales* is inductive, Leicester would say; structurally the voice of the tales precedes the voice we hear in the frame, even though in the logic of the fiction, the actions and dialogues of the frame become the context of each tale, and often its efficient cause.

In many respects the 'Clerk's Tale' supports these implications of Leicester's theory; the style of the tale does seem to generate the portrait of the man we find in the General Prologue. But as a general principle of Chaucerian characterization, Leicester's view is too narrow. Character in the *Canterbury Tales* is deductive as well as inductive. There are figures in the General Prologue like the Yeoman, the Plowman, and the Five Guildsmen for whom no tale exists. But if tales did exist, and we thought they suited their tellers, each would have had to conform to the traditional, pre-existing qualities we find in their individual portraits. A tale may create the particular qualities of character, but why these qualities and no others? Why is the Clerk a combination of lucubratious spirituality and worldly vivacity, rather than merly studious or high-spirited? Why is he not proud, as clerks often are in what Jill Mann calls estates satire,[57] or wanton, they are in the Miller's and Reeve's tales? By focusing exclusively on the text, Leicester has ignored what Geoffrey of Vinsauf called the 'archetypus,' the mental conception of a work an author must have before he begins to write. In Chaucer, as well as in Ovid and Boccaccio, long-standing conventions determined the 'archetypal' nature of any character. Clerks were thought to act in certain ways, and the medieval elaborations of the rhetorical doctrine of 'genera dicendi' would have required that the character's words be consistent with his actions. And, as we have seen, in Chaucer, the Clerk, the Miller, and the others behave most typically in the frame.

In truth, therefore, the Canterbury pilgrims are twice-formed at least; once by their tales and once by their frame. Though interrelated in effect, these are independent processes and should be differentiated when we analyse character in Chaucer. Most often, those tales for which there is a direct source provide the best opportunity to see Chaucer at work on narrative characterization. The changes Chaucer made frequently point in a consistent direction and become the basis of the teller's disposition. Thus the worldly and spiritual elements of the Clerk emerge from the tale he tells.

But these qualities of character remain unactualized until we see them articulated as motives in the frame. Unlike the *Decameron*, so many Canterbury Tales are told for purposes that extend beyond the mere fulfilling of an agreement. One story is prompted by revenge, another by self-aggrandizement, another by envy, still another by piety. More often than not, these motives spring from the commonplace propensities reeves and pardoners, lawyers and nuns were supposed to have. Behind the Clerk's decision, both spiritual and world, to tell the tale of Griselda and to direct it against the Wife of Bath, we discern the traditional debate of knights and clerks in love. Behind the Man of Law's indictment of Chaucer we see the traditional rivalry between lawyers and poets.

Kenneth Burke has shown that in drama, the nature of acts and agents should be consistent with the nature of the scene. The scene, as it were, contains the act, 'expressing in fixed properties the same quality the action expresses in terms of development.'[58] The *Canterbury Tales*, of course, is not drama, but it shares many characteristics with it: the same principle which relates scene to action relates character in the frame to character that emerges from the narrative. As the pilgrims ride to Canterbury, what they do and say becomes the scene for the tale they tell. And just as it would be futile to divorce a character from his scene, so is it impossible to talk of character in Chaucer without considering both the tale and what the teller does in the frame. For it is by means of this double perspective that Chaucer's characters manage to be discrete yet universal at once. The tale determines what the Clerk is, but his actions on the road to the shrine of St Thomas show us that all clerks make the pilgrimage with him.

On a different level, this double perspective offered Chaucer the chance to exploit the distance that can separate a narrator from what he says, to grant something like symbiotic autonomy to each. By allowing the Clerk to comment on Griselda, Chaucer ironically distances him from the tale, even though he and Griselda are cut from the same cloth. The Clerk's patience, in fact, fails to measure up to that of his fiction. This very failure, however, is what most engages the reader. We rush in and supply the details which make the Clerk a human being. In the 'Clerk's Tale,' as throughout the *Canterbury Tales*, Chaucer beguiles us into filling the gap between a character's perception of what he says and our perception of it. In Chaucer's maturest fiction, as in Ovid's and Boccaccio's, we are as much interpreted by our reactions to his characters as they are by what they say.

I have called this study the Cast of Character; it could as well be called Casts of Character. Although the representation of personality in late antique and medieval literature became a fixed set of rhetorical instructions, for many of the authors examined here the traditions and conventions of the schoolmasters were the material, rather than the guiding idea, for the construction of character. Ovid, Chrétien, Boccaccio, and Chaucer all found different ways to create figures who express a great deal more than their typicality. This book has been an inquiry into some of those ways. And it is precisely this quality which makes characters the spokesmen of other aspects of their fiction that allows us to treat these poets together. In a real sense, these chapters on character are a prolegomenon to a more detailed study of medieval narrative. Yet for all they tell us about the fiction they populate, Troilus and Criseida, Yvain and Alcyone, ser Ciappelletto and the Clerk demand attention in and of themselves. And when we consider how these figures were made, consider that is their rhetoricity but most of all their poetry, we sense that an abiding glory of medieval literature truly is its diversity of character.

Notes

ABBREVIATIONS

Chau R	*Chaucer Review*
CQ	*Classical Quarterly*
CP	*Classical Philology*
CW	*Classical World*
CFMA	*Classiques Français du Moyen Âge*
CCSL	*Corpus Christianorum Scriptorum Latinorum*
CSEL	*Corpus Scriptorum Ecclesiasticorum Latinorum*
ES	*English Studies*
FMLS	*Forum for Modern Language Studies*
GRLMA	*Grundriss der romanischen Literaturen des Mittelalters*
GSLI	*Giornale Storico della Letteratura Italiana*
JRS	*Journal of Roman Studies*
MLN	*Modern Language Notes*
MLR	*Modern Language Review*
MP	*Modern Philology*
PL	*Patrologia Latina*
PQ	*Philological Quarterly*
PMLA	*Publications of the Modern Language Association*
RES	*Review of English Studies*
SATF	*Société des Anciens Textes Français*
SP	*Studies in Philology*
TSLL	*Texas Studies in Language and Literature*
UCPCP	*University of California Publications in Classical Philology*
UTQ	*University of Toronto Quarterly*
WSt	*Wiener Studien*

INTRODUCTION

1 Aristotle's *Poetics*, of course, was not widely known in the Latin West during the Middle Ages: the single translation by William of Moerbecke (1278) had no apparent influence on contemporary writers, while the importance of Averroes's version of the *Poetics* translated by Hermann the German, which survives in twenty-four mss, is a matter of some debate. Averroes had rendered character 'consuetudines'; according to O.B. Hardison, medieval philosophers in general distorted Aristotle by making 'character rather than action the object of imitation.' They stressed 'the moral overtones of this revision by making virtue and vice the specific qualities of character to be imitated.' See O.B. Hardison, Jr, 'The Place of Averroes' Commentary on the *Poetics* in the History of Medieval Criticism' in *Medieval and Renaissance Studies*, ed John Lievsay, no 4 (Durham, N.C. 1970), 70ff. Judson Allen, however, in 'Hermann the German's Averroistic Aristotle and Medieval Poetic Theory,' *Mosaic* 9 (1976), 67–81 and most recently in *The Ethical Poetic of the Later Middle Ages* (Toronto 1982), 19ff, makes some sense of Averroes by viewing what he says in terms of medieval ethics, rather than as a distortion of Aristotle. Although I feel Allen over-emphasizes the influence of the Averroistic *Poetics*, the idea of character presented here agrees with his evidence. See also Robert Edwards, *The Montecassion Passion and the Poetics of Medieval Drama* (Berkeley and Los Angeles 1970), 159–92. So too have I omitted from this study of character the idea of 'persona' as an actor in the theatre. See Mary Hatch Marshall, 'Boethius' Definition of *Persona* and Medieval Understanding of the Roman Theater,' *Speculum* 25 (1950), 471–82.

Much interesting work, especially by Hans Robert Jauss, has recently stressed the potential complexity of those simpler allegories Dante would have called poetic. While I have reservations about the emphasis 'aesthetic experience' receives in Jauss's reading of medieval texts, I agree that to some extent at least we must recognize the alterity of the Middle Ages in relation to antiquity and the modern world. When I say 'characters without substance,' I mean substance in the Aristotelian sense (*Catagoriae*, 5) the Middle Ages were familiar with. See H.R. Jauss, *Alterität und Modernität der mittelaltlichen Literatur*, (München 1977), 9–47 and the section reprinted from GRLMA VI/I, 'Zur allegorischen Dichtung,' 153–307.

2 Kenneth Burke, *A Grammar of Motives* (Berkeley and Los Angeles 1945), 503ff.

3 For ancient literature, see Francis Cairns, *Generic Composition in Greek and Roman Poetry* (Edinburgh 1972) and F. Quadlbauer, *Die antike Theorie der 'genera dicendi' im lateinischen Mittelalter*, Osterreichische A. d. W. Ph.-hist. Kl. Sitzungsber. 241, 2 (Graz, Vienna, Cologne 1962), and H.R. Jauss, 'Theorie der Gattung und Literatur des Mittelalters,' in *Alterität und Modernität*, 327–48.

4 See Leo Spitzer, 'Note on the Poetic and the Empirical "I" in Medieval Authors,'
Traditio 4 (1946), 414–22; Martin Stevens, 'The Performing Self in Twelfth-
Century Culture,' *Viator* 9 (1976), 193–212. Others have dealt with the historical
audience in Ovid, Boccaccio, and Chaucer. For a good review of this kind of
audience and the theoretical literature on the place of the reader's response in the
evaluation of texts, see W. Daniel Wilson, 'Readers in Texts,' *PMLA* 96 (1981),
848–63; my own approach is closest to that of Wilson himself.
5 Colin Morris, *The Discovery of the Individual* (London 1972); Robert Hanning,
The Individual in Twelfth-Century Romance (New Haven and London 1977).

CHAPTER ONE

1 All quotations from the *Metamorphoses* are from Ovidius, *Metamorphoses*, ed
William S. Anderson (Leipzig 1977).
2 All quotations from the *Amores* and the *Ars Amatoria* are taken from P. *Ovidi
Nasonis Amores, Med. Fac. Fem., Ars Amatoria, Remedia Amoris*, ed E.J. Kenney
(Oxford 1968).
3 Richard Heinze, 'Ovids elegische Erzählungen,' *Ber. der Sach. Akad. d. Wiss. Kl.
71, 7* (1919); rpt in *Vom Geist des Römertums* (Stuttgart 1960), 308–403.
4 The two versions of the Mars and Venus offer perfect evidence for Heinze's conclusions. After saying that Leuconoe tells the story of the adulterous deities 'not
because she herself wanted to, but as an introduction to the story of the Sun's
love for Leucothoe,' Heinze compares the account in the *Ars*: 'so sieht man, was
dem Elegiker erlaubt schien, und was der Epiker sich versagte: die Erzählung der
ars ist durchaus frivol ... die der *Metamorphosen* demgegenüber, so weit das ein so
heikler Stoff zulässt, zurückhaltend und ehrbar; sie verweilt nicht bei dem Bild
des ertrappten Paares, sondern nur bei der Schilderung der zauberhaften Kunst
Vulcans, und wenn auch die lustige Klausel der homerischen Erzählung nicht
ganz fehlt, ist sie doch mit *"aliquis ... turpis"* so dezent wie möglich wieder-
gegeben. / So one sees what seems allowed to the elegiac poet, and what the epic
poet denies himself. The narrative of the *Ars* is frivolous throughout ... that of
the *Metamorphoses*, on the contrary, so far as the delicate nature of the material
permitted, is reserved and dignified. It lingers not over the picture of the two
captured deities, but on the description of the wonderous art of Vulcan, and if the
lusty codicil of the Homeric version is not entirely lacking, it still with the
phrase "aliquis ... turpis" has been rendered as decent as possible.' Heinze, 318. For
a recent assessment of these distinctions, see T.F. Brunner, '*Deinon* vs. *eleeinon*:
Heinze Revisited,' *AJP* 92 (1971), 278–84.
5 See further L.P. Wilkinson, 'The Augustan Rules for Dactylic Verse,' *CQ* 34
(1940), 30–43, and *Ovid Recalled* (Cambridge 1955), 27–43. See as well M. Plat-

nauer, *Latin Elegiac Verse* (Cambridge 1951), 36–8; 72–3, and R.D. Anderson, P.J. Parsons, and R.G.M. Nisbet, 'Elegiacs by Gallus from Qasr ibrîm,' *JRS* 69 (1979), 125–55, esp 148–49.

6 Otto Stern Due, *Changing Forms: Studies in the Metamorphoses of Ovid. Classica et Mediaevalia,* Diss x (Copenhagen 1974), 129.

7 Ibid, 124.

8 See Horace, *Ars Poetica,* 140ff. All quotations from the *Ars* are taken from Q. Horatius Flaccus, *Briefe,* erklärt von A. Kiessling, neue besorgt von R. Heinze, 5th. Aufl. (Berlin 1957).

9 One might also note that the shared outrage of the Sun, Vulcan, and Leuconoe occupies the analogous position in the structure of the passage that the description of Mars's ardour and Venus's acquiescence has in the *Ars.*

10 The change is intentional, since, as Bömer says, '*Iunonigena* is without parallel among the epithets of the gods' (my translation). See *P. Ovidius Naso, Metamorphosen: Kommentar von Franz Bömer,* Buch IV–V (Heidelberg 1976), 71.

11 See the analysis of Leuconoe's transition from the Venus and Mars to the story of the Sun and Leucothoe, IV, 190–7, p 67ff below.

12 In the following discussion I rely heavily on Alfred Korte, '*XAPAKTHP,*' *Hermes* 64 (1929), 69–86, and Warren Anderson's introductory essay in *Theophrastus: The Character Sketches* (Kent, Ohio 1970), i–xvii.

13 See Plato, *Republic,* Book x, 603C–607D.

14 W.D. Ross, *Aristotle,* 5th ed (London 1968), 187.

15 Ibid, 188.

16 Aristotle, *Nicomachean Ethics,* tr J.A.K. Thomson, Penguin Classics (Baltimore, Md 1970), Book II, ch 6.

17 Ross, *Aristotle,* 115.

18 Aristotle, *Rhetoric,* tr Lane Cooper (Englewood Cliffs, N.J. 1932), Book I, ch 2. Future citations are given by book and chapter number within the text. For an important analysis of this concept, as well as of many others, see Wesley Trimpi, 'The Ancient Hypothesis of Fiction,' *Traditio* 27 (1971), 1–78.

19 Aristotle, *Poetics,* ed and tr S.H. Butcher (New York 1951), VI, 17. Future citations are given within the text.

20 See Ross, *Aristotle,* 285ff and the analysis of David Jones, *Aristotle and Greek Tragedy,* and Trimpi, 'Ancient Hypothesis,' 43–55.

21 Warren Anderson, *Character Sketches,* xvii.

22 Korte, '*XAPAKTHP,*' 78.

23 Cicero, *Orator,* xi, 36. I quote from *Brutus and Orator,* ed and tr H.M. Hubbell, Loeb Classical Library (Cambridge, Mass 1939). Cicero's use of Greek 'ethikon,' 'that which expresses character,' is also typical. In *Orator* XXXVII, 128, he defines the term as 'ad naturas et ad mores et ad omnem vitae consuetudinem accom-

modatum / that which is related to men's nature and character, their habits and all the intercourse of life' (Hubbell's translation).

24 In what follows I have relied chiefly on J.F. D'Alton, *Roman Literary Theory and Criticism* (London 1931), 114–29; 423ff. See as well George Kennedy, *The Art of Rhetoric in the Roman World 300 BC–AD 300* (Princeton 1972), and Fabio Cupaiuolo, *Tra Poesia e Poetica* (Napoli 1966), esp chs 3 and 6.

25 Cicero, *De Oratoria*, II, 184. See F. Solmsen, 'Aristotle and Cicero on the Orator's Playing upon the Feelings,' *CP* 33 (1938), 390–404.

26 This important rhetorical precept stems from Aristotle's *Rhetoric*, I, 2, 3. See D'Alton, *Roman Criticism*, 125, and esp Trimpi, 'Ancient Hypothesis,' 65–71.

27 See Cicero, *Pro Caelio*, ch 3; Quintilian, *Institutio Oratoria*, III.8.48; Aristotle, *Rhetoric* III, 7. 6, and D'Alton 125.

28 Cicero, *Brutus*, ii, 8.

29 Cicero, *Orator*, xxxvi, 138. Another important source of rhetorical characterization for Ovid would have been Virgil's speeches, which were studied by Roman critics and imitated by Roman writers. See Gilbert Highet, *The Speeches in Vergil's Aeneid* (Princeton 1972).

30 D'Alton, *Roman Criticism*, 117.

31 H.R. Fairclough's translation. Horace, *Satires, Epistles, Art of Poetry*, tr H.R. Fairclough, *Loeb Classical Library* (Cambridge, Mass 1931).

32 See Pierre Grimal, *Essai sur l'Art Poétique d'Horace* (Paris 1968), 127ff for a discussion of possible intermediary influences between Aristotle and Horace in this particular passage.

33 Gordon Williams, *Tradition and Originality in Roman Poetry* (Oxford 1968), 329–57, esp 330–47.

34 In what follows I rely greatly on A.W. Allen, 'Sincerity and the Roman Elegists,' *CP* 45 (1950), 145–60.

35 Richard Heinze, 'Fides,' *Hermes* 64 (1929); rpt in *Vom Geist des Römertums*, 25–38

36 A.W. Allen, 'Sincerity,' 147, who quotes Quintilian, *Inst. Or.*, VI, 2. 18. Future citations from the *Institutes* are given in the text and are taken from Quintilian, *Institutio Oratoria*, ed H.E. Butler, *Loeb Classical Library* (Cambridge, Mass 1936).

37 All quotations from Propertius are taken from *The Elegies of Propertius*, ed H.E. Butler and E.A. Barber (Oxford 1933).

38 A.W. Allen, 'Sunt Qui Propertium malint' in *Critical Essays on Roman Literature: Elegy and Lyric*, ed J.P. Sullivan (Cambridge, Mass 1962), 108. For a review and bibliography of various aspects of elegy, see R.D. Anderson et al, 'Elegiacs by Gallus from Qasr Ibrîm.'

39 On the troublesome phrase 'ut iam ...' (v 3), see Hans-Joachim Newiger, 'Zum Epigramm der Amores Ovids,' *Hermes* 92 (1964), 119–21.

40 All quotations from Catullus are taken from *C. Valerii Catulii Carmina*, ed R.A.B. Mynors (Oxford 1958).

41 See Arthur Leslie Wheeler, *Catullus and the Traditions of Ancient Poetry*, Sather Classical Lectures, IX (Berkeley and Los Angeles 1934), 21ff for a discussion of the debate.

42 Deprecation of this sort is a commonplace, though Catullus's poem is interesting in that it is not a conventional 'recusatio.' Nowhere does he apologize for not writing an epic, as later poets invariably would. There is even a discernible measure of poetic pride: only the work of Nepos, not poetry at all, dwarfs Catullus's undertaking. For the reverse situation, see *Odes* II, i, where Horace tells Pollio that when Pollio's history of the Civil Wars has been written, he should return to his true calling, which is poetry. The poem, one should note, also begins a section of Horace's work. On the 'recusatio,' see p 30ff and note 69.

43 Wheeler, *Catullus*, 222.

44 'Expolitum,' 'lepidum' (related to Greek 'leptos' by sound, though not etymologically: cf Callimachus, *Aetia*, V 11, the famous 'kata lepton'), and 'doctis' are all adjectives fit to recall Callimachus, whose poetry prided itself on its elegance and learning. Even more than they reveal Catullus's character, the adjectives announce, with justifiable pride, the style and tradition in which Catullus writes.

45 The juxtaposition between Catullus's work and Nepos's, at first glance so disadvantageous to Catullus, on closer examination reveals an implied comparison. Catullus's phrases of admiration for Nepos, 'Iuppiter, unus Italorum, doctis … laboriosis,' are carefully balanced when he refers to himself: 'patrona virgo, uno … saeclo, lepidum.' The tension of the poem arises when we measure this implicit balance and equality against the patent disparity which the poem avows on its surface.

46 See Wheeler, *Catullus*, 174 for a discussion of this motif in relation to Catullus 67.

47 This according to the *Concordance* of Ovid, ed R.J. Deferrari et al (Washington 1939).

48 Pseudo-Cicero, *Rhetorica ad Herennium*, ed H. Caplan, *Loeb Classical Library* (Cambridge, Mass 1954). All translations are Caplan's. I use the *Rhetorica* since the work was both typical of Roman rhetoric and highly influential in the Middle Ages. All citations are given book and chapter numbers in the text, and in the following notes, parallel passages in other Roman rhetorical works are noted.

49 'ut adtentos, ut dociles, ut benivolos auditores habere possimus.' Cf Cicero, *Part. Orat.* VII, 28. This, of course, is the often-counselled 'captatio benevolentiae.'

50 'si nostrum officium sine adrogantia laudabimus … item si nostra incommoda proferemus.'

51 Cf. Cicero, *De Inv.*, I, xvii, 24.

52 Martial, *Epigrams*, tr W.C. Ker, *Loeb Classical Library* (Cambridge, Mass 1968), III, 9.

53 'Si defessi erint audiendo, ab aliqua re, quae risum movere possit ...'

54 There is something undeniably salacious in the way Ovid lures his readers, which Chaucer exploits with equal deftness in the Introduction to the 'Miller's Tale':

> And therfore, whoso list it nat yheere,
> Turne over the leef and chese another tale;
> ...
> Blameth nat me if that ye chese amys.
> The Millere is a cherl, ye knowe wel this;
> So was the Reve eek and othere mo,
> And harlotrie they tolden bothe two.
> Avyseth yow, and put me out of blame;
> And eek men shal nat maken ernest of game.
>
> (A 3176–7; 3181–6)

55 Compare the famous passage in the third book of the *Ars*:

> prisca iuuent alios, ego me nunc denique natum
> gratulor; haec aetas moribus apta meis
> ...
> ... quia cultus adest nec nostros mansit in annos
> rusticitas priscis illa superstes auis.

Let others take pleasure in ancient days: I rejoice that I was born now. This age suits my character ... because culture now rules, nor does that rudeness of our ancient grandfathers survive in our day.   (III, 121–2; 127–8)

56 Aristotle here is speaking of enthymemes, that is, of the species of proof rhetoricians are to use. This was a particularly important section of the *Rhetoric*.

57 *Tristia*, IV, x, 48. All quotations from the *Tristia* are taken from Ovid, *Tristia and Epistolae ex Ponto*, tr A.L. Wheeler, *Loeb Classical Library* (Cambridge, Mass 1959).

58 William K. Wimsatt, *Philosophical Words* (New Haven 1948), 113.

59 One way Propertius makes his love seem the model of all love is through his use of mythology. For examples, see A.W. Allen, 'Sunt qui Propertium malint.'

60 *Aeneid*, IV, 23.

61 Even the ardour itself is presented not as direct experience but as a literary metaphor: 'saucius arcu,' wounded by the bow of Cupid. This is more a conceit than a passion.

62 Ovid makes the comparison explicit in the *Remedia Amoris*: 'tantum se nobis elegi debere fatentur, / quantum Vergilio nobile debet epos. / As much as the noble epic owes to Virgil, so much elegy confesses it owes to me' (393–4).

63 Hermann Fränkel, *Ovid: A Poet Between Two Worlds*, Sather Classical Lectures, XVIII (Berkeley and Los Angeles 1945), 11.

64 James Joyce, *A Portrait of the Artist as a Young Man* (New York 1966), 256. The line from Ovid comes from the story of Daedalus, *Metamorphoses*, VIII, 188.

65 This is a point often made that deserves to be made again. See A.W. Allen, 'Sunt qui Propertium malint,' 117 and Gordon Williams, *Tradition and Originality*, 515. I differ from Williams in taking Ovid's pretensions as more than a pose.

66 Compare *Ars Poetica*, 315–16: 'ille perfecto / reddere personae scit convenientia cuique / He surely knows how to give each character his fitting part.' See Grimal, *Essai*, 109ff, 217ff, and Cupaiuolo, *Tra Poesia e Poetica*, 43–125. 'Convenientia,' of course, was a topic of rhetorical thought Horace himself drew on, but as poet of greatest influence, he would be the man whose ideas Ovid would most likely want to address. Horace is what Due, *Changing Forms*, calls a 'model of reading.'

67 Compare *Ars Poetica*, 73–4.

68 Another point often made. See the commentary in the fine edition of the first book of the *Amores* by John Barsby, *Ovid: Amores Book I* (Oxford 1972), 43ff.

69 For the 'recusatio,' see the discussions of Cupaiuolo, *Tra Poesia e Poetica*, 48–50; Williams, *Tradition*, 46ff; and esp W. Wimmel, *Kallimachos im Rom*, Hermes Einzelschriften, Heft 16, (Wiesbaden 1960), 300ff.

70 Callimachus, *Aetia*, 1–39.

71 Williams, *Tradition*, 46.

72 In a second reading of the *Amores*, one would also think of the gigantomachia Ovid says he was writing in *Amores*, II, i. In any case, this is exactly the sort of poem Callimachus upbraided his Alexandrian rivals for writing.

73 Virgil, *Eclogues*, VI, 1–8 pictures himself singing of 'reges et proelia,' kings and battles, and Propertius, III, ii: 1–12 just sets his lips to the 'fountain of Bellerophon's steed.' Neither extols the merit of what he has written, as Ovid does: 'et satis oris erat.' 'My diction soared to the occasion' is Guy Lee's translation of the key phrase. See *Amores*, tr Guy Lee (London 1968).

74 See Williams, *Tradition*, 47ff, and esp J.K. Newman, *The Concept of Vates in Augustan Poetry*, Collection Latomus LXXXIX (Brussels 1967), 100–14.

75 See Barsby, *Ovid*, 45ff. I.M. Le M. DuQuesnay, 'The Amores' in *Critical Essays in Roman Literature: Ovid*, ed J.W. Binns (London 1968), 1–47 also analyses this passage, though in a somewhat different way.

76 'armis uictis,' 22.

77 This is a favoured technique of characterization in Ovid: see below, pp 51ff and 60ff.

78 On the political aspects of this poem, see Karl Galinsky, 'The Triumph Theme in the Augustan Elegy,' *WSt* 82 (1969), 75–107, esp 91–4.

79 See E.J. Kenney, 'Nequitiae poeta' in Ovidiana: Recherches sur Ovide, ed N.I. Herescu (Paris 1958), 201. Kenney is examining Ovid's allusion to Virgil in Ars Am. II, 453.

80 John E. Sandys, A Companion to Latin Studies, 3rd ed (New York 1963), 627.

81 Jean-Marc Frécaut, L'Esprit et l'Humour chez Ovide (Grenoble 1972).

82 The poets Ovid chooses to keep company with are interesting. Naming Virgil makes explicit the rivalry announced with the first word of the Amores. Catullus certainly was the neoteric most concerned with his art, and therefore a great kindred spirit. The absence, however, of Gallus, Tibullus, and Propertius is striking. As if by default Ovid suggests his pre-eminence in elegy matches Virgil's in epic and Catullus's in love poetry.

83 A possible exception (the only one) is Amores, II, xviii, 8: ' "me miseram, iam te" dixit "amare pudet?" / "Alas," she said, "you are shy to love now?" ': one line, and we cannot be sure the 'puella' who says it is Corinna.

84 The phrase is Barsby's, Ovid, 71. See as well on this poem Georg Luck, Latin Love Elegy (London 1959), and Williams, Tradition, 511–12.

85 Charles Paul Segal, Landscape in Ovid's Metamorphoses, Hermes Einzelschriften, Heft 23 (Wiesbaden 1969), 76.

86 Although ostensibly addressed to Corinna, the distance of the first three lines of the poem ought to be noted. Phrases such as 'tantum patiatur amari / let her only permit me to love her' are not likely to be directly spoken to one's lover.

87 It is also to remain true to these series of allusions that Ovid attacks Corinna in I, v in a fit of passion that is little less than rape.

88 See the discussion in Barsby, Ovid, 60ff.

89 The most famous example of this conceit is Amores, III, xiv.

90 The mention of Paelignum recalls the last poem of Book I: Ovid says through geography that this is the same poet; one should expect the same subject matter. On 'nequitia,' see R.D. Anderson et al, 'Elegiacs by Gallus,' 140.

91 Quintilian, Inst. Or, x, 1, 88.

92 Ovid similarly translates metaphor into reality at the end of the second book of the Ars. Here, as Robert Durling says, Ovid claims to have fulfilled the promises he made at the beginning of the poem, 'and extends even further the humorous application in literal statement of what began as metaphor ... The successful teaching of the art ... is identified with its successful application; previously the steps in the instruction were metaphorically seen as steps in the pupil's love affair, but now the (metaphorical) success of the pupil is seen as the teacher's own amatory prowess.' Robert Durling, The Figure of the Poet in the Renaissance Epic (Cambridge, Mass 1965), 31–2.

93 Barsby, Ovid, 95.

CHAPTER TWO

1 See A.W. Allen, 'Sunt Qui Propertium malint' in *Critical Essays*, 107–48.
2 Of the numerous examples, I will cite only George Kennedy, *The Art of Rhetoric in the Roman World*, 412 ff, and A.F. Sabot, *Ovide, Poète de l'Amour dans ses Œuvres de Jeunesse* (Paris 1976), 226–42; 296–348.
3 All quotations from the *Fasti* are from Ovid, *Fasti*, ed and trans Sir J.G. Fraser, *Loeb Classical Library* (Cambridge, Mass 1976).
4 Richard Heinze, 'Ovids elegische Erzählungen' in *Vom Geist des Römertums*, 308–43.
5 Ascra, of course, is Hesiod's locale.
6 See Robert Durling, *The Figure of the Poet in the Renaissance Epic*, 26–43; John Fyler, *Chaucer and Ovid* (New Haven and London 1979), 1–22; Richard Lanham, *The Motives of Eloquence* (New Haven and London 1976), 48–64; Joseph Solodow, 'Ovid's *Ars Amatoria*: The Lover as Cultural Ideal,' *WSt* 11 (1977), 106–27.
7 Brooks Otis, *Ovid as Epic Poet*, 2nd ed (Cambridge 1971), 273. My reading of character in the *Metamorphoses* agrees generally with Galinsky's point that Ovid was not so much concerned with mythological metamorphosis as he was with the transformation of myth. The characters in the *Amores* are part of the same 'game' of alteration and parody that finds its most complex expression in the *Metamorphoses*. See Karl Galinsky, *Ovid's Metamorphoses: An Introduction to the Basic Aspects* (Oxford 1975)
8 Otis, *Ovid*, 261–3. For a discussion of the sources, see 421–3 and A.H. Griffin, 'Ovid's Treatment of Ceyx and Alcyone' in *Ovidianum: Acta conventus omnium gentium ovidianis studiis fovendis*, ed N. Barbu et al (Bucharest 1976), 321–4.
9 Otis, *Ovid*, 233.
10 Ibid, 234.
11 Ibid, 238–46. In addition, the passage might well have been modelled on the storm in *Aeneid* I. This tempest seems to reflect the distemper on Olympus, and the confusion of the hero who is first seen and heard in the midst of it. The fact that Virgil himself followed *Odyssey* VI would have doubled the literary attractiveness of the passage for Ovid.
12 Otis, *Ovid*, 240.
13 See J.J. Moore-Blunt, *A Commentary on Ovid's Metamorphoses: Book II* (Uithoorn 1977), 114–37.
14 The entire Orpheus interlude deserves to be compared to its Virgilian counterparts. As A.G. McKay has pointed out to me, Ovid seems to undercut the sentimental episode in the fourth *Georgic* deliberately. Virgil sidestepped the rhetorical aspect of Orpheus's style, that is, the techniques by which he seduced the powers of

death, but Ovid, with typical panache, designs a pompous, rather ineffective bit of fustian which is full of wit, sophistication, and artificial emotion. The pathos of tragedy has been transformed into the bons mots of verbal repartee. In the period after his mourning, when Orpheus transfers his love to young men, Ovid's creation brilliantly parodies Virgil's penchant for shade ('umbra'), nature's complementary gift to poets. And the epic catalogue of trees in the Cyparissus story is yet another hilarious parody of the catalogue in the *Georgics*.

15 For a somewhat similar reading of this episode see Viktor Poeschl, 'L'arte narrativa di Ovidio nelle *Metamorfosi*' in *Atti del Convegno Ovidiano* II (Sulmone 1958), 295–306. In addition, we should note again the borrowing and parody of Virgilian elements. Cyparissus's deer definitely recalls Silvia's in *Aeneid* VII. The excessive love that led to war in Virgil leads to the beginning of reconciliation in Ovid.

16 P. Ovidius Naso, *Metamorphosen: Kommentar von Franz Bömer*, Buch IV–V, 70. Horace, of course, addresses a famous ode (I, 11) to a Leuconoe, and Ovid plays wittily with this figure who has been enjoined to seize the day since life is short. Unlike Horace's girl, Ovid's Leuconoe is not wise ('sapias, vina liques,' Horace has commanded: 'Be wise; strain your wines'); instead our prig remains sober, though ironically she is just as unaware of her impending doom as her Horatian counterpart. Ovid's woman exemplifies the ambiguity of her name. If we etymologize Leuconoe as 'leukos' (white) and 'noos' (the mind), the name may signify 'clear-headed' or 'silly-minded' according as 'leukos' is taken in a good or bad sense. Ovid's Leuconoe tries to appear high-minded, but her kind of probity proves silly indeed.

17 Bömer, *Kommentar*, 75.

18 Scholarship on the *Metamorphoses* is vast: one need only look at Alison Elliott's 'Ovid's *Metamorphoses*: A Bibliography, 1968–1978,' CW 73 (1980), 385–412 to realize how much has been done. A number of studies explore concerns similar to mine, but time has prevented me from reading them all. I beg the indulgence of readers and authors for the omissions.

CHAPTER THREE

1 All quotations from *Tristan* are from Gottfried von Strassburg, *Tristan*, ed Karl Marold (Berlin 1969); future references are given their verse numbers within the text. Translations are my own, but I have consulted A.T. Hatto's version, Gottfried von Strassburg, *Tristan*, Penguin Books (Baltimore 1960).

2 W.T.H. Jackson, *The Anatomy of Love: The Tristan of Gottfried von Strassburg* (New York 1971), 193.

3 Tristan himself is quite aware how complicated the question of his paternity is: at 4365ff he says, in translation: 'I hear my father say that my father was killed

long ago ... O father, and belief that I had a father, how you have been taken from me.'

4 The main events of the Tristan story, of course, already existed before Gottfried came to tell it. See the studies in *Arthurian Literature in the Middle Ages*, ed Roger S. Loomis (Oxford 1959), by Helaine Newstead, 'The Origin and Growth of the Tristan Legend,' 122–33, and Frederick Whitehead, 'The Early Tristan Poems,' 134–44. The harp-playing, for instance, was in Thomas; at least it appears in Brother Robert's translation of Thomas's version into Old Norse, where, it is interesting to note, Mark says Tristan should play at night when Mark himself lies awake: 'pa (er) ek [Mark] ligg vakandi!' *Tristrams Saga ok Isondar*, ed Eugen Kölbing (Heilbronn 1878), ch 22, p 24. The parallel to Saul is even closer. As will be explained, literary typology can invest a character with a thematic dimension which points to a similarity in the moral direction of two texts without affecting the plot of either. Nor is literary typology at all incompatible with the kind of patterning Vinaver discerns in the Arthurian Cycle in general, with its 'fascination of tracing a theme through all its phases, of waiting for its return while following other themes, of experiencing the constant sense of their simultaneous presence.' Eugene Vinaver, Presidential Address, Modern Humanities Research Association, 1966, quoted in Urban T. Holmes, *Chrétien de Troyes* (New York 1970), 104. If this was, in fact, a technique native to material spread over many tales, literary typology could meet it more than half way, organizing even further a particular telling by setting it to an external, highly recognizable pattern.

5 In the following discussion, I rely on the works of Singleton, Freccero, and other Dantists, as well as standard works on biblical exegesis. See Charles S. Singleton, *Dante Studies I: Commedia, Elements of Structure* (Cambridge, Mass 1954), and *Dante Studies II: Journey to Beatrice* (Cambridge, Mass 1958), but also Phillip Damon's note of dissent, 'Dante's Canzoni and the Allegory of Poets' in *Modes of Analogy in Ancient and Medieval Verse*, UCPCP 15, 6 (Berkeley and Los Angeles 1961), 329–34. See also Erich Auerbach, 'Figura' in *Scenes from the Drama of European Literature* (New York 1959), 1–63; Jean Daniélou, *From Shadows to Reality* (Westminster 1960); Henri de Lubac, *Exégèse Médiévale, les quatre sens de l'écriture*, 4 vols (Paris 1959–64); Angus Fletcher, *Allegory: The Theory of a Symbolic Mode* (Ithaca 1964); M.D. Chenu, *La théologie au 12ᵉ siècle* (Paris 1957); see also *Nature, Man, and Society in the Twelfth Century*, selected, ed, and tr J. Taylor and L. Little (Chicago and London 1968); Beryl Smalley, *The Study of the Bible in the Middle Ages* (Notre Dame 1970). In the following discussion, I am not dealing so much with the four senses of Scripture as with the mechanics, one might say, of allegory and typology. Morton Bloomfield's caveat should be kept in mind. See 'Symbolism in Medieval Literature,' *MP* 56 (1958), 73–81. See as well Robert Hollander, 'Typology and Secular Literature,' and Karlfried Froeh-

lich, 'The State of Biblical Hermeneutics at the Beginning of the Fifteenth Century,' both in *Literary Uses of Typology*, ed Earl Miner (Princeton 1977), 3–19; 20–48.

6 Dante Alighieri, *Il Convivio, ridotto a miglior lezione e commentato*, 2 vols, eds G. Busnelli and G. Vandelli (Firenze 1934–7), 2:1.

7 Dante Alighieri, *Epistola ad Can Grande* in *Opere di Dante*, 2nd ed, *Società Dantesca Italiana, Epistole*, ed Ermenegildo Pistelli (Firenze 1960), Ep. XIII, 7. Compare Thomas Aquinas, *Summa Theologica*, I, 1, 10.

8 This interpretation is from Augustine, *De Trinitate*, xv, ix, 15; PL 43, col 1068.

9 See Augustine's discussion in *De Doctrina Christiana*, ed J. Martin, CCSL 32 (Turnholt 1962), I, 3.

10 This is not to suggest that Christian ideas of allegory were solely derived from Jewish tradition. As is well known, the classical tradition of allegorical interpretation was also highly influential. See Ernst R. Curtius, *European Literature and the Latin Middle Ages*, tr Willard R. Trask (1958; rpt New York 1963), 203ff et passim.

11 W.T.H. Jackson discusses this passage in connection with Gottfried's appropriation of the language of Christian mysticism in 'Gottfried von Strassburg,' in *Arthurian Literature*, 145–56.

12 See Curtius, *European Literature*, 60.

13 See Edmond Faral, *Les Arts Poétiques du XIIᵉ et du XIIIᵉ Siècle* (Paris 1958), 75. The relevant classical texts concerning character which were known in the Middle Ages are: Cicero, *De Inventione*, I, 24–5; the anonymous tract *De attributis personae et negotio* in C. Halm, *Rhetores latini minores* (Leipzig 1863), 305ff; Cornificius, *Rhetorica ad Herennius*, IV, 49–50; Quintilian, *Inst. Or.*, VIII, 64–73 (cf the commentary by C. Julius Victor, 22, in Halm, *Rhet. min.*, p 436); Priscian, *Praeexercitamina*, 7 (*De laude*), 10 (*De descriptione*) (cf *De ethopoeia*, and Emporius, *Praeceptum demonstrativae materiae*, in Halm, p 562); Horace, *Ars Poetica*, 114–27, 158–78.
   The relevant portions of the medieval treatises Faral prints are: Matthew of Vendôme, *Ars Versificatoria*, I, 41–92; Geoffrey of Vinsauf, *Documentum de modo et arte dictandi et versificandi*, II, 138–9; the anonymous tractate *Debemus cunctis proponere*.

14 Faral, *Arts Poétiques*, 79.

15 Matthew of Vendôme, *Ars*, I, 65: 'Verbi gratia, in ecclesiastico pastore fidei consonantia, virtutis appetitus, illibata religio, et blandimentum pietatis debent ampliari ...' Cf Matthew's description of a Pope, I, 50.

16 Matthew, *Ars*, I, 60; Faral, 79.

17 Wesley Trimpi, 'The Quality of Fiction: The Rhetorical Transmission of Literary Theory,' *Traditio* 30 (1974), 1–118.

18 See ibid, 85ff.

19 Vittore Branca, *Boccaccio medievale* (Firenze 1970), 109. See also Trimpi, 'Quality of Fiction,' 90ff.

20 Erich Auerbach, *Mimesis: The Representation of Reality in Western Literature*, tr W.R. Trask (Princeton 1953), 4ff.

21 All quotations from *Yvain* are from Chrétien de Troyes, *Yvain*, ed W. Foerster (Halle 1912); future references are given their verse numbers within the text.

22 Auerbach, *Mimesis*, 73.

23 See Charles Singleton, *Dante Studies I and II*, and the forthcoming collection of Freccero's articles from University of Minnesota Press.

24 All quotations are from the text prepared for the *Società Dantesca Italiana*, Dante Alighieri, *La Commedia*, a cura di Giorgio Petrocchi (Verona 1967); future references are given their line numbers within the text.

25 The literature on the tenth canto of the *Inferno* is huge; see Michele Barbi, 'Il canto di Farinata' in *Dante: Vita, opere e fortuna* (Firenze 1952), 207–70; Siro A. Chimenz, 'Il disdegno di Guido e i suoi interpreti,' *Orientamenti culturali* I (1945), 179–88; Letterio Cassata, 'Il disdegno di Guido,' *Studi Danteschi* 46 (1969), 5–49; Charles Singleton, 'Inferno X: Guido's disdain,' MLN 77 (1962), 49–65. I am also relying on verbal communications from John Freccero.

26 See Auerbach's analysis, *Mimesis*, 174–203.

27 See besides Cassata, 'Il disdegno,' the commentary on this verse in Dante Alighieri, *The Divine Comedy*, tr, with a commentary by Charles S. Singleton, *Inferno* 2. *Commentary* (Princeton 1970), 152ff. Central to my point, of course, is the fact that such possibility for misunderstanding exists in the first place.

28 Singleton, *Divine Comedy*, 153 also notes the similarity of the two pasages, but does not draw the conclusions I have.

29 See G. Mazzotta's recent *Dante, Poet of the Desert* (Princeton 1979) for a detailed reading of this theme.

30 Auerbach, *Mimesis*, 9ff; 66ff; and especially *Literary Language and its Public in Late Latin Antiquity and in the Middle Ages*, tr Ralph Mannheim (Princeton 1965). Auerbach, of course, relied on a great deal of scholarship concerned with the classical and biblical styles. See the general observations and bibliographies in Martin McGuire and Hermigild Dressler, *Introduction to Medieval Latin Studies*, 2nd ed (Washington 1977), ch 3: 'The Period of Late Latin: The Age of Transition from Antiquity to the Middle Ages; The Constituent Elements of Medieval Latin c. 200 A.D.–c. 500 A.D.,' 15–58. Studies I have found especially helpful: E. Löfstedt, *Late Latin* (Oslo 1959); Eduard Norden, *Die Antike Kunstprosa vom VI Jahrhundert v. Chr. bis in die Zeit der Renaissance*, 2 vols (1915; rpt Darmstadt 1958), 573ff; Christine Mohrmann, *Études sur le latin des chrétiens*, I, 2nd ed

(Rome 1961); and of course Joseph Schrijnen, *Charakteristik des altchristlichen Latein, Latinitatis Christianorum Primaeva* I (Nijmegen 1932); see also the Italian translation with an afterward by Christine Mohrmann, 'Dopo quarant' anni' in *I Caratteri del latino cristiano antico* (Bologna 1977).

31 Auerbach, *Mimesis*, 74.

32 Augustine, *De Doctrina Christiana*, IV, 17. Future references are given their book and chapter number within the text. See Auerbach, *Literary Language*, 35ff.

33 Auerbach, *Mimesis*, 75. Of the many works on Augustine's style, compare H. Marrou, *Saint Augustin et la fin de la culture antique* (Paris 1938); Wilhelm Süss, *Studien zur lateinischen Bibel, I: Augustins Locutiones und das Problem der lateinischen Bibelsprache* (Tartu 1932); Melchior Verheijen, *Eloquentia Pedisequa: Obervations sur le style des Confessions de Saint Augustin*, Latinitatis Christianorum Primaeva, x (Nijmegen 1949).

34 I quote from Augustine, *Confessionum libri tredecim*, ed P. Knöll, CSEL 33 (Prague, Vienna, Leipzig 1896).

35 Kenneth Burke, *The Rhetoric of Religion: Studies in Logology* (Berkeley and Los Angeles 1970), 43–171.

36 Compare Augustine's remarkable description of his recitation of a psalm by heart, *Confessions*, XI, 19.

37 Eduard Norden, *Die Antike Kunstprosa*. The term appears as a general rubric throughout his discussion of Late Medieval Latin, and reflects widely held opinion.

38 See the general observations in McGuire and Dressler, *Introduction to Medieval Latin*, 32, and the bibliography that follows.

39 See McGuire and Dressler, *Introduction*, 27, and the bibliography that follows.

40 See Auerbach's discussion in *Mimesis*, 77–95, and *Literary Language*, 103–12; also P. Taylor, *The Latinity of the Libri historiae francorum* (New York 1924). See as well Robert Hanning's discussion of the use of typology by medieval historians in *The Vision of History in Early Britain* (New York and London 1966), passim.

41 This is one of the major points of Auerbach's long chapter 'Latin Prose in the Early Middle Ages,' in *Literary Language*, 85–179.

42 Dag Norberg, 'A quelle époque a-t-on cessé de parler latin en Gaule?' *Annales economies sociétés civilisations* 21 (1966), 346–59.

43 Auerbach, *Literary Language*, 201ff.

44 E. Talbot Donaldson, 'Four Women of Style' in *Speaking of Chaucer* (New York 1970), 46–64. See also his 'Chaucer and the Elusion of Clarity,' *Essays and Studies 1972*, 23–44.

45 Chrétien's imagery may well recall Paul's in 2 Corinthians 3:2–3: 'You are our

epistle, written in our hearts, which is known and read by all men; Being manifested that you are the epistle of Christ, ministered by us, and written not with ink, but with the Spirit of the living God, not in tables of stone, but in the fleshy tables of the heart.' In the same chapter (2 Corinthians 3:14–17), Paul speaks of 'lifting the veil' of holy Scripture, by which later commentators universally understood the allegorical method of reading the Bible. Chrétien's very words suggest the probability that his narrative will be structured according to the same principles.

46 This, of course, is an old thesis: cf Myrrha Lot-Borodine, *La Femme et l'Amour au xiie siècle ...* (Paris 1909), 237ff; Gustave Cohen, *Un Grand Romancier d'Amour et d'Adventure au xiie Siècle: Chréstien de Troyes et son Oeuvre* (Paris 1948), 303ff. One should, however, see as well the more recent studies of A.H. Diverres, 'Chivalry and *fin' amor* in *Le Chevalier au Lion'* in *Studies in medieval literature and languages in memory of Frederick Whitehead*, ed W. Rothwell, et al (Manchester 1973), 91–116; and T. Hunt, 'Tradition and Originality in the Prologues of Chréstien de Troyes,' *FMLS* 8 (1972), 320–44.

47 Chrétien refers to the *Lancelot* directly three times in *Yvain*: 3706–15; 3918–39; 4740–5; none of them flatters Arthur's or Lancelot's conduct. The similarity of the titles *Chevalier de la Charette* and *Chevalier au Lyon* makes it probable that Chrétien wished the two romances to be read side by side.

48 In *Owein*, the Welsh counterpart of Chrétien's tale, the Black Man, who corresponds to the 'vilain,' is surrounded by many animals. Chétien seems to have taken pains to emphasize the bulls' significance. This might be cited as an instance of Jauss's notion that beast poetry marks the threshold of individuality in medieval literature. See 'Untersuchung zur mittelalterlichen Tierdichtung' in *Alterität und Modernität*, 50–125.

49 For a summary of these views, which centre chiefly about the significance of the lion, see Edward Schweitzer, 'Pattern and Theme in Chrétien's *Yvain*,' *Traditio* 30 (1974), 145–90.

50 For a summary of the views, see Joseph Reason, *An Inquiry Into the Structural Style and Originality of Chrétien's Yvain* (Washington, D.C. 1958), 48. See also W.R. Ryding, *Structure in Medieval Narrative* (The Hague 1971), 139–40 and the article by Hunt, n 49. Most recently, see the fine study of rhetoric in Old French romances by Douglas Kelly, 'Topical Invention in Medieval French Literature' in *Medieval Eloquence: Studies in the Theory and Practice of Medieval Rhetoric*, ed James J. Murphy (Berkeley and Los Angeles 1978), 231–51. After completing this chapter, I read Rainer Warnung, 'Formen narrativer Identitätskonstitution im höfischen Roman,' in *GRLMA* IV/I: *Le roman jusqu'à la fin du xiiie siècle*, ed J. Frappier and R. Grimm (Heidelberg 1978), 25–59. Warnung is interested in narrative theory generally and in the historically determined characteris-

tics and structures that constitute the 'genre' of the courtly romance. In his discussion of Chrétien, and especially of the *Lancelot* and *Yvain*, Warnung points to the structural pattern of an event that recalls earlier events ('steigernde Reprise'), which he relates to figural exegesis, as I do.

51 See Jean Frappier, *Chrétien de Troyes: l'homme et l'œuvre* (Paris 1957), 227. See also Frappier, *Étude sur Yvain ou le Chevalier au Lion de Chrétien de Troyes* (Paris 1969), passim.

52 As Hanning argues, Yvain's responses are all his own. See *The Individual in Twelfth-Century Romance*, 151ff and 209ff.

53 See, for example, Madeleine Doran, *Endeavors of Art: A Study of Form in Elizabethan Drama* (Madison, Wisc 1954) and Richard Levin, *The Multiple Plot in English Renaissance Drama* (Chicago 1971).

54 Mark Rose, *Shakespearean Design* (Cambridge, Mass 1972), 9.

CHAPTER FOUR

1 Wesley Trimpi, 'The Quality of Fiction: Rhetorical Transmission of Literary Theory,' 41.

2 Ibid, 61.

3 See Ibid, 43–51 and the bibliography listed there.

4 Cicero, *De natura deorum*, 1.12, quoted in Trimpi, 45.

5 Cicero, *Tusculan Disputations*, II.9; see Trimpi, 44.

6 Cicero, *De natura deorum*, III.72–3; see Trimpi, 44.

7 Trimpi, 'Quality of Fiction,' 45–6.

8 Ibid, 99.

9 The final paragraphs of the *De Amore* make this clear. In the first part of the work, Andreas says 'we set down one point after another the art of love, as you so eagerly asked us to do.' By practising this system, Walter 'will obtain all the delights of the flesh in fullest measure ...' In the latter part of the book, however, Andreas was 'more concerned with what might be useful to you ...' Translated by J. Parry, *The Art of Courtly Love* (New York 1969), 211.

10 See Trimpi's analysis, 'Quality of Fiction,' 90.

11 See Vittore Branca, 'Le nuovi dimensioni narrativi' in *Boccaccio medievale*, 109ff; P. Rajna, 'L'episodio delle questioni d'amore nel *Filocolo* del Boccaccio,' *Romania* 31 (1902), 28–81; Trimpi, 'Quality of Fiction,' 85ff. For a different approach, see Virginia Kirkham, 'Reckoning with Boccaccio's *questioni d'amore*,' MLN 89 (1974), 47–59.

12 All quotations from the *Filocolo* are from Giovanni Boccaccio, *Il Filocolo*, a cura di S. Battaglia (Bari 1938). Graziosa's question is from Book IV, Questione XI, p 353.

13 All quotations from the *Filostrato* are from *Tutte le opere de Giovanni Boccaccio*, II: *Filostato*, a cura di V. Branca (Milano 1964).

14 Aldo Scaglione, *Nature and Love in the Late Middle Ages* (Berkeley and Los Angeles 1963).

15 Robert Hollander, *Boccaccio's Two Venuses* (New York 1974).

16 All quotations from the *Decameron* are from Giovanni Boccaccio, *Decameron*, a cura di V. Branca. *Accadamia della Crusca* (Firenze 1976).

17 *Vita di Dante*, 22. All quotations from the *Vita* are from *Vita di Dante e difesa della poesia*, a cura di C. Muscetta, *Edizioni dell'Ateneo* (Roma 1963).

18 Trimpi, 'Quality of Fiction,' 100. Salvatore Battaglia also stresses the ethical neutrality of exempla, which in Roman and medieval rhetoric could illustrate either good or bad actions. See 'Carattere paradigmatico e qualità realistiche dell'esempio medievale' and 'Dall'esempio alla novella' in *Giovanni Boccaccio e la riforma della narrativa* (Napoli 1969), 1–81. For a theoretical discussion of how Boccaccio makes problematic the little genres of antiquity and the Middle Ages, see H.J. Neuschäfer, *Boccaccio und der Beginn der Novellistik* (München 1969).

19 See Branca's note, '*Immagine popolaresca, di tradizione canterina*' in his edition of the *Filostrato*, 851, and his *Il cantare trecentesco e il Boccaccio del Filostrato e del Teseida* (Firenze 1936).

20 See for instance the preface to the legend of St Margaret in the *Legenda Aurea*: Margarita dicitur a quandam pretiosa gemma, quae margarita vocatur, quae gemma est candida, parva, et virtuosa. Sic beata Margareta fuit candida per virginitatem ...' *Vitae Sanctorum*, tom 3 (Coloniae Agrippinae 1618), 242. ('Margaret takes her name from a certain precious gem which is called the pearl [Latin 'margarita'], which gem is white, small and of great merit. Thus St Margaret was white in her virginity ...'). The tradition was a commonplace throughout the Middle Ages. See E.V. Gordon's introduction to his edition of *Pearl* (Oxford 1953), xxviiff.

21 Troiolo's change of heart parallels the narrator's; in this we see that the arguments advanced in the *Proemio* are not the final word in this question of love. There is no final arbiter in the *Filostrato*.

22 For Boccaccio's other view of Dido, see p 117ff.

23 Branca is cautious, saying this is 'forse reminiscenza del simulato tossire ... / perhaps a reminiscence of the simulated cough ...' But as he himself points out, Boccaccio would have known of Malehaut not only from the *Lancelot du Lac*, but from Dante, *Paradiso*, XVI, 13ff as well.

24 All quotations from the *Teseida* are from *Tutte le opere di Giovanni Boccaccio*, II: *Teseida delle nozze d'Emilia*, a cura di A. Limentani (Milano 1964).

25 Henri Hauvette, *Boccace* (Paris 1914), 98. Among others who argue similarly,

see J. Hulbert, 'What was Chaucer's aim in the Knight's Tale?' *SP* 26 (1929), 375–85, and R. Pratt, 'Chaucer's Use of the *Teseida*,' *PMLA* 62 (1947), 603.

26 J. Whitfield, 'Boccaccio and Fiammetta in the *Teseida*,' *MLR* 33 (1938), 22–30. Among others, see R.K. Root, *The Poetry of Chaucer* (1906; rpt Gloucester, Mass 1950), 163–73.

27 F. Torraca, *Per la biografia di Giovanni Boccaccio* (Napoli 1912). Among others who refuse to express an opinion are V. Crescini, *Contributo agli studi sul Boccaccio* (Torino 1887), 215 and G. Koerting, *Geschichte der Literatur Italiens im Zietalter der Renaissance*, II (Leipzig 1880), 618n. A review of the evidence is found in S. Battaglia, 'Elementi autobiografici nell'arte di Boccaccio,' *La Cultura* 9 (1930), 241–54. I cite these older critics to show how successfully Boccaccio has presented Palemone and Arcita as equal voices in a 'disputatio in utramque partem.' After the studies of Branca, Billanovich, and others, few today would maintain that events in Boccaccio's actual life are conterminous with those in the *Teseida* or any of his other works.

28 Among others see H.S. Wilson, 'The Knight's Tale and the *Teseida* Again,' *UTQ* 18 (1949), 136.

29 See also *Teseida*, III, 16–17, where both knights are shot with the arrows of love; also III, 36, which describes the effects of love on both of them:

> Era a costor della memoria uscita
> l'antica Tebe e 'l loro alto legnaggio,
> e similmente se n'era partita
> la 'nfilicità loro, e il dammaggio
> ch'avevan ricevuto, e la lor vita
> ch'era cattiva, e 'l lor grande eretaggio;
> e dove queste cose esser soleano
> Emilia solamente vi teneano.

Ancient Thebes and their noble lineage had slipped from their minds, and similarly their happiness was gone, and the injury they had received, and that their life was wretched, and their great heritage; and where these things were wont to be they held only Emilia there.

30 As has been observed many times, Boccaccio is recalling Dante's statement, 'Arma vero nullum latium adhuc invenio poetasse / Indeed, I find no Italian has yet sung of arms,' both here and at the end of the poem (XII, 84). See Dante, *De Volgari Eloquentia*, a cura di A. Marigo, 3rd ed (Firenze 1957), I, II, 9–10, 180.

31 See G. Boccaccio, *Genealogie Deorum Gentilium Libri*, a cura di V. Romano, 2 vols (Bari 1951), Book X, ch 49; also Pratt, 'Chaucer's Use of the *Teseida*,' 603.

32 The typical view is expressed by W.P. Ker, *Epic and Romance* (New York 1908), 364. More recently see Robert Hollander, *Boccaccio's Two Venuses*, 54ff.

33 Compare Ovid, *Amores*, I, ii, 27–8: 'ducentur capti iuuenes captaeque puellae; / haec tibi magnificus pompa triumphus erit. / Captive youths and maidens are led; this procession will be a magnificent triumph for you [Amor].' The idea is common in French, Italian, and English poetry.

34 All quotations from the *Roman de la Rose* are from Guillaume de Lorris and Jean de Meung, *Le Roman de la Rose*, ed E. Langlois, 5 vols, SATF (Paris 1914–24). The tone of Book III of the *Teseida* is derived I feel almost totally from this definition of friendship. Although the passage in the *Roman* is modelled closely on Cicero's *De amicitia* (see Langlois, II, 337ff or parallels), there is no reason to believe Boccaccio did not rely on the *Roman* as a guide. See V. Crescini, *Contributo*, who argues that the *Roman de Thebes* had great influence on the *Teseida*; also P. Savj-Lopez, 'Sulle fonti della Teseida,' *GSLI* 36 (1900), 57–78, esp 68ff. The influence of the *Roman de la Rose* has been recognized by Crescini, Savj-Lopez, and others, though the resemblance has been limited to aspects of the garden, the temples of the gods, etc. For the influence of Statius as well, see A. Limentani, 'Boccaccio "traduttore" di Stazio,' *La Rassegna* 8 (1960), 231–42.

35 This advice, of course, is the courtly basis for Pandaro's behaviour in the *Filostrato*, a definition of friendship he cunningly plays on to get his way.

36 After Arcita is banished from Athens, the course of the *Teseida* becomes rather like a debate fashioned after Graziosa's question in the *Filocolo*, the same question, as we have seen, which structures the *Filostrato*. Cf Chaucer, who ends the first part of his 'Knight's Tale' with an explicit question of love:

> Yow loveres axe I now this questioun:
> Who hath the worse, Arcite or Palamoun?
> That oon may seen his lady day be day,
> But in prison he moot dwelle alway;
> That oother wher hym list may ride or go,
> But seen his lady shal he nevere mo.   (A 1347–52)

37 Book VII, note to stanza 30.

38 *Summa Theologica*, I, q. 81, a. 2, 3. The translation is by A.C. Pegis, *Introduction to St. Thomas Aquinas* (New York 1948).

39 Augustine, *De Trinitate*, XII, xii, 13.

40 Ernst R. Curtius, *European Literature and the Latin Middle Ages*, tr W. Trask, 475–6.

41 Curtius, *European Literature*, 228.

42 See Tzvetan Todorov, *Grammaire du Décameron* (The Hague 1969), 77–82, and 'Structure of Narrative' in *Novel: A Forum for Fiction* 3 (1969), 70–6. The article was translated by Arnold Weinstein and is reprinted in Giovanni Boccaccio, *The Decameron*, ed and tr Mark Musa and Peter Bondanella, *Norton Critical Editions* (New York 1977), 250–8. See esp 255.

43 All quotations from the *De Mulieribus* are from *Ioannis Boccatii de Certaldo insigne opus De claris mulieribus* (Beinae Helvet: M. Apiarius 1539), ch 40, fol xxix.

44 All quotations from the *Esposizioni* are from *Tutte le opere de Giovanni Boccaccio*: vi, *Esposizioni sopra la Comedia di Dante*, a cura di G. Padoan (Milano, 1965). Canto v, 65.

45 See D.C. Allen, 'Marlowe's *Dido* and the Tradition,' in *Essays on Shapespeare and Elizabethan Drama* (Baltimore 1962), ed Richard Hosley (New York 1962), 55–68. For Boccaccio, see G. Padoan, *Esposizioni*, 859–60.

46 See Trimpi, 'Quality of Fiction,' 101–4.

47 *Boccaccio medievale*, 201. For Fiammetta as a person of high character, see *Filocolo*, IV, 43; v, 30ff; *Comedia*, XVIII, XXXVI; *Filostrato* and *Teseida*, Introductory letters, *Amorosa Visione*, and *Elegia di Madonna Fiammetta*, passim. For Fiammeta as wanton, see *Filocolo*, III, 36; v, 8, 39ff; *Rime*, LXXII, LXXIV, LXXXIX.

48 For a good account of Fiammetta's character in the *Elegia*, see Robert Griffin, 'Boccaccio's Fiammetta: Pictures at an Exhibition,' *Italian Quarterly*, 18 (1972), 75–94. As Griffin says (p 76), the 'objectifying of feeling in *Fiammetta* owes less to medieval allegory per se than to the *pro et contra* argumentation that characterized much Silver Age drama and rhetoric.' I agree, and would say that the exposition of Fiammetta's character itself depends on the same technique.

49 See Branca, *Boccaccio medievale*, 202–3, and Robert Hollander, 'The Book as Galeotto' in *Boccaccio's Two Venuses* for a more detailed discussion of the inconsistencies in the narrators who stand for Boccaccio.

50 G. Billanovich, *Restauri boccacceschi* (Roma 1947), 161.

51 Walter Pabst, 'Venus als Heilige und Furie in Boccaccios Fiammetta-Dichtung' Schriften und Vorträge des Petrarca-Instituts Köln, XII (Krefeld 1958).

52 Quaglio's reviews appeared in *GSLI* 137 (1960), 435ff and *Lettere Italiane* 12 (1960), 221–6; Hollander reviews the debate in *Boccaccio's Two Venuses*, 160–1.

53 See again Battaglia's *Giovanni Boccaccio e la riforma della narrativa*, esp 'Carattere paradigmatico e qualità realistche dell' esempio medievale.'

54 Branca, *Boccaccio medievale*, 22. As contemporary spokesman for this view, Branca stands in the great tradition that began with DeSanctis.

55 This is not to deny that aristocratic ladies did not exert strong influence on the kind of literature written in fourteenth-century Florence. See G. Padoan, 'Mondo aristocratico e mondo comunale nell-ideologia e nell' arte di Giovanni Boccaccio,' *Studi sul Boccaccio* 2 (1964), 91ff.

56 See G. Mazzotta, 'The *Decameron*: The Marginality of Literature,' *UTQ* 42 (1972), 64–81.

57 The phrase is Mazzotta's, 'Marginality of Literature,' 65. See 64–6 for a discussion of the antipathy between history and Boccaccio's literature.

58 Andres Jolles, *Einfache Formen* (1929; rpt Darmstadt 1958). Cf H.R. Jauss, *Alterität und Modernität*, 47.

59 See, for example, M. Baratto, *Realità e stile nel Decameron* (Vicenza 1974), 56; G. Getto, *Vita di forme e forme di vita nel Decameron* (Torino 1958), 30; A. Lipari, 'Donne e muse,' *Italica* 15 (1938), 132–41; G. Mazzotta, 'Marginality of Literature,' 76–7; E. de' Negri, 'The Legendary Style of the *Decameron*,' *Romanic Review* 43 (1952), 175–8.

60 For an analysis of marriage as a major form of accommodation in the *Decameron*, see Thomas Greene, 'Forms of Accommodation in the *Decameron*,' *Italica* 45 (1968), 297–313.

61 Wayne C. Booth, *The Rhetoric of Fiction* (Chicago 1962), 9–16.

62 See A. Lipari, 'The Structure and Real Significance of the *Decameron*' in *Essays in Honor of Albert Feuillerat*, ed Henri Peyre (New Haven 1943), 43–83. According to Lipari, Panfilo represents the innate 'gentilezza' of the humanist poet, Filostrato his 'passione amorosa,' etc. Needless to say, Lipari's view is controversial. The more traditional reading is expressed by Padoan, 'Mondo aristocratico,' 144. See as well M. Janssens, 'The internal reception of the stories within the *Decameron*' in *Boccaccio in Europe: Proceedings of the Boccaccio Conference, Louvain, Dec. 1975*, ed G. Tourney (Leuven 1977), 135–48. To me, the 'brigata' seems just another vehicle for expressing one more view in Boccaccio's exposition: with the possible exception of Dioneo, they strike me, in Padoan's words, as a 'personaggio collettivo.'

63 See the long review of Cesare di Michelis in *Studi sul Boccaccio* 5 (1968), 341–64, esp 348. This 'recensione' is a good introduction to much recent critical work on the *Decameron*.

64 See Branca, *Boccaccio medievale*, 43 and Padoan, 'Mondo aristocratico,' 161–6.

65 V. Branca, 'Registri narrativi e stilistici nel *Decameron*,' *Studi sul Boccaccio* 5 (1968), 29–76.

66 I am of course referring to F. DeSanctis's influential reading in *Storia della letteratura italiana*, a cura di B. Croce, 4th ed (Bari 1949), I, 318. This view has been opposed by Croce, Momigliano, and others, but their amazement at the friar's credulity still colours their readings. (The friar isn't a blockhead ['un babbeo'], says Momigliano, even if he sometimes appears to be one; see Giovanni Boccaccio, *Il Decameron, 49 novelle commentate* da A. Momigliano, a cura di E. Sanguinati [Torino 1964], 47). See in addition Guido Almansi, *The Writer as Liar: Narrative Technique in the Decameron* (London 1975) 24–55; G. Getto, *Vita di forme*, 55ff; and L. Fasso, 'La prima novella del Decameron e la sua fortuna' in *Saggi e ricerche di storia letteraria* (Milano 1947), 33ff.

67 See Getto, *Vita di forme*, 69ff.

68 On the legendary elements see E. de' Negri, 'Legendary Style,' 186 and Branca,

'Registri narrativi,' passim. The mixture of styles is one of the most compelling features of the novella. The creation of audiences corresponding to the styles of the tale is an aspect of the novella Millicent Marcus examines very well. See 'Ser Ciappelletto: A Reader's Guide to the Decameron,' *Humanities Association Review* 26 (1975), 275–88 and her book *An Allegory of Form, Literary Self-Consciousness in the Decameron*, Stanford French and Italian Studies 18 (Saratoga 1979).

69 Musciatto must find someone who 'was so wicked a man ... that he might be able to offset the wickedness of the Burgundians / chi tanto malvagio uom fosse ... che oppore alla loro malvagità si potesse' (I, 1, 8). Ser Cepperello is Musciatto's man.

70 A point Mazzotta makes exceedingly well: see 'The Marginality of Literature,' 70ff.

71 See Getto, *Vita di forme*, 47.

72 G. Petronio, 'Introduzione' in Giovanni Boccaccio, *Il Decameron* a cura di G. Petronio (Torino 1950), 55.

73 Mazzotta, 'Marginality of Literature,' 70.

74 Branca, *Boccaccio medievale*, 14.

75 Thomas Bergin, 'An Introduction to Boccaccio' in *The Decameron*, ed Musa and Bondanella, 165. On this tale see as well M. Baratto, *Realità e stile*, 342–5; M. Cottino-Jones, 'Fabula vs. Figura: Another Interpretation of the Griselda Story,' *Italica* 50 (1973), 38–52; Getto, *Vita di forme*, 77ff; M. Marti, 'Introduzione' in Giovanni Boccaccio, *Decameron* a cura di M. Marti (Milano 1958), 18ff; V. Pernicone, 'La novella del marchese di Saluzzo,' *La Cultura* 9 (1930), 961–74; L. Russo, *Letture critiche del Decameron* (Bari 1967), 315–28.

76 G. Mazzotta, 'The *Decameron*: The Literal and the Allegorical,' *Italian Quarterly* 18 (1975), 53–73, esp 66ff.

77 Ibid, 67ff.

78 Ibid, 66.

79 Padoan, 'Mondo aristocratico,' 120. As if to emphasize how much human beings are bound to interpret the phenomena of their world' in utramque partem,' without ever reaching final certainty, Boccaccio describes one last time the group's reaction to Dioneo's tale: 'e assai le donne, chi d'una parte e chi d'altra tirando, chi biasimando una cosa e chi un'altra intorno ad essa lodandone, n'avevan favellato ... / And the ladies, some taking one side and others another, some finding fault with one of its details and others commending another, had discussed it thoroughly ...' (*Conclusione*, 1).

80 French romances of the thirteenth and fourteenth centuries also made great use of rhetorical debate. See Marc M. Pelen, 'Machaut's Court of Love Narratives and Chaucer's *Book of the Duchess*,' *Chau R* 11 (1976), 128–55 for an analysis which

deals chiefly with Machaut, but glances at Froissart, Jean de Condé, and Baudoin de Condé as well. Carlo Muscetta, *Boccaccio*, Letteratura Italiana Laterza, VIII (Bari 1972) has emphasized the great influence of the French 'romanciers' on the 'opere minori.' Boccaccio's characters have literary as well as rhetorical ancestors. Indeed, many of the qualities Hanning has said characterize twelfth-century romance – the emphasis on wit ('engin'), the sophisticated use of perspective to fashion character – apply as well to Boccaccio. See Robert Hanning, *The Individual in Twelfth-Century Romance*, passim.

CHAPTER FIVE

1 John Dryden, *Preface to Fables in Geoffrey Chaucer: A Critical Anthology*, ed J.A. Burrow (Baltimore 1969), 66–7. Critics through the centuries have shared Dryden's enthusiasm. John L. Lowes, to cite one example, speaks for most Chaucerians today when he says 'Chaucer's ultimate glory is not his finished craftsmanship but the power by virtue of which he creates, through speech and action, living characters.' *Geoffrey Chaucer and the Development of his Genius* (Boston 1934), 229.

2 Dryden's assumption has been amply demonstrated. See John M. Manly's seminal essay, 'Chaucer and the Rhetoricians,' *Proceedings of the British Academy* 12 (London 1926) and especially Robert Payne, *The Key of Remembrance: A Study of Chaucer's Poetics* (New Haven 1963). See also Payne's 'Chaucer's Realization of Himself as Rhetor' in *Medieval Eloquence, Studies in the Theory and Practice of Medieval Rhetoric*, ed James J. Murphy (Berkeley and Los Angeles 1978), 270–87 and the bibliography on p 281, and 'Chaucer and the Art of Rhetoric' in *Companion to Chaucer Studies*, ed Beryl Rowland (Toronto, New York, and London 1968), 38–51. Note also should be taken of Murphy's caveat, 'A New Look at Chaucer and the Rhetoricians,' *RES* ns 15 (1964), 1–20.

3 The classical concept of 'genera dicendi' – of high, middle, and low styles – in the Middle Ages was applied to the characteristic types of persons, their attendant paraphernalia, and their actions. See F. Quadlbauer, *Die antike Theorie der 'genera dicendi' im lateinischen Mittelalter*, and Douglas Kelly, 'Topical Invention in Medieval French Literature,' 236.

4 As Payne says, the net effect of any of the pairings of the *Parliament* – the two inscriptions, the over-rich temple of Venus and the open-air hill of Nature, the aristocratic and common birds – 'is that each makes the other look inadequate, if not silly.' *Key of Remembrance*, 141. That is exactly one result of rhetorical debate as handled by poets like Boccaccio and Chaucer: the truth emerges, if at all, from a multiplicity of viewpoints. For an analysis of the esthetics of multiple

perspective in Chaucer, see Donald Howard, *The Idea of the Canterbury Tales* (Berkeley, Los Angeles, London 1976), 188ff et passim.

5 No aspect of the *Troilus* has received more attention than its characterization. In general I agree with Ida Gordon's analysis in 'Processes of characterisation in Chaucer's *Troilus and Criseida*' in *Studies in Memory of Frederick Whitehead*, 117–131: 'Chaucer develops the story that he found to hand in Boccaccio's *Il Filostrato* in a series of situations in which the actions of the characters realise, or particularise, different aspects of the problem of love by revealing their attitudes and motives on the important issues raised' (119). Cf her remarks about Troilus as exemplum (122), and her conclusion that in Chaucer 'the character of his persons does not determine their behavior, but rather the other way around (125). This is quite similar to what I call narrative characterization in the *Canterbury Tales*. See also Donald Rowe, 'Psychological and Sacramental Characterization' in *O Love, O Charity: Contraries Harmonized in Chaucer's Troilus* (Carbondale and Edwardville 1976), 57–91.

6 The Black Knight almost becomes a personification when, like Hamlet, he identifies himself with grief itself: 'For whoso seeth me first on morwe / May seyn he hath met with sorwe, / For y am sorwe, and sorwe ys y' (595–7).

7 The dreamer's tact, or stupidity, of course, has been the central subject of debate ever since Kittredge's discussion, *Chaucer and his Poetry* (Cambridge, Mass 1915), 37–73. See D.W. Robertson's review 'The Book of the Duchess' in *Companion to Chaucer Studies*, 332–40. One should note that the dreamer as reader appears to be an innovation of Chaucer's: see Marshall W. Stearns, 'Chaucer mentions a Book,' *MLN* 57 (1942), 28–31.

8 All quotations from the *Paradys d'Amour* are from *Oeuvres de Froissart: Poèsies*, ed A. Scheler (Brussels 1870), I, 1. For good recent discussions of Chaucer's use of his sources, see John Fyler, *Chaucer and Ovid*, 66ff; Marc M. Pelen, 'Machaut's Court of Love Narratives and Chaucer's *Book of the Duchess*,' and James I. Wimsatt, *Chaucer and the French Love Poets: The Literary Background of the 'Book of the Duchess,'* UNCSCL 43 (Chapel Hill 1968).

9 Many have seen the *Book of the Duchess* as a dialectic between 'ernest' and 'game.' See Fyler, *Chaucer and Ovid*, 17 and Charles Muscatine, *Chaucer and the French Tradition* (Berkeley and Los Angeles 1957), 101–7.

10 John L. Lowes, *Geoffrey Chaucer*, 101. See as well John Lawlor, 'The Pattern of Consolation in the *Book of the Duchess*' in *Chaucer Criticism*, ed R. Schoeck and J. Taylor, II (Notre Dame 1961), 243ff.

11 The relationship between the story of Ceyx and Alcyone and the poet's dream has been mentioned by every critic of the poem since Wolfgang Clemen, *Der junge Chaucer* (Bochum-Langendreer 1938), 39ff (cf *Chaucer's Early Poetry* [London

1963], 39ff). For a new interpretation of the changes Chaucer made, see John Fyler's fine chapter in *Chaucer and Ovid*, 70ff.

12 All quotations from *La Fonteinne Amoureuse* are from *Oeuvres de Guillaume de Machaut*, ed E. Hoepffner, III *SATF* (Paris 1921).

13 In Machaut, Juno instructs Iris to have Morpheus show Alcyone 'Ceys le roi, / Et la maniere / Qu'il fu peris, et comment, et pourquoy / Ceyx the king, and the manner in which he perished, and how and why' (581–3).

14 Questions such as those the dreamer asks at 1130ff, which seem to show his fascination with the Black Knight's courting of Blanche, make me disagree with J. Burke Severs, 'Chaucer's Self-Portrait in the *Book of the Duchess, PQ* 43 (1964), 27–39, who argues that the narrator's condition at the opening of the poem was not due to unrequited love, and that he never speaks as a lover.

15 In this regard, see the discussion of the *House of Fame* and the *Book of the Duchess* in Payne, *Key of Remembrance*, 112–46.

16 For a discussion of the debate genre, see Hans Walther, *Das Streitgedicht in der lateinischen Literatur des Mittelalters* (München 1920); Peter Dronke, *Medieval Latin and the Rise of European Love-Lyric* (Oxford 1968), 229ff; Charles Outmont, *Les Débats du clerc et du chevalier* (Paris 1911); Edmond Faral, *Recherches sur les sources latines des contes et romans courtois du Moyen Âge* (Paris 1913), 191–203, and R. T. Lenaghan, 'The Clerk of Venus' in *The Learned and the Lewed*, ed. L. Benson (Cambridge, Mass 1974), 37ff.

17 On the relation between the tales of the Knight and Miller, see D. S. Brewer, 'The Fabliaux' in *Companion to Chaucer*, 247–67; Paul Beichner, 'Absalom's Hair,' *MS* 12 (1950), 222–33; W.F. Bolton, 'The *Miller's Tale*: An Interpretation,' *MS* 24 (1962), 83–94; and Charles Muscatine, *Chaucer and the French Tradition*, 223–39.

18 Literary suppositions of debate such as these support Kittredge's notion of a marriage-group.

19 There is, of course, another side to the portrayal of clerks in the Middle Ages. See Jill Mann, Chaucer and Medieval Estates Satire (Cambridge 1973), who stresses the admirable: 'The Clerk is an ideal representative of the life of study' (73). As we shall see, the Clerk is actually a combination of earnest and game. Mann's book is an important contribution to the study of Chaucerian character, supplementing with new material and insights the other important studies of the General Prologue, Muriel Bowden, *A Commentary on the General Prologue to the Canterbury Tales* (New York 1948), and Harold F. Brooks, *Chaucer's Pilgrims: The Artistic Order of the Portraits in the Prologue* (London 1962).

20 This is a central point of Payne's book. See *Key of Remembrance*, esp chs 2, 3 , and 4.

21 The similarity of the Miller and Reeve to Palamon and Arcita has frequently been noted. See, for instance, Charles Owen, Jr, 'Chaucer's Canterbury Tales: Aes-

thetic Design in the Stories of the First Day,' *ES* 35 (1954), 49–56 and more recently *Pilgrimage and Storytelling in the Canterbury Tale*, (Norman 1977), 99.

22 It is interesting to note that Chaucer's famous apology for the less salubrious material in the *Canterbury Tales* appears here. Chaucer's defence is quite similar to Boccaccio's, though more arch. In both, the reader has been alerted that he will be interpreted by his reaction to what follows.

23 Hugh of St Victor, *Eruditionis didascalicae*, liber VII, PL 176, col 814.

24 Warren Ginsberg, 'Preaching and Avarice in the Pardoner's Tale.' *Mediaevalia* 2 (1976), 77–99.

25 Some in fact have suggested that the catalogue be moved to either of the two tales Chaucer tells. See Robinson's note, *The Works of Geoffrey Chaucer*, 690.

26 'Oure text' is usually explained as an 'actual textbook of the lawyers' (Robinson, 690), and the *Digesta* of Justinian has been cited as an example. It also is possible to see the phrase as the terms of agreement that bond the Man of Law and the Host. The Many of Law recasts what Harry has said into legal form, just as he will recast Chaucer's own words. That the Lawyer claims a man should 'practise what he preaches' has an ironic relevance to the character I think Chaucer is presenting.

27 See Skeat's note, *The Complete Works of Geoffrey Chaucer*, v (Oxford 1900), 137.

28 I take the odd form 'Metamorphosios, commented on by Robinson 691, as a further, not quite correct instance of the Man of Law's desire to let the pilgrims know he is a man of considerable learning.

29 John M. Manly, *Some New Light on Chaucer* (1926; rpt New York 1952), 131ff.

30 Gordon Williams, *Tradition and Originality in Roman Poetry*, 10.

31 See, for example, Gower's *Vox Clementis*, VI, 1–6, and Bowden, *Commentary*, 169; Rodney Delasanta, 'And of Great Reverence: Chaucer's Man of Law,' *Chau R* 5 (1971), 288–310; Jill Mann, *Estates Satire*, 80.

32 Quintilian, *Inst. Or.*, x, 5, 8, tr Butler.

33 Boccaccio, *On Poetry*, tr Charles Osgood (Indianapolis 1956), 22–3.

34 Ibid, 23.

35 Ibid, 24.

36 E.T. Donaldson, *Chaucer's Poetry: An Anthology for the Modern Reader*, 2nd ed (New York 1975), 1050.

37 Murray, who compiled the letter 'T' for the OED, cites this line from the Man of Law's portrait as evidence for its meaning a work of literature. He could just as well have cited the *Legend of Good Women* (G 420) where Alceste says Chaucer 'hath maad many a lay and many a thyng.'

38 Martin Stevens, 'The Royal Stanza in Early English Literature,' *PMLA* 94 (1979), 62–76.

39 In addition to Stevens, see Alfred David, 'The Man of Law versus Chaucer: A Case in Poetics,' *PMLA* 82 (1967), 217–25; Rodney Delasanta, 'Chaucer's Man of Law'; Chauncey Wood, 'Chaucer's Man of Law as Interpreter,' *Traditio* 23 (1967), 149–90.

40 Stevens, 'The Royal Stanza,' 72.

41 Thomas R. Lounsbury, *Studies in Chaucer*, III (New York 1892), 340. Scholarship on the 'Clerk's Tale' is vast; the following studies proved particularly helpful: J.V. Cunningham, 'Ideal Fiction: the Clerk's Tale,' *Shenandoah* 19 (1968), 38–41; E.T. Donaldson, *Chaucer's Poetry*, 1080ff; Joseph Grennen, 'Science and Sensibility in Chaucer's Clerk,' *Chau R* 6 (1971), 81–93; Robert Jordan, *Chaucer and the Shape of Creation* (Boston 1967), 198–207; Alfred L. Kellogg, 'The Evolution of the "Clerk's Tale": A Study in Connotation' in *Chaucer, Langland, Arthur: Essays in Middle English Literature* (New Brunswick 1972), 276–329; John McNamara, 'Chaucer's Use of the Epistle of St. James in the Clerk's Tale,' *Chau R* 7 (1973), 184–93; Charles Muscatine, *Chaucer and the French Tradition*, 190–7; Elizabeth Salter, *Chaucer: The Knight's Tale and the Clerk's Tale*, Barron's Studies in English Literature, v (New York 1962); James Sledd, 'The Clerk's Tale: The Monsters and the Critics,' *MP* 51 (1953), 73–82.

42 For the origins and subsequent history of the Griselda legend, see Francis L. Utley and W.E. Bettridge, 'New Light on the Origin of the Griselda Story,' *TSLL* 13 (1971), 153–208.

43 I translate from the text established by J. Burke Severs, 'The Clerk's Tale' in *Sources and Analogues of Chaucer's Canterbury Tales*, eds W.F. Bryan and G. Dempster (New York 1941), 288–331.

44 Salter, *Clerk's Tale*, 38.

45 Compare this with the contemptuous cynicism of the corresponding passage in Boccaccio: 'My friends, you constrain me to do what above all else I had decided never to do, considering how hard it is to find someone whose customs well match one's own, and how many thousands there are whose are just the opposite, and how hard life is for the man who comes up against a woman ill suited to him. And to say you believe you will be able to know the manners of the daughters from those of their mothers and fathers ... is ridiculous. For I don't know how you are to know the fathers, nor how you can know the secrets of the mothers; and even if you did, daughters very often are different from either parent.'

46 See Augustine, *Confessions*, x, 35. Augustine, of course, was Petrarch's favourite Church Father, and Petrarch quotes him more often in his work than any other author save Cicero.

47 According to Lewis and Short, 'gurges,' besides meaning 'raging waters,' 'whirl-pool,' also carried connotations of 'insatiable craving,' a human trait that well describes Walter.

48 DuCange, *Glossarium Mediae et Infimae Latinitatis* (Niort and London 1884–7), s.v. 'Exiguus.'

49 Salter, *Clerk's Tale*, 50.

50 Particularly interesting is the rhetorical form of the last of these asides. This is nothing less than a 'demande d'amour: cf 'Knight's Tale,' 1347–8; 'Franklyn's Tale,' 1621–4.

51 Jordan, *Chaucer*, 201.

52 Salter, *Clerk's Tale*, 58.

53 John Wyclif, *Sermones*, ed Iohannes Losert, IV (London 1887–90), Sermon XXXI, p. 271. For a general survey of the controversy, see J.W. Atkins, *English Literary Criticism: the Medieval Phase* (1934; rpt Gloucester, Mass 1961), 143–62. The theme of simple and humble speech runs throughout the Middle Ages. See Auerbach, *Literary Language*, 27–66.

54 On Wyclif and the poor preachers see Edward Block, *John Wyclif: Radical Dissenter*, Humanities Monograph Series, I (San Diego 1962), 36–9; George Trevelyan, *England in the Age of Wycliffe* (1912; rpt New York 1966), p. 177 et passim.

55 *The Text of the Canterbury Tales*, 6 vols, ed J. Manly and E. Rickert (Chicago 1940), II, 244, 265, 500–1; III, 473.

56 H. Marshall Leicester, 'The Art of Impersonation: A General Prologue to the Canterbury Tales,' PMLA 95 (1980), 213–24. See 217. One must hasten to say that Leicester is concerned with the idea of 'impersonal artistry' within the confines of a single narrative, not with the formation of character in general. I find I am much more in agreement with Leicester's theory than not.

57 See Jill Mann, *Estates Satire*, 74–85 for examples.

58 Kenneth Burke, *A Grammar of Motives*, 3.

Index

Lightning Source UK Ltd.
Milton Keynes UK
UKHW010650160122
397192UK00001B/87